BLESSED ARE
THE BROOD MARES

BLESSED ARE THE BROOD MARES

SECOND EDITION

M. Phyllis Lose, V.M.D.

HOWELL
BOOK HOUSE

Macmillan General Reference
A Simon & Schuster Macmillan Company
1633 Broadway
New York, NY 10019-6785

Library of Congress Cataloging-in-Publication Data
Lose, M. Phyllis.
  Blessed are the brood mares / M. Phyllis Lose.—2nd ed.
    p. cm.
  Includes index.
  ISBN 0-87605-848-9
  1. Horses—Breeding. 2. Mares. 3. Horses—Reproduction.
4. Foals. 5. Veterinary gynecology. 6. Veterinary pediatrics.
I. Title.
SF291.L58 1991
636.1'082—dc20   91-6557   CIP

10

Designed by Nancy Sugihara

Printed in the United States of America

For My Mother
and My Father

Blessed are the Brood Mares . . . For they shall bear Foals

Though we be sick, and tired, and faint, and worn,
Lo, all things can be borne!

—ELIZABETH AKERS ALLEN (1832–1911)
Endurance

Contents

Acknowledgments

How can I ever thank
my sister, Norma;
my niece, Margaret;
and my dear friend Suzanne Hineman Jenkins . . .
together they have made
my dream come true.

Foreword

I HAVE ALWAYS WANTED to write a book about the equine fair sex, and particularly about the mysterious brood mare. So, after twenty years of the exciting but grueling pursuit of veterinary practice, I have gathered some of my case notes together, turned on my tape recorder while driving from farm to farm, and recorded random and specific recollections. With the help of the devoted members of my all-important team of assistants, this book has finally been brought to life.

It is difficult to maintain absolute clarity of expression and direction in a book that is intended to be read by a widely varied audience—hunting people or riders who simply enjoy hacking through the countryside, children just starting their pony club experience, advanced pony club riders, professional or amateur show-ring competitors, eventers, owners of show stables, one-horse owners, neophytes interested in breeding for a first foal, professionals already engaged in large-scale breeding—any and all of those people who have or will be looking forward to the pleasures (and pains) of caring for a mare and her foal.

The mystery of life—that door that never has been unlocked—is shown to us by every creature that is able to reproduce. But of all the animals with which we are in close touch in our daily living, none is more straightforward, more impressive than the female horse who delivers—if all goes well—with such relative ease and comparative swiftness. After a brief rest, she rises in dignity from her couch of straw, greets her twenty-minute-old offspring in a loving, maternal manner, has a quiet bite of supper or breakfast after she has licked her foal relatively dry. Then she goes about the business of feeding her newborn.

Very soon she resumes her normal pattern of eating, drinking, moving about quietly in her stall, and resting—but always her attention is focused on the new foal.

There are things that the veterinarian and the attendant or owner can do to see that the mare and her young are well looked after. These things are what this book is about, as are the provisions for her health during any stage of her life, and her excellence of condition at the time she is presented to the stallion to whom she is to be bred.

Problems encountered at any time can be solved in almost every case, *if* the owner or caretaker will learn what things not to do, how to prevent mistakes, and, most important, when to summon the veterinarian. This book is intended to inform, prepare, and warn the average mare owner of the eventualities that may be encountered, and to suggest workable solutions.

Not everyone is within reach of my hospital gates or the services of a veterinarian. How I wish they were! I would like to help every animal, solve every problem. But, since this is impossible, I want to describe for you the perfect, natural process and ideal care of mare and foal from breeding to the end of the foal's first year.

Some of the sad incidents I have described may seem fictional. I promise you they actually happened. Some could have been prevented had the persons in attendance not been frightened into making mistakes by unfamiliar events. Others could not have been prevented. From each situation we do learn, however: even from tragedy.

If, with the help of you who read this book, I have saved any brood mare pain or eased any foal's introduction to this world, I will have been well rewarded.

M.P.L.

BLESSED ARE
THE BROOD MARES

1

By Way of Introduction

At this speed it was difficult to keep the car, heavily ladened with drugs, equipment, and supplies, on the road. Poorly inflated tires were a greater concern than traffic at 2:00 A.M. on a back country road—eight miles seemed more like eighty. The expected but feared telephone call at 1:55 A.M. was an indication of serious trouble. My anxiety increased because I knew this farm handled all routine foalings with competence, although I had been alerted. Just that afternoon the farm manager had drawn my attention to the extremely valuable old matron who was overdue. This last foal: then the old mare's owner planned for her retirement after her outstanding career. . . .

That devilish turn at the end of the long lane was always a challenge and the last, long eighth of a mile was punishing for any car, even when negotiated at a sane speed. At the stable entrance at last, it seemed an eternity and a series of unnecessary delays to stop the car, open the door, turn off the ignition, release the seat belt, grab the medical bag, and run.

When the barn door was flung open, the steam-filled stable made it impossible to see, although I could hear quiet voices. Anxious eyes in exhausted faces met me as I was hurriedly led down the aisle. Suddenly, a beautiful shrill baby foal's whinny filled the air.

The realization that the foal had arrived brought all of us humans literally to our knees. As I rushed to the mare's side, I could see the farm manager's broad grin as he, covered with blood and urine, vigorously

1

toweled the struggling, resentful foal. I carefully examined the mare and her newborn with a great sense of relief and a feeling of pride in the grand old, competent mare. I glanced around the barn. It was a sight to behold—the happily excited people, the wet and lively foal kicking its tired mother—a wonderful climax to the eleven-month wait.

Listening intently to the awesome tale, I continued routine treatment. The mare had been found down, wringing wet and near exhaustion. As the foaling attendant watched several strenuous, prolonged straining efforts with no water bag in view, he shouted to the night watchman, "Call the veterinarian!" and forced the unwilling mare to her feet. It had been a struggle to keep the distraught mare up, for she repeatedly threw herself to the ground and, rolling in pain, had to be forced to her feet again.

Finally it became impossible to keep her up any longer. In spite of the combined strength of the men, she refused to rise. Suddenly she turned on her side and, miraculously, her efforts assumed a different rhythm. With quiet, businesslike labor she delivered a live foal just as I had entered the door.

Apparently the foal had been presented in a position that made normal delivery impossible. Acting upon his previous experience, the attendant waited until he was certain that the mare needed assistance. He then took the initiative, forced the mare to stand, and the fetus was allowed to fall back by gravity into the huge abdomen. Fortunately nature prevailed, the foal's position altered, and natural delivery proceeded smoothly.

By the time I was ready to leave the stall the mare was on her feet, quietly eating hay. As I took one final look at the peaceful pair, I noticed the mare's surprisingly intelligent eye regarding me as if in quiet agreement that all was well.

When the car was headed back down the rough lane, the sun was beginning to lighten the sky and activity seen and heard from the scattered dairy barns nearby confirmed the early hour. In spite of the effort required to keep my eyes open and concentrate on driving, I found myself grateful and pleased—with God, the world, with everything—even my car.

Another new foaling season had begun.

Near tragedies with successful endings such as this, I suppose, are what make it all worth while for the harassed practitioner. Nature *will* prevail.

In most cases nature will prevail—if given a chance. Nearly every mare delivers in a very capable manner; the exception results from only a slight change or minute aberration that may "throw a cog" into the beautiful, complex machinery of parturition. Suddenly the mare's innate efficiency is replaced by chaos: then everyone is called into action.

The first week in January heralds the foaling season. This means catch-as-catch-can sleep, catch-as-catch-can meals consisting of cold sandwiches at best, and swift "pit stops" to replace drugs and equipment. Try to visualize the foaling hassle, which usually encompasses the entire night, then add to this the breeding season onslaught, which usually takes up the entire day. The whole scene resembles a production line without shift changes. We strive all night to deliver foals, harvesting the results of last year's efforts, then we fight all day to settle mares to assure next year's crop, with little time left to treat other medical problems.

No wonder practitioners question the importance of a rigid and short-calendar breeding season.

Veterinary school emphasized knowledge and academic standards, but no one stressed physical strength and, most of all, endurance—the endurance needed by the veterinarian to sustain the breeding season activities superimposed on the normal year-round demands of practice.

Limitless energy is required to assist a mare during a difficult delivery, administer supportive therapy to a weak foal, help initiate a newborn's respiration, apply casts to crooked legs, examine mares and determine breeding dates, meet the challenges of "problem" mares, run fertility tests, and assist with stallion efficiency. All this, when added to routine calls, necessitates squeezing in treatment of a case of colic, X-raying the ankles of a race horse, and suturing, in a cosmetic manner, a show filly's facial laceration barely in time to return for the twelve-hour check on a weak foal. Now comes the moment to bathe, eat, and lean toward a bed. Then a voice on the telephone pleads, "Please come! My mare is foaling." An endless cycle indeed, but one we either learn to love—or leave to become a nine-to-five secretary or accountant.

Long hours and added demands mean hiring additional help during this season, with its increased number of late-hour farm calls. The number of enthusiastic young people who apply in a constant stream for jobs with horse doctors never ceases to amaze me. Their obviously superficial impression of the practice and its glamour invariably changes into an awareness and deep appreciation of animal needs. Without exception, all new assistants wish to witness foalings and anticipate them with great expectation.

To the contrary, these young people soon learn that the only deliveries they will observe are the difficult ones. The rapidity of the normal delivery, plus delay in summoning the veterinarian until the water bag is presented, are the usual reasons why the foal arrives before the veterinarian. Any trouble or suspected problem is rarely recognized early enough to place a well-timed call.

If all is normal, when the veterinarian arrives, the foal should already be there.

The difficult deliveries that my helpers do observe are not very pleasant to watch. It is always an ominous sign when my car comes screeching to a stop and the foal has not yet been delivered. As the new assistants accumulate experience and put on mileage in the line of duty, they are automatically thrilled to find the foal already on the ground, because they have become aware of the threatening implications of a yet-undelivered foal.

If the foal wins the race, everybody is the winner.

The owner, interested in breeding and raising horses, can expect to share in the disappointment of failures and the satisfaction of successes. To have a healthy foal, regardless of color or sex, is a triumph and an event that requires careful planning. If you are one of the many people who have an interest in breeding horses, you should have a desire for more than *just a foal.* You undoubtedly want one to be proud of—one to suit a need or realize a dream.

Let us pause here to consider a few facts. Visualize the foal as the end product. Remember that science has proved that equal chromosomal contribution of each parent is a fact. Why begin, as most neophytes do, with an inferior mare?

This is a common pitfall. Most beginners have been given a mare, one unwanted for various and sundry reasons, or have inherited dear old Auntie's aged mare, or purchased a neighbor's mare that was for sale "cheap." Do not allow such temptations to persuade you into unsound thinking. Remember that 50 percent of your future foal is represented by the mare at which you are now gazing. Yes, she *could* possess a treasure of hidden, recessive genes, but the odds are tremendously against this happening. Unfortunately, in breeding, what you see is most likely what you will get.

The exception to this rule does exist. However, the percentages are so low that you may well waste your precious time and dollars in backing a thousand-to-one bet. Instead, why not stack the odds in your favor by spending in the mare's interest an equal amount of time, research, and energy as you will spend on the selection of the sire of her future foal?

Select your mare with the same objectivity, vigor, and care as you will the stallion.

The time spent and the modest inconvenience will represent an investment that, hopefully, will be returned to you in self-fulfillment, satisfaction, and even financial reward. Don't view your mare merely as an oven from which magically pops a miniature of the flashy stallion you selected. Remember that the progeny inherits two equal genetic contributions, so it is not an immaculate conception. Your foal will be a composite of literally hundreds of genes allied with a few chromosomes from each parent; and, like a roll of the dice, its characteristics, abilities, and its future will be instantly determined by both dominant and recessive traits.

The serious breeder should search beyond the individual at hand and scrutinize its pedigree, for each parent represents a composite of *its* sire and dam, thereby broadening the potential for desirable as well as undesirable characteristics in your future foal.

Of course, the influence from earlier generations in the pedigree is proportionately diluted, so that greater attention should be focused upon the individual you are considering. And remember that the mare, in addition to her equal genetic influence, makes a more powerful contribution to your foal because of her continuous, daily influence, her habits, her disposition, and her personality. Remember, too, that her stable vices, if any, are a consideration: many foals are mimics.

By now it should be clear that very careful selection of your mare constitutes a major factor in the enterprise of foal raising, because she represents a permanent resident. If she fulfills your expectations, she may be the mother of your many future foals; don't weaken your potentially strong breeding structure by unwise concessions such as obligations to friends or needless financial restrictions. An inadequate mare may result in a rudderless venture with only luck for your salvation.

Any offensive or undesirable feature in a mare, no matter how minute, will invariably be seen when her foal first stands to nurse. We have found from research statistics that *most* gross undesirable characteristics are dominant. Thus, unequal emphasis upon stallion selection over choice of the mare is a vogue that should be abandoned.

The task of stallion selection is somewhat easier than that of the mare. All data, pertinent information, and achievements are readily available in periodicals or promotional flyers, available at saddlery and equipment stores, that describe the horse's virtues. This individual's right to stand at stud is based upon his pedigree, accomplishments, and conformation. When you visit a breeding farm to examine and select a horse most suitable for your mare, the candidate paraded before you is likely to be exceptional in one or more ways. Had he not excelled, he undoubtedly now would be a gelding filling another role in life.

Select the horse best suited to your mare's pedigree, conformation, and disposition in your attempt to combine and complement desirable characteristics and to dilute and minimize the undesirables. You can save time by studying pedigrees and performance records before deciding upon which farms to visit.

Stallion owners are business people, so each stallion obviously will be presented in a fashion most flattering to him. Do not allow the glamour of the stallions parading by to influence your judgment. As you see each horse, mentally compare, contrast, and correlate all conformational features with those of your mare. It is all too easy to be distracted by admiration for an individual horse and so lose sight of your original plan.

Stallion fees are an important consideration. The cost of a service or "cover" in relation to the purchase of your mare, her board, and eighteen months of maintenance expense is proportionately low, so why not select the very best stallion you can afford? Do not allow a small dollar difference to tilt the balance and dictate your choice. Considered from a business viewpoint, the best result that can be expected is one foal each year, and the worst that can be expected is no foal at all. Each year represents quite an investment when raising horses, compared with other domestic animals. Twins, triplets, and litters are commonplace in other species, but a twin pregnancy in the mare is considered a potential disaster.

Select the best horse possible within your budget and, at the same time, strive always for improvement.

A built-in protection exists in the horse industry against the small breeder who overrates his mare and tries to breed her "up." The balance is maintained by a ceiling that exists to protect the mare owner from investing large, disproportionate sums for stallion fees. Syndicate members and stallion owners are highly selective when signing contracts because they have large monetary investments in the balance. *One* mare of inferior quality can affect a stallion's yearly statistics and averages. These figures and percentages bear upon the stallion standings and directly affect the stallion ratings. Stallion owners hold these figures dear to their hearts, both as a matter of pride and as an influence upon future income.

Much to the amazement of inexperienced owners, the advertised stud fee is of secondary consideration to the owner of an excellent stud horse. Primarily, the mare's quality and breeding potential are the major consideration when deciding whether or not she can be booked to a specific horse. The large farms will not allow an inferior mare to be covered by one of their horses, regardless of the amount of money offered. If they placed stud fee offers ahead of mare quality, their horse's reputation could suffer greatly when foals of questionable quality reached market age. Further, because of the large number of stallions standing in America, the market is highly competitive for outstanding brood mares and considerably less so for the mediocre mare. Good mares make good stallions, it is said.

Before making an important commitment, an aspiring brood mare owner should seek out advice and knowledge on which to base his or her decisions, for early mistakes can be both costly and discouraging.

The most common mistake is to acquire a mare without proper guidance and a veterinary medical examination. High hopes and great expectations can be changed quickly by the sobering realization that your mare is substandard from the breeding farm viewpoint or, even worse, if the medical examination discloses fertility problems.

Do avoid this disappointment. At a relatively minor expense these questions can be answered before you write the purchase check. Somehow a mare that is being resold never possesseses value equal to when she was first purchased.

It is nothing short of a calamity if you discover that the mare you purchased at such a reasonable price wasn't the steal you believed. Backward steps are costly, so it is wise to ask a professional horseman, as well as individuals engaged in the breeding business, to discuss the do's and don't's when embarking on this lengthy journey. You might be pleasantly surprised by their response and find their tales of pitfalls and heartaches interesting and informative. You might even receive some moral support and make new friends with a common interest with whom to celebrate or commiserate.

Most people in this field are anxious to share their knowledge and help the newcomer along; however, be careful to avoid the person willing to give advice only in a biased fashion—biased in favor of his horses, his farm, and, especially, *his* stallion. Base your decisions on facts gathered from many sources and on advice from honest people with no conflict of interest. Only a fool fails to utilize available knowledge.

Perhaps it's the mare's unusually long gestation period that causes people, for the most part, to become impatient and anxious to see what they have indirectly created as the end result of all their planning. For some reason, they expect to realize a dividend at the end of the eleventh month. True, a live foal is a dividend; but it is the better part of two years before you can, if you wish, realize a return on your investment.

Commercial breeders have learned that profits are greater and it is a sounder business venture when foals are grown and conditioned to be sold as yearlings at summer sales rather than attempting a quick profit by selling them early as weanlings, privately or at fall auctions. The select summer sales represent a seller's market, whereas open fall sales are commonly to the buyer's advantage.

But the exception is dictated at any time by "private treaty." You can advertise, arrange with a dealer to act as your agent, or discover your own purchaser without using a middleman.

If the mare is fertile and bred back successfully, there exists a period of doubled productivity. This is an overlapping term during the growth of your first foal. Your mare is preparing to produce another offspring just as your first foal is ready to begin its first schooling.

Obviously, the first foal presents the longest dry wait. It's a different story once it's on the ground: then the pace quickens and exciting events occur in rapid succession.

No matter where your interest lies—be it racing, hunting, showing, eventing, or with a particular breed that attracts you (Thoroughbred, Standardbred, Morgan, Arabian, Quarter Horse, or simple pleasure horses)—an old rule of thumb is: "Breed the best to the best and then hope for the best."*

It is a good adage, but more is required than hope. The mare and the stallion are the first concern, management and husbandry the second, then—balanced precariously—comes the foal. If the precious foal topples, for the moment all is lost.

Finally, I have a message for a very special group of horse owners—a group for whom this book was certainly intended, although it may sometimes seem not to have been written with these people in mind. I refer to those of you who already have been blessed with a totally satisfactory member of the equine family: it may be a mare, a pony, or a donkey. No matter. This beloved creature may not fulfill all the requirements I have recommended for selection of a brood mare, with an eye to profitable sale of the offspring. But if you own a proven, safe, and useful mount—ideally suited to your needs—from which you and/or your children desire to raise a foal for your own pleasure, one to remain in your family, by all means have her examined and breed her to a stallion of your choice.

Follow, to a reasonable extent, the suggestions I have made for selection of the stallion that might diminish her faults, if any, or enhance her looks, if possible.

Once your mare is settled in foal, all the other chapters covering the period dating from her first visit to the stallion to her postnatal care will be applicable to your particular pet.

---

*I must confess that determination of the "best" has eluded me through the years; there is such an enormous range of opinions.

2

Preparations

Although the mare owner occupies a position of only modest importance during the breeding season's intense activity, the owner's prime obligation is to present an acceptable mare in good health and accompanied by the required certificates to the stud farm manager. Most breeding farms require:

1. Health certificate or interstate health certificate;
2. Current negative Coggins Test (EIA);
3. Current negative Contagious Equine Metritis Test (CEM);
4. Current negative Equine Viral Arteritis (EVA);
5. Certificate certifying gynecologic health status plus a current negative cervical culture certificate;
6. Up-to-date vaccination certificate.

Required vaccinations vary somewhat in accordance with the breed of horse and geographical areas. The most commonly used vaccines are listed below:

- Influenza A-1 and A-2;
- Eastern Equine Encephalomyelitis Vaccine (EEV) (PHP)*;

*Public Health Problem.

- Western Equine Encephalomyelitis Vaccine (WEV) (PHP);
- Venezuelan Equine Encephalomyelitis Vaccine (VEE) (PHP);
- Strep-equi bacterin (Strangles);
- Rabies Vaccine. Endemic and increasing in incidence. No treatment; prevention only. (PHP);
- Potomac Fever Vaccine. Endemic in coastal areas. Newly developed vaccine;
- Lyme Disease. Newly developed vaccine. (PHP);
- Botulism Bacterin. Endemic in heavy horse-populated areas. High mortality; associated with "Shaker Foal Syndrome" in suckling foals. (PHP);
- Tetanus Toxoid (Lockjaw). No treatment; prevention only;
- Rhinopneumonitis. Abortion in mares; upper respiratory infection in young horses;
- Enterotoxemia Vaccine—FDA approval forthcoming.

All of these documents can be arranged for by enlisting the help of your equine veterinarian.

Communication between the mare owner and the stud farm personnel is intermittent at best; occasionally it breaks down completely during the busy breeding season. Understandably so, because so many records must be kept—and kept accurately—including the daily "teasing," which must be recorded on the chart for each mare. All this additional paperwork is loaded onto an already packed daily schedule. Such endless recordkeeping comes on top of an exhausting routine of physical activity each day.

Imagine a late-night phone call (9:00 P.M. *is* late for breeding farm people) to the farm owner, a bright, eager voice on the line saying: "Hello. This is Mrs. Jones. How is my mare?"

After teasing and caring for as many as one hundred mares from before sunup until final night check at 9:00 P.M., the weary manager finds it impossible to identify Mrs. Jones's nameless mare. Groping for the teasing chart in order to give an accurate and intelligent report, the tactful manager must interrupt seemingly endless chitchat to extract the mare's name from the talkative owner, only to find the chart information unnecessary this time—the call was purely a social one.

Farm personnel, over the years, cultivate a deep appreciation for the owner who shows them consideration by placing calls during working hours and giving them the pertinent information immediately. How much less frustrating such a call would be if presented as: "Hello, Mr. Smith, this is Mrs. Jones. Are you near your records? How is my maiden bay mare, Baby's Dream? If you remember she was delivered by Brown's Transportation Company four weeks ago. Has she been covered yet?" This would delight any hardworking farm employee and immediately place both you and your mare in very good standing.

Pregnancy Determination

There are many ways to determine your mare's pregnancy status, but there is no way to predict its outcome! For years horsemen have depended upon veterinary rectal palpation of the mare's uterus performed as early as the eighteenth post-ovulatory day. Serum, blood, and urine tests have been abandoned and are outmoded. All have seemingly taken a back seat to today's state-of-the-art technology, the ultrasound machine.

This small portable machine is expensive, easy to operate, and can determine pregnancy, or its absence, as early as the eleventh post-ovulatory day. This new knowledge is of particular value when dealing with the infamous "progesterone" mare. Her schedule of either I.M. injections or oral dosages can be greatly enhanced with this early evaluation.

The ultrasound machine can simultaneously produce a permanent readable image of the precious embryo or embryos floating inside of its little vesicle, still unattached to the lining of the uterus.

Oftentimes when twin images are discovered an agonizing decision compels us to act in ways not always in our best interest. Termination of a pregnancy (pinching off or flushing out) based upon ultrasound findings can be premature. It is a known fact that mares who ultrasounded with twins on the eleventh day have been reexamined on the eighteenth post-ovulatory day and found to be pregnant with one single embryo.

Examination of thousands of placentas has proven that the mare does possess the inherent ability to arrest fertilized ova and perhaps select a viable embryo to progress and develop. Thus in more cases than not the mare should be given the chance before invasive intrusion by humans.

Check your mare again at her eighteenth post-ovulatory day and if a twin conceptus has persisted, there is then plenty of time to abort the pregnancy and start again. With this knowledge, please do not be hasty and possibly wash away a fine viable pregnancy. While ultrasound is wonderful and exciting, the effects of sound waves on an early pregancy have yet to be established.

Early, Premature and Abortion—Deliveries

There is a fine line separating early parturition, premature, and in fact abortion. In the event that the foal is viable, keep it as warm as possible and whisk it off to the nearest state-of-the-art neonatal critical care center, commonly found in state veterinary universities. Good work is being done but it can easily become "cost prohibitive" and with varying degrees of success.

Twin and Multiple Pregnancies

It has been erroneously perceived and accepted by horse people that the brood mare develops and ovulates a single ovum (egg), with of course an occasional double ovulation. Years of placental membrane studies and the ultrasound data prove this theory false. The brood mare does, in fact, release double, multiple, and sometimes "litter-sized" numbers of ova, all of which can be fertilized on one single cover. Mares possess a superior ability to conceive, but most are unable, and thus fail, to carry, support, or care for more than one conceptus. It is the rare mare that deviates from this status, and most will abort the conceived twins around the seventh or eighth month of gestation.

Consequently, seldom if ever do twins endure the long eleven-month gestation period and deliver alive and well.

Gestation

The normal gestation period of the brood mare can extend from 330 to 350 days, and the majority of mares foal between 332 and 348 days. An extension or undue shortening of this time span is cause for concern and necessitates careful observation of the mare.

However, no fixed, normal gestation period can be calculated because each mare is affected both by the external environmental and hereditary influences from her own genetic background and by those same influences received from the stallion to which she was bred.

Climatic conditions characteristic of certain geographical areas and certain years can be documented as a particular year when *all* mares carried beyond their due date, delivered early, or—amazingly—delivered precisely on time.

Other domestic animals have a relatively fixed gestation period that permits last-minute preparation and is thus more convenient for the people concerned with their care. But the brood mare's varying length of gestation results in unavoidable inconvenience and apprehension, as well as great anticipation.

While the mare is doing her essential part in the production of your foal, you, the conscientious owner, can do many things to ensure the safety, health, and well-being of both the mare and her expected offspring.

Overdue Date

When, however, a mare begins to either "shape up" too early in her pregnancy, delays parturition, or goes extremely overdue, even the cool learned horse people take a wary eye. It is the wise horseman who checks on due dates, and then consults with the veterinarian, perhaps for reevaluation. There are four valid and likely reasons for the aforementioned:

1. Uterine infection with septicemic foal;
2. Twin pregnancy;
3. Ruptured uterus, with intact umbilical cord (maintaining oxygen and nutrition to the foal);
4. Ruptured prepubic tendon, predominantly in older mares.

Feeding

Nutritional requirements of the adult horse, as well as the pregnant mare, have not yet been scientifically established, in spite of the research undertaken for other species' needs. Understandably, most research has been directed toward the care and improvement of food-production animals. But horses are either athletes or beasts of burden. Their nutritional requirements, therefore, are not the same as for food-producing animals.

Understanding the nutritional requirements of the herbivore horse is of major importance and concern for all involved horse people. Shockingly, this is a relatively unknown fact with little consideration . . . to the contrary, to be successful, this must be understood. This basic husbandry knowledge combined with the sharp eye of an experienced horseman can prevent insidious myopathies and gastrointestinal disturbances (colic, founder, and a multitude of related problems).

> FACT: The equine is a herbivore, *not* a ruminant. Thus, vast differences are present in the digestive tracts. Danger can exist in feeds, feed preparation, and storage.

> FICTION: Do not treat the equine as a ruminant in any dietary situation, and keep this thought foremost when preparing the equine's diet.

> CAUTION: Feed only feeds that have been researched and marketed specifically for the equine.

In lieu of adequate scientific information, an educated guess is the only guide we have at present. Your mare's dietary demands during the early gestation period will be much the same as before she was bred. No great changes are necessary, provided she is turned out regularly and exposed to some grass and some sun. The regular ration of approximately 8 quarts of grain each day for the average-size Thoroughbred should be supplemented with well-cured, leafy green hay, *absolutely* free of dust, and *absolutely* free of even the slightest hint of mold.

Mares of other breeds—Morgans, Arabians, Quarter Horses, and other smaller breeds—should be fed an amount proportionate to their size and breed requirements.

Around the middle of September the change in climatic conditions and the increase in size of the growing fetus, for the mare due to foal in January, justifies the addition of a reliable vitamin-and-mineral supplement (feed one half of recommended dosage), as well as the beginning of a gradual monthly increase in daily grain intake.

A satisfactory and safe way to increase grain intake is to add *1 additional quart a month* through the ninth month of gestation, but *never* to exceed a daily total of *14 quarts for a 1,000-pound Thoroughbred mare*, provided she has access to good-quality hay.

If simple horse sense rules are abided by, the fear of causing founder by overfeeding a pregnant mare should be put to rest. Its incidence is negligible—except for feed-room accidents or actual stupidity on the part of an uninformed attendant. Founder in brood mares develops *after* delivery only. Such a misfortune is a completely separate clinical entity, involving the placenta and incorrect postpartum care.

Careful observance of monthly increases in feed, combined with choice legume hay and adequate exercise, should maintain your healthy mare and produce a vigorous foal. *Throughout her entire pregnancy the mare should have free access to hay, water, and a salt-and-mineral block.*

To avoid creating vitamin and mineral imbalances, especially the delicate ratio of calcium and phosphorus, keep a mineral salt lick within reach of your mare and foal at all times and thus allow them to *select* the amount of salt rather than eat a man-made mixture!

The necessity for continuously available protein cannot be overemphasized—growth demands are occurring in both the mare and her fetus. In addition to this vital need for protein, vitamins and minerals are essential. Such an urgent need is best met by feeding as much as *20 to 40 pounds daily* of quality, green, clean, and well-cured legume hay. Alfalfa and clover hay are excellent sources.

The need for vitamin A is intensified during the long winter months:

even the average "well-fed" animal suffers to some degree from vitamin A deficiency because the daylight hours are shorter and the pastures deficient in edible cover. Rich, highly palatable hay supplies a good portion of the mare's daily requirements of minerals, calcium, and vitamins.

Some written work and experimental evidence have clearly demonstrated that for the mare who is fed properly cured hay, the minerals, vitamins, and protein are more accessible and more readily assimilated than when fed in the form of commercial preparations.

It is wise for the owner to seek out a source in advance, for this scarce food is difficult to find. Often the only supplier, other than the less desirable commercial feed companies, is your local dairy farmer. And the amateur mare owner, when approaching the farmer, is often confronted by a jaundiced eye. The farmer seems to hold his home-grown hay so close to his heart that only visions of many dollar signs can pry it loose from his barn.

Dairy farmers who depend upon milk yield for their income have learned that what they feed is in direct ratio to what they receive. The same principle applies to the producing brood mare.

The type of hay that is required is naturally green, leafy, and high in moisture content. Obviously it takes special care to cure this lush hay properly because it bales tight and heavy, predisposing it to mold growth. Whereas cows tolerate a small mold content quite well, the highly sensitive equine will react to *minute* quantities of it and may become seriously ill —or even abort.

Further, a shocking number of pregnant mares, even today, are unintentionally underfed and suffer varying degrees of malnutrition. Unfortunately, old and inaccurate beliefs still prevail, controlling the feeding procedures in many barns today.

I recall one sad episode that occurred because two intelligent, affluent amateur owners, following the advice of an old-time, dyed-in-the-wool professional horseman, were disastrously misled.

I was called in to see a seriously malnourished mare in the tenth month of her pregnancy. The owners sensed, but did not know, that everything was not as it should be.

They had been told the exact amounts of grain and hay to feed her and had been cautioned not to allow the mare to put on any weight because "there is more room for the foal to grow outside than inside the mare." *This quotation should be eradicated from our hearts and minds forever.*

For twenty years or more I have observed well-fed brood mares and have not seen one foal that was too large to be delivered because of the quantity of nourishment provided. The size of the foal is genetically controlled; barring monstrosities and genetic anomalies, in spite of the narrow margin nature provides for safe delivery, foals are not too large to be delivered by their dams.

It is essential to be careful to avoid frank obesity. That *is* undesirable, for it is a hindrance rather than a help to any mare.

In this case, my first look at the malnourished mare revealed an impending tragedy. Backlighted from the stall window, the silhouetted form of a skeletal frame with a huge balloonlike sack suspended beneath it was an unforgettable sight. Irreparable damage had been done: in spite of my efforts to provide nutrients by injections, supplements, and specially prepared feedings during the final month of pregnancy, both the mare and foal were lost.

True, this case is an extreme one, yet it is a vivid example of what can and does happen, even to well-meaning people. It should also serve as a lesson and reminder of the damage that ignorance and repetition of old adages founded on myth continues to cause—even today.

Overfeeding

By trying to grow a "super colt," a man-made monster was created that was directly responsible for abortions, intrauterine fetal contraction, gastrointestinal disturbances (colic, laminitis, founder), obesity, and even death. An abundance of dietary protein causes equine tendon contraction in utero and nutritional contraction in young growing horses. Never exceed 14 percent protein content in your grain mixture.

The misuse of high percentage protein concentrates and highly advertised but unnecessary additives contributed to the modern mare's "man-made" dilemma. Remember, when you feed your equine, sharpen your eyes and mind, and follow old-time feeding methods.

Exercise

Exercise is as imperative a need as food. Without proper exercise all vital body functions are affected to some degree. The mare's heart, lungs, digestive system, muscle tone (which is directly involved with circulation), even her feet are benefited. Fresh air, sunshine, and freedom to roam in a pasture or large paddock encourage appetite as well as a sense of good health and contentment.

The pregnant mare should be turned out only with other pregnant mares or alone, for her safety and well-being. The exception is the companionship of an old friend—usually a foundered pony or an arthritic donkey.

Mixed company often ends in disaster—a lesson most horse people learn at a price. Geldings are the worst offenders, for they present the greatest danger to the mare. Some old geldings retain their amorous ways throughout their lives and therefore pose potential problems forever. Of next concern is the false gelding who outwardly appears to be a neuter, but who behaves as if he were a stallion: he is the result of an abdominally retained testicle or an incomplete castration. In the case of the true gelding, such bizarre behavior is inexplicable.

The hazards are evident. Maiden mares and barren mares are more active and competitive than pregnant mares: the pregnant mare will be at a distinct disadvantage in their company. She surely deserves the consideration of compatible companions at this time.

The Stall

The owner should see that a suitable stall is prepared to serve as the mare's delivery room and as a nursery for the newborn. Size is an essential consideration. The mare will need ample room to get down to foal and sufficient room to permit someone to assist her if it becomes necessary. In addition, the mare and her foal will share these quarters until weaning time. Twenty by twenty feet is ideal. Usually foaling stalls of this dimension are found at large breeding farms. But a solution for the owner of a small barn is to remove the partition between two existing stalls and so double the space.

The stall should have a smooth interior, free of all projections; the walls should be solid to a level of at least three feet, with no holes or openings through which a foal could place a tiny foot.

Do not overlook the doors: they should be solid from the ground surface up. Stall screens are a potential disaster unless they are carefully secured and have a board at the bottom to prevent a foal's foot, leg, or head from being wedged underneath. Feed tubs and water pails should be removable and hung high enough to prevent injury. Hay racks, metal or wooden, should be removed from the stall. "An ounce of prevention is worth many a pound of cure."

Very early one morning I was summoned from bed to hurry to a farm in answer to an urgent call. There I saw an outstanding foal hopelessly wedged under a wooden stall door. Most of the door's weight was directly over her heart, ribs, and lungs.

I asked the barn men to break the hinges and carefully lift the heavy door from the limp body. The foal was in shock. Emergency fluids and supportive therapy were administered immediately. Unfortunately, her ribs were fractured: they had punctured the lungs and a massive pulmonary hemorrhage resulted.

A beautiful chestnut filly needlessly lost her life under a door.

As I left the farm I made a solemn vow that I would tell this story to everyone possible, with the hope that this sad accident would never happen again.

A stall should be as foolproof and safe as humanly possible; yet it should not be so solid as to interfere with proper ventilation. Adequate movement of air, even in cool weather, is essential and should be so arranged that the foal is never in a draft or in a direct air current, whether it is up and playing or sleeping in the straw bedding.

In addition to the necessary adjustments to the stall, an adequate sleeping area for the attendant should be prepared for future round-the-clock surveillance; it should be adjacent to the mare's stall and equipped with some sort of small, unobtrusive observation window. Some sort of communication system also should be provided because one person should not be expected to assume full responsibility for the unpredictability and complexity of the foaling process. In lieu of a telephone, a bell, buzzer, or gong should be at arm's length to notify others and summon assistance in order to avert a possible tragedy.

Your stall must be clean. Scrub the stall floor, walls, and ceiling with hot *soapy* water (detergents are not harmful). Use a wire brush, when necessary, to remove all organic material and visible dirt. If the floor is clay, a layer should be scraped away and the floor leveled.

When the stall is thoroughly clean and dry, it should be disinfected. A garden pressure-tank spray with an adjustable nozzle set on "fine spray" does a good job. The spray reaches cracks and crevices that might otherwise be neglected. Recommended solutions of Lysol, pine oil, or, preferably, one of the newer povidone-iodine compounds are suitable; however, any disinfectant with a satisfactory phenol coefficient will do. Do not neglect tubs, pails, or screens. Today we have available machines that can be rented, which are water under pressure or steam sterilizing. An old-fashioned method of disinfecting whitewashed walls is to incorporate the disinfectant solution into the whitewash. In your attempt to clean the area effectively, apply a fresh coat of paint or creosote. That will be both efficient and attractive.

Consult your paint dealer to be positive that the paint is safe to use in animal quarters. *Avoid lead-based paints.*

After the stall is thoroughly disinfected, it should be left open to air, with no bedding present. The floor and the lower portion of the walls, ordinarily covered, will benefit particularly from the fresh air and whatever sunlight reaches them. Most harmful bacteria found in stalls are anaerobic in nature and thrive in warm, moist, dark areas where there is little or no oxygen available.

One of the most dreaded diseases affecting the horse is botulism. It is caused by ingestion of a minute quantity of neurotoxin produced by bacteria belonging to an anaerobic family. By thoroughly cleansing the corners formed between the wall and floor, and allowing exposure to air, these lethal bacteria are reduced in number and, most important, are prevented from producing their harmful toxins.

Be especially diligent when cleaning under the feed tubs and water pails. The conditions required for spilled grain to germinate are also the precise environment required for these deadly bacteria to propagate. Hence, grain sprouting in these moist warm areas is the signal for immediate removal, scraping, and thorough disinfecting.

Bedding should be absorbent, clean, and dust-free. Wheat and rye straw are the beddings chosen by most well-informed people. Bright, clean, long-stemmed, dust- and mold-free straw has become increasingly difficult to find and increasingly costly. But try your hardest to find it.

Oat and barley straw are usually chaffy, dusty, dark, and undesirable as bedding for a brood mare. The most unattractive feature of such straw is that mares are inclined to eat it—sometimes to the exclusion of their nutritious hay.

Substitute beddings such as peat moss, Staz-Dri, shavings, or processed wood by-products, while satisfactory for other horses, should not be used for the mare and foal. They do not afford adequate cushioning or essential warmth, nor do they provide a place in which the foal can snuggle down. Most of these substances are irritating to the ocular, nasal, genital, and navel membranes of the foal.

The unprotected newborn with its open navel (a portal for infection) is delivered into straw teeming with millions of bacterial, viral, and fungal enemies. When a matron, down in the bedding, presents a foal and rises, the downward pull of the heavy placenta opens the vulva and allows an inrush of air into the vacuum created by negative pressure in the recently vacated and enlarged uterus. This inrush of contamination occurs when the vulnerable uterus is at its lowest ebb of resistance to infection. *A clean, disinfected stall is therefore essential for the well-being of both the post-partum mare and her new foal.*

A small night-light should be positioned so that the foaling attendant can observe the mare; to turn on the lights in a quiet, dark stall suddenly startles a sleeping or resting mare. It is not unusual for the attendant, when looking through the peephole, to find a large, dark eye carefully watching him or her in the dim light. Sometimes I wonder who is watching whom.

The mare becomes accustomed to a steadily burning light and, after she delivers, it will help her not to lose sight of her newborn. Such an arrangement is especially useful in the case of a maiden or *prima* mare who may not recognize her foal immediately, or of an overpossessive mare who panics when she cannot see her foal.

In cold weather, heat lamps can be a tremendous help in dispelling chill and dampness from the foaling stall. Cold temperatures are an added stress upon the newborn. The proper use of heat lamps can eliminate this unnecessary strain on the foal's endurance. When comfortably warm a foal will be more relaxed, function more normally, and be more contented.

The indiscriminate use of heat lamps, however, can overdry the atmosphere in the stall and consequently dry out the nasal mucosa and respiratory tract of young ones.

It is important that heat is used carefully and in moderation in the neonatal stall. The infrared heat lamps that can be purchased at most drugstores serve the purpose very well. But be certain to specify "infrared." *Never use ultraviolet lamps.* Although they are bacteriocidal, they do not produce heat and can do irreparable damage to an animal's eyes.

Infrared lamps have a standard base and should be used in the regular heat-resistant receptacle. One or more lights placed in sockets in the ceiling, if positioned high enough, are a simple solution. Photographic light reflectors with clamps can be used on top of the stall partitions, as long as they are out of reach of the mare and foal and are protected from accidental breakage.

If an electric extension cord is used, it is vital to see that it is safely secured, well out of reach. These lights are heat-producing and become very hot when used for extended periods of time. They should *never* be placed where they could possibly touch any flammable material. However, lights on an extremely high ceiling are too far away to function properly. Lowering a heat lamp on a chain is an acceptable method of bringing the heat source to within an effective distance.

The entire stall does not have to be heated: in fact, it is unhealthy to do so. Foals will seek out a warm spot when they feel chilly or move from the warmth to a cooler spot in the stall if they become overheated. It is much better that the stall be a little on the cool side rather than too warm.

All these precautions are essential: I beg you to follow them with care.

The Paddock

As well as preparing the stall, consideration should be given to a small paddock in which the mother and her newborn can stretch their legs in protected privacy. For a period of from seven to ten days the pair should have an opportunity to exercise alone, before they are turned out with other brood mares and foals.

Remember that the foal requires from two to three days for its vision to develop enough to be trusted beyond the safe confines of the stall. Even when it is ready to be exposed to the outside world, it should be protected from other horses. The new mother will not be especially anxious to have others present, for she is extremely possessive and jealous of her new baby.

An existing paddock can be subdivided into a private paddock as long as there is no possibility of an inquisitive friend reaching over the fence for a closer look at the new arrival. Double fencing is one way to solve this problem. A small area adjacent to the barn is ideal, if it has not been overused for pasture.

Pastures can become what is known as "horse-poor" or overgrazed and parasite-infested; then they are of little or no value except as a place for exercise. If your pasture falls into this category, it is unsuitable; perhaps a part should be renovated for the new occupants. One year's rest is the minimum required for a horse-poor pasture to rejuvenate and allow for parasitic eggs and larvae to die. (It is wise to communicate with a state official, who will then want to visit and conduct a routine soil analysis. The results of his examination will provide you with the necessary information and enable you to correct the situation.)

Medical Box

A medicine chest or box of supplies should be prepared in advance and positioned so that it is handy to the foaling stall. The list is not long but *everything included in it is vital*. All contents should be fresh and scrupulously clean.

For treatment of the foal's navel you will need a wide-mouthed, 4- to 5-ounce *sterile jar* with an efficient lid. Boil it, air-dry it, then fill it with 7 to 10 percent tincture of iodine.

Tail bandages, even if new, should be freshly laundered; but *3-inch gauze bandages,* which can be disposed of after use, are preferable. A roll of sterile cotton, a package of gauze squares (bandages), and a roll of adhesive tape may also be useful.

Obtain a pint of *Therapogen or povidone-iodine compound* to serve as an antiseptic for cleaning your hands and the mare's perineal region. (Its effectiveness is not decreased by suitable mildness.) About six to eight clean towels will be needed to dry off and stimulate the circulation of the foal when it arrives.

An *enema can* with attached rubber tube is safe to use on the foal and can be readily obtained from any drugstore.

Last but far from least for the mare's postpartum discomfort, a bottle of *colic medicine* is an absolute necessity and can be obtained from your veterinarian.

The use of a *small oxygen cylinder* is becoming increasingly popular on large farms to help sustain small, weak foals.

A *seamless pail,* thoroughly scrubbed and dried, can be used as the storage container. Small items placed in small plastic bags can be packed; the pail and its contents should be protected by a large plastic bag that is securely closed.

If you do not already have one, a *large animal thermometer* (rectal) is an asset in any medicine chest.

Well in advance of parturition, request from your veterinarian a large vial of injectable *Dipyrone.* This is an essential part of your armamentarium for use in *any* mare to safely dispel pain before, during, and after foaling. It also aids in smooth placental cleansing and increased flow of milk. Dipyrone is safe, reliable, and a drug that every horseman should keep in the stable refrigerator.

DOSAGE: 30cc administered IM and repeat every half hour if mare's discomfort persists.

Another important reminder: If your mare is notoriously high-strung or unpredictable, make arrangements well in advance of parturition time for a suitable mild tranquilizer already prepared in a sterile syringe with a sterile needle. This also should go into your refrigerator for emergency use.

Her Temperament

Owners should be prepared to anticipate and, thus, better cope with the habits, whims, and expectations of a heavy brood mare who is quite a different creature from horses that are in active use in competition, performance, or mere daily work. In the absence of discipline and daily demands made by close contact with humans, brood mares go through a transitional phase and gradually acquire a new, distinctive personality.

Horsemen recognize that when a young active mare enters the stud, she should be allowed a period of acclimatization so that she can safely and successfully enjoy her new role. With so little being asked of her, enjoying almost unlimited freedom, the average mare becomes increasingly haughty and independent. With each ensuing pregnancy she becomes more demanding and less responsive.

Some mares, who have absolutely no talent other than their personal appeal, are fortunate enough to have inveigled for themselves a lifetime of love and affection. But most brood mares have earned their lofty place in the sun by virtue of outstanding performance or choice bloodlines. The average mare has sufficient idiosyncrasies, more than enough God-given problems, and an overabundance of peculiarities.

The pregnant purebred brood mare is one who expects meals served on time, to be turned out to enjoy total freedom, and to be "put up" at midafternoon in a well-bedded stall provisioned with quality hay, fresh water, and a large meal served promptly. If things are not to her liking, her patience is sorely tried. Her independence and freedom are foremost in her mind and she seems to resent any interruption in her daily schedule.

She usually commandeers her stable mates with her special ability to threaten with pinned ears, reaching teeth, and lifted foot: there is seldom need for her to follow through. Most stable mates bow and step back.

Her capabilities and self-reliance never cease to amaze me when she is compared with her equine counterparts. The purebred brood mare of any breed is an independent, self-reliant, efficient complex of behavior patterns. She is a creature of habit, not particularly responsive to anyone— a demanding soul who looks upon people as her servants and is annoyed when asked to change ever so slightly from her regular daily schedule.

During her last trimester of gestation, she is naturally overweight, assumes a swaggering stride, and because of her pendulous abdomen is only just able to fit through stall doors. Responsible owners and caretakers make sure that she receives adequate exercise and the finest nutrition so essential for the health of the heavy mare and the increasing inner demands of her growing fetus.

Once she foals, the selfish, independent brood mare temporarily becomes completely maternal. Her all-consuming interest in her new foal causes a profound personality change; but, even before the foal reaches weaning age, a gradual metamorphosis can be seen and our original self-centered individual reappears.

3

The Elusive Term Mare

As a child, living on our parents' farm, I wanted to see a mare foal more than anything else in the world.

I watched a favorite mare become huge and approach term. Then my mother permitted my sisters to accompany me to the barn with a cot and blankets. We prepared our unobtrusive grandstand seat next to the big, heavy mare's stall and started our watchful wait.

After ten long nights we were exhausted and bleary-eyed during the day, for we barely slept at night from excitement and anticipation.

On the eleventh night we sensed a slight change in the mare's attitude. Her full udder seemed very tense. Mother called us in to dinner and within twenty minutes we were headed back toward the barn, provisioned with sandwiches to fortify us through the night's vigil.

To our dismay, as we walked in the barn we heard a shrill whinny! We raced to the stall to see a new colt, soaking wet and unbelievably perky.

The mare turned and looked at us with an expression that seemed to say, "Foxed you, didn't I!" I'll never be convinced that she did not carefully wait for us to leave and then, in privacy, deliver her foal.

Not until the next year did I see my first foaling.

During the last two months of gestation, the normal, healthy matron rapidly gains in weight and size as the fetus doubles its weight and demands in this final eight-week period. By this time the mare's daily intake of 8 to 10 quarts of quality concentrates or grain of the finest quality available, abundant free-choice hay (as much as 20 to 40 pounds) that is clean and leafy, and a limitless supply of clean, cool water is well developed.

The value of incorporating a large, warm bran mash into her daily diet is evident in her pre- and postparturient health. Let me suggest that for the last two months of gestation she be fed an evening meal consisting of a 4-quart bran mash; over a period of two weeks you may gradually increase the amount to 8 quarts.

The mash should be made from equal parts of concentrate or grain, with wheat bran mixed with hot water. If a bran mash is properly prepared, its digestibility and palatability are greatly enhanced:

RECIPE FOR BRAN MASH (8 QUARTS)

4 quarts concentrate (grain)
4 quarts wheat bran

Place the concentrate in a clean metal pail. Add boiling water slowly, stirring all the time until the mixture is *light and fluffy, not wet and soggy.* Add the bran, continue stirring to retain the light texture. Cover the pail with a clean towel until it has cooled enough to be fed.

Many people prefer to cook the concentrate first in a *small* amount of water—being very careful not to burn it. Using a pan with a tight cover will preserve most of the nutrients.

The dry bran is then added to the cooked concentrate. Extra boiling water may be added if the mash is too dry.

Set the mixture aside to cool.

A few slivers of carrots may be added to tempt a finicky eater. Do NOT add apples or salt.

As a child I remember seeing large grain cookers steeping all day long at some of the better-managed farms. I am sorry to say that this practice has been abandoned today in favor of a quicker method that, while satisfactory, is not comparable.

The bran mash benefits both the mare and the foal. It provides additional protein for the rapidly growing foal and adds the bulk needed to condition the mare's gastrointestinal tract in preparation for the approaching periods of intermittent stress. This late, warm, and filling meal offers the special advantage of satisfying the mare's by-now voracious appetite. She becomes more relaxed, hence more contented.

We must assume at this time that the mare has been properly cared for during her pregnancy (see later chapters). Diet, exercise, effective parasite control, appropriate vaccinations, dental care, and proper trimming of her feet have been important throughout her gestation in order to maintain her health and sense of well-being. All of this is necessary so that she will approach the last few weeks in the best possible condition.

Definite external changes can be observed during the last few months of pregnancy: the enlarging abdomen, gradually gravitating toward the ground, rides below sprung ribs projecting out on each side. It is interesting to look from back to front and measure the degree of rib expansion occurring as she adjusts to the rapidly growing fetus.

The mare's stride slowly changes to accommodate her increased circumference and weight. The average foal is too large to lie in a side-to-side position, and because it occupies the body and only one of the two horns of the uterus, each mare's abdomen is lopsided when viewed from front or back.

Each mare has her own individual way of "shaping up" to foal, although it will vary from pregnancy to pregnancy. This is quite understandable when you consider that your mare is often bred to a different horse each year. One should realize, too, that what we term "inconsistency" may, in fact, be the influence of each sire. What you will cope with may be a perfectly normal pattern resulting from the sire's genetic contribution, which itself combines with external influences upon the mare to affect each unique countdown to parturition.

Clear, precise stages can be observed in some mares, while others seem to slip through these stages, showing only intermittent changes. "Textbook" cases do exist, but they are in the minority.

The mare prepares herself to deliver in a much less obvious fashion than do other species. It requires an astute observer to perceive each early change. As the countdown slowly but steadily progresses, whether obvious to the beginner's eye or not, each precise, complex step is continuously developing and taking shape so that this birth—this wonder of nature—can take place.

However, once delivery begins it is a totally different story. Her whole world knows then, because the process is irreversible and explosive.

I would like to invite you to read the following description of the last few weeks of pregnancy in the hope that you will one day add your own personal, daily observation of your own mare. If you do not experience a deep sense of learning and adventure, or feel privileged by the possession of this new knowledge, you will have lost a unique opportunity for personal enrichment and I will have failed in my descriptive attempt.

As the fetus grows, the maternal system prepares itself by means of musculoskeletal relaxation and simultaneous mammary development. Each step is accomplished steadily, without interruption.

Great preparation is necessary to enable the mare to deliver the full-size fetus. Nature provides for the propagation of the breed by adequately preparing the mare for an efficient delivery of the full-term foal. The innate physiologic and anatomic peculiarities specific to the mare create a unique, explosive, dynamic delivery with very little margin for error.

With the benefit of abundant natural measures to ensure protection of the reproductive tract, the large, leggy foal leaves the uterus and is transported through the birth canal into the external world without injury to the mare or the foal. But, without efficient preparation for this rapid journey by the fetus, the reproductive tract can suffer severe injury, resulting in irreversible genital damage.

The mare's future fertility, breeding efficiency, and even her life are at stake with every parturition. Usually brood mares live out their lives with limited serviceability for any other purpose, so reduced fertility suggests an ominous future. The mare's value is greatly lowered and her usefulness is in jeopardy if irreparable damage is sustained.

On breeding farms parturition is often referred to as "the moment of truth."

About three weeks prior to her due date, a phenomenon of major and highly integrated changes is experienced by the expectant mare.

At this time the pituitary gland is activated. The exact manner of its initiation is not understood, but one can safely assume that some fetal or placental change must trigger the pituitary to begin the elaboration of its hormones directly responsible for preparations for delivery. Some of these changes can be readily recognized externally; others, although present, are subtle in nature and hardly evident. The pituitary affects its target glands, which in turn respond with their respective secretions.

The pituitary gland can be envisaged as the leader of the entire endocrine orchestra: one can easily picture all the endocrine glands suddenly reacting to the pituitary baton, resulting in a beautiful, harmonious melody. As each gland responds, it affects *its* target gland, which in turn reacts with the others. The harmonious interplay of ductless glands and their products creates the three-week phenomenon in the mare.

Meanwhile, other awesome and unseen preparations silently progress within the mare, the ultimate goal being the delivery of a live foal and provision of adequate food for the newborn. But this three-week phenomenon and its manifestations are completely dependent upon the degree of efficiency of the pituitary gland and the other components of the endocrine system.

The relative inconsistency of the mare's ability to "shape up" correctly and deliver on time is related directly to her unstable hormonal system. Unfortunately, a small percentage of mares, usually maidens, suffer hormonal inadequacies, and when fetal development is completed, will foal, ready or not, at the expense of the mare's genital tract. It is interesting to note that this same hormonal system is responsible for some of the fertility problems encountered during the breeding season.

During the critical three-week period, hormone action is exerting a softening effect upon muscle, tendon, ligament, and bone tissue—specifically upon the pelvic symphysis. These changes account for the progressively unsteady gait seen in the mare approaching term. As well, these influences permit the large, well-developed fetus to pass from the uterus through the cervix into the bony pelvis and birth canal, then on through the vagina and into the outside world.

Miraculously, successful parturition leaves in its wake tissue that can swiftly recover, regenerate, repair itself, and return to normalcy in preparation for subsequent pregnancies.

If the hormones do their job properly, the birth canal is prepared so that birth is smoother and easier. Hormone action is also responsible for mammary gland development and the production of milk precursors—wax and, ultimately, the critical colostrum.

This period also exhibits itself in udder formation: gradual enlargement should be visible, followed by very slow relaxation of the pelvic ligaments and associated muscle masses. Such masses include the large gluteal muscles, the biceps femoris muscles, and the caudal coccygeal and sacrosciatic ligaments on each side of the tail head.

The softening is manifested by an appearance of looseness and the inability to hold the tail down firmly. The degree of flaccidity progressively increases in some mares. In older mares some degree of locomotion is actually lost when parturition is imminent.

However, most young or maiden mares may not show evidence of extensive muscle relaxation until just before delivery. Some young mares, whose hormonal system is less active and who deliver without the advantage of this softening syndrome, suffer varying degrees of damage to the reproductive tract as a consequence. But it is safe to say that the amount of muscle relaxation indicating parturition varies with each individual.

Generalized tissue changes in the perineal region, including the dock or base of the tail, the vulva, and the immediate surrounding muscles, will advance rapidly and show profound atonicity just before or at the moment of delivery. It is normal in the average mare to see the musculature fall away from the vertebral column in the lumbosacral area.

A relatively consistent finding is that the degree of softening and falling away of this area is directly related to the number of pregnancies and the age of the matron.

In some mares unfortunate enough to receive poor nutrition during gestation, not only do they show hormonal muscular relaxation, with bony pelvic involvement, but the entire perineal area and tail head seem to fall away. These individuals assume a very weak stance approaching delivery: a mare in this condition represents a grave risk. Poor nutrition is a severe disadvantage under any circumstance, but when seen in an approaching-term mare, it can be disastrous.

In over twenty years of practice, I have yet to see a strong, well-grown foal produced by a malnourished mare (although well-managed mares, with a more than adequate diet, can and sometimes do produce weak or small foals that are undoubtedly the result of genetic structure, rather than nutritional deficiencies).

It is well known that if borderline nutrition exists during pregnancy, the foal's demands are met first—at the expense of the dam. Should this occur, the number of pregnancies, subsequent fertility, and general health of the brood mare all become questionable.

Approaching Parturition

After the 300th day of gestation the mare should be examined daily—especially in the evenings—for gradual changes that indicate approaching parturition.

Since normal gestation is highly variable and the calculated due date usually cannot be relied upon, it is important to observe the mare on a daily basis. It is to her advantage to make the necessary changes slowly as she approaches parturition.

Lack of outward signs of readiness or bizarre behavior is most commonly seen in maiden mares. However, such deficiencies are found to be a constant factor in some older mares throughout the whole of their reproductive lives. An accurate history of a mare's behavior pattern is a valuable tool to the veterinarian—if she is consistent enough to have a pattern—although such information is often received by knowledgeable horsemen with tongue in cheek.

> *Warning*: any mare can deliver without any sign;
> any mare can deliver without wax;
> any mare can deliver with a small bag!

"Shaping up" is the pattern followed by the majority of mares; but some mares foal without *any* obvious outward indication of hormonal influence upon muscle relaxation. Maiden mares, in particular, may foal with a small udder and without wax or milk. Other mares make sudden changes and go through the whole countdown in a matter of hours.

Some mares gradually shape up over a period of three to four weeks; some mares require only three to four days; and a small percentage makes all of the necessary changes in three to four hours.

Mares approaching their due date should be scrutinized several times each day and have a night attendant on duty, in spite of lack of external evidence.

Your powers of observation truly will be tested by the "sneaky" mare. The owner who walks out to the barn in the morning to find that his mare has unexpectedly foaled invariably will say that she foaled in the absence of any changes. His mare undoubtedly falls into the category of the three- to four-hour mare—and *went through all her changes unobserved*.

As I mentioned earlier, the majority of mares foal between the 332nd and the 348th day from the time of conception. This period varies greatly with the individual mare, resulting in an inconsistent intrauterine period for the foal.

After eleven months of protected environment afforded by the mare's abdominal muscle tone and the security of her uterus, suddenly the fetus must survive an abrupt excursion into unprotected surroundings. Emerging from its watery nest out the cervical door and over the pelvic threshold, the foal passes through the vaginal vault and into its new, outside world.

All the needed changes for performance of this dynamic, physiologic miracle vary in intensity with each mare. And her functional efficiency is affected by both hereditary and external environmental influences.

There are so many variables and inconsistencies in the intricate physiologic makeup of the pregnant mare that it is impossible to predict the foaling date with any certainty. Only "green" or inexperienced people offer forecasts; their foolhardy attempts merely reveal their lack of experience.

Slight mammary gland enlargement may be noticed four to six weeks prior to delivery: this is the first indication of approaching termination of pregnancy. "Bagging up," as it is called when the udder begins to appear full, occurs about three weeks from foaling. From this time on, the mare's udder should be inspected daily for visible changes in size, shape, texture, and temperature. During the early stages, the udder will be soft, flabby, varying in size, and cool to the touch. When turned out in the morning, the mare's bag will be larger after the quiet night; when she is brought in from pasture in the afternoon, as a result of exercise her bag will be smaller. Udder development may regress intermittently.

But the afternoon the mare comes in from pasture with an udder as large as it was when she went out in the morning is the first signal that closer observation is needed and a warning that parturition is near.

At this time, in addition to regular daily checkups, added trips to the mare's stall are in order to observe any changes.

The udder is one of the cardinal indicators, among many, of continuing changes taking place within the mare's body. When the udder remains constant or increases in size, a progressive tenseness and increased warmth develops. The small teats are deflected outward by pressure from within the udder. The teats then expel the dry plugs from their openings: soon, wax will appear on the ends of the teats. This wax appears as a honey-colored, sticky substance. It is a product of the activated ducts and tubules of the milk gland—all of which are under hormonal control.

I remember that old-timers relied upon the presence of wax as a reliable sign that the mare would foal within three days. I have never found this to be true and consider it to be an old wives' tale. Wax may form, then fall away, only to reappear and be replaced by a stringy, sticky, less viscous substance that is a precursor of milk and is present for varying periods of time.

The appearance of the first milk is unmistakable. Large drops of white milk gather on the end of the enlarged, full, dark teats; at this time the udder becomes dark and shining, glistening as if wet. The disappearance of the dimple at the base of each teat is an additional significant change.

Some mares will stream milk from the udder so profusely that the hind legs become coated with the strong, sweet fluid. The appearance of milk is a sign of imminent delivery. *From this time on, the mare should not be left unattended.*

Unfortunately, there are some mares who lose milk into the straw bedding or in the pasture for periods of from several days to several weeks before delivery. This essential first milk, or colostrum, is a uniquely valuable substance for the future of the yet-to-be-delivered foal. It will provide the *only* antibody source available for the newly born, completely unprotected foal.

Colostrum is highly nutritious and contains a laxative substance vital to the foal's gastrointestinal functioning.

Currently, mares who have lost foals at delivery are hand-milked to collect the precious colostrum, which may then be processed and frozen. This hand-milking lasts from 48 to 72 hours after delivery.

When the production of colostrum ceases and the normal milk begins to flow, these mares are no longer milked, so that stimulation of milk production is stopped and efforts are then made to dry the mare up, unless she is needed for an orphan foal.

The hormones that activate the complete process of birth are normally well synchronized. Each step is interrelated with the others, so that when the foal arrives the essential colostrum is its first food. Those mares that continue to lose large quantities of first milk before they foal are not in hormonal balance and their foals are denied the fundamental benefits that many times are so desperately needed.

A colostrum substitute is available commercially, but it is composed of universal nutrients and does not contain specific antibodies.*

Experienced horsemen know that a pregnant mare may suffer colic for many reasons. It is not uncommon for a heavy mare to show mildly colicky symptoms any time from the tenth month to the time of delivery. Restlessness, pawing, looking at her side, rising and then lying down again, are all reactions to pain caused by pockets of gas trapped by the gastrointestinal tract as a direct result of the large fetus crowding the normal intestinal space. If an oral dose of colic medicine, followed by a warm bran mash, does not relieve the symptoms, it would be wise to call your veterinarian.

Contrary to some beliefs, mares approaching term *do* lie down to sleep. The grunts and groans emitted by the sleeping mare are not true signs of discomfort; they are caused by pressure on the epiglottic closure and should not be confused with the characteristic sounds of labor.

The resting or sleeping mare is relaxed, with no change in her postural attitude.

Personality changes can be expected near the end of the period of gestation. These changes may be indicated by irritability, abnormal sensitivity or hostility when near other members of the horse community, or the individual mare may become timid and attempt to isolate herself from other mares.

---

*The careful horseman should inquire into the location of now-existing programs and stations that have colostrum, and should help by collecting and processing this unique and irreplaceable substance, which will otherwise be lost.

Some mares will come to the pasture gate, stand looking at the barn, or walk the fenceline, expressing a desire to be brought into the barn earlier than the regularly scheduled time.

Heavily pregnant mares deserve consideration and should have their whims catered to at this time. But other calmer mares will follow their routine right up to the moment they foal, undaunted by the inconveniences of their condition.

A small percentage of mares lose their appetites a week or two before foaling. Every effort should be made to make the meals more enticing and palatable. Sliced carrots may be introduced, *but no other tidbits*. A veterinarian's visit and examination to eliminate the possibility of a pathologic cause of such lack of appetite will normally be reassuring.

The absolute opposite extreme of the mare who goes "off her feed" is the mare with a voracious appetite who may stop in the middle of a hastily consumed meal to drop down to foal, then get up to devour the remainder of her dinner—and remain completely unperturbed.

Perhaps nature signals the mares in some way that we do not understand, but we do know that the mare who continues to eat is better able to withstand the foaling process. The mare who decreases her food intake is at a definite disadvantage.

Older mares, late in term, occasionally stock up behind and may have well-delineated ventral abdominal edema that becomes a well-delineated or rectangular swelling as it progresses toward the front legs. Some of these mares show a reluctance to move and appear weak. These manifestations of circulatory changes may be seen individually or in combination. The condition is more prevalent in older mares who have had multiple pregnancies, but it may also be seen in young matrons.

Although the underlying cause of either edema or weakness is commonly related to age, diet, and exercise, the appearance of one, the other, or both indicates the need for examination by your veterinarian to eliminate the possibilities of anemia, infectious disease, a foal being carried in a poor position, or a heart condition. Only rarely is this combination of symptoms related to the size of the fetus.

In spite of a relatively proficient endocrine system—as evidenced by a smooth easy delivery and an abundant supply of milk—these mares are slow to rebound from delivery and go through a negative postpartum stage.

Some mares will stand with their rumps against the stall wall, as if to counteract the pressure of the fetus during the last week of gestation. This is not significant other than as an indication of how uncomfortable the mare feels.

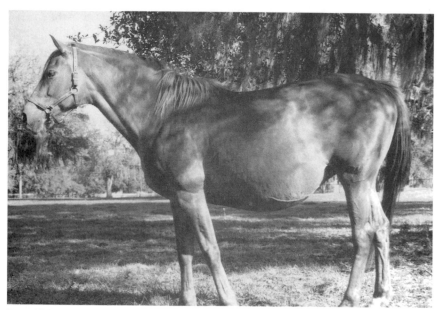

Beautiful matron ten days from delivery.

Foal is still in transverse position. Mare has not begun Stage I.

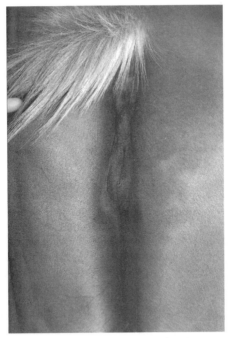

Mare's vulva three weeks from due date.

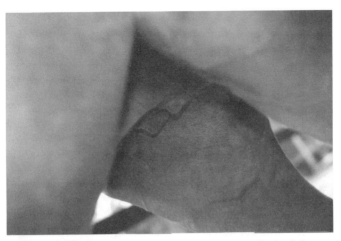

Mare's udder three weeks from due date. Note small glandular development with well-defined teats and strong dipples.

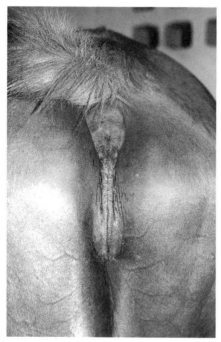

Strong hormonal influence on
vulva—tailhead musculature and
total relaxation of tail—no tone, no
resistance when elevated.

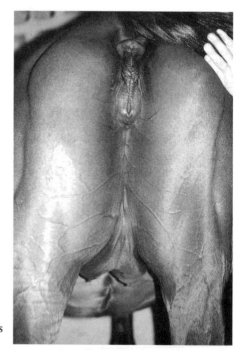

Hormonal influence on skeletal
muscle. Vulvar relaxation and
mammary buildup. Although the
nipples are small and well-formed
with dipples in evidence, this mare is
considered imminent.

Occasionally, from the tenth month on, a worried owner will find a small pool of blood—about the size of a saucer—in the bedding of a term mare's stall. This is the result of rupturing of minute, superficial vaginal capillaries caused by fetal pressure and approaching parturition.

When the mare shows any or all of these signs of imminent parturition, the owner or conscientious attendant should alert his veterinarian so that appropriate schedule adjustments can be made to provide for immediate veterinary service, should it be needed. Additional telephone calls reporting on the mare's progress will help assure the owner of the veterinarian's availability.

The following list of observable physical changes should clarify, yet not oversimplify, signs of approaching delivery:

1. A very large and pendulous abdomen;
2. Udder enlargement, with changes in size, shape, texture, and temperature;
3. Straw- or honey-colored wax on teats, with subsequent appearance of milk;
4. Muscular and ligamentous relaxation in hindquarters and around the tail head;
5. Enlarged abdominal milk veins;
6. Personality changes;
7. Lack of appetite;
8. Circulatory disturbances;
9. Behavioral peculiarities;
10. Changes in gait and posture.

Your mare *may or may not* exhibit any or all of the conditions listed. As a general rule, the longer a mare goes beyond her due date, the more obvious the changes become.

Recently I was attending two pregnant mares on farms separated by only a few miles. Both inexperienced, apprehensive owners wanted me to be in attendance when their mares foaled and both were keeping a careful watch.

One mare was an old matron who had successfully delivered eight previous foals, but now her age was a consideration. Her due date was one week off when the huge mare waddled in from pasture with a full, tense udder streaming milk.

My office was alerted and the owner, equipped with a cot and sleeping bag, moved into the stall next to the mare to begin her nightly vigilance. For three weeks the ponderous mare continued to come in from pasture each afternoon streaming milk and the weary owner crawled into the sleeping bag for another sleepless night of observation. Each day I received a call reporting that there was nothing "new or different."

Finally, after twenty-one days of attentiveness, the owner walked into the mare's stall to give her a pat on the neck before retiring. The experienced old mare was quietly eating hay, but the owner was startled to find that the animal was sticky and sweating slightly in spite of the near-freezing temperature.

The calm owner's call to my office was relayed over the car's radio-telephone and I received the message between calls while I was only minutes away. Just as I walked into the barn, the mare went down into the straw. Immediately she quickly and efficiently delivered a fine-looking, strong colt.

The next afternoon I answered a call from the owner of the second mare. She had requested that I examine the mare to determine whether it was time to start her careful observation of the young maiden, by now several days past her expected date of delivery.

When I saw the mare, her udder was large and fresh drops of milk could be seen on her teats. It seemed that the mare would foal within a matter of hours and I suggested that the owner prepare to stay with her. She immediately made elaborate preparations for her night in the barn —with a thermos of hot black coffee, sandwiches, blankets, pillows, books, and a radio. After she had carefully arranged her observation post and turned on the night-light, she peeked in at her mare.

Her expectant charge had become restless and was walking in circles around and around the stall. As the owner watched, a cloud of steam began to rise from the mare's body. The owner's excited call was relayed to me when I was about thirty minutes away.

I arrived to find the mare down on her side in the large stall, soaked with sweat. A gray bulge visible beneath her tail indicated the presence of at least one small foot already. I scrubbed hurriedly, cleansed the mare, opened the gray membrane, and slid my hand into the shiny envelope to check the foal's position.

The second foot with the foal's nose close behind it was reassuring, but the size of the feet and legs instantly revealed that the foal was unusually large. A quick evaluation of the pelvic canal quelled the momentary concern I felt. With the help of slight assistance from me, a large chestnut filly rapidly appeared on the straw bedding.

The history of these two mares demonstrates the vast difference in the time required for mares to prepare themselves for effective and safe delivery of a live foal, and indicates the importance of watchfulness on the owner's part.

Had either mare been in serious trouble and required professional help, rather than mere reassurance to the owners, the willingness of the two owners to involve themselves on behalf of their mares would have made it possible for skilled help to arrive in time.

4

The Three Stages of Labor: The Foal Arrives

Parturition represents the period of greatest danger of death for all animals.

Time is of the essence in equine deliveries, so early decisions must be made rapidly. Therefore it is of utmost importance that the people in attendance be familiar with a normal delivery as it occurs in mares in order to recognize instantly any pathologic symptoms or abnormalities that require immediate veterinary assistance.

To watch a mare foal when each stage of the process is perfectly co-ordinated is an exciting and unforgettable experience; yet many people who have had this experience are unaware of what they are actually witnessing. It might almost be worth while to arrange for them to see a tragically "difficult" delivery.

One inexperienced young woman described the first foaling she had attended:

> When I checked on her the mare was pawing a large hole through the bedding in the middle of her stall. As had been prearranged, I called the veterinarian to alert him that I thought my mare was foaling, and returned to watch from outside the stall.
>
> In a few minutes the mare lay down and seemed fairly quiet. Then there was a sound of rushing water and she went flat on her side. I went quietly into the stall and crouched behind the mare. She pushed down and sud-

denly a shiny sac appeared with a little foot inside. I was momentarily startled and fearful that seeing only one foot was an indication that the foal was not properly positioned, but the mare pushed again and a second foot and the nose quickly appeared. She pushed once more and the whole head with a little of the neck was outside.

The sac was not broken and I almost panicked again. It seemed to me to be the proper thing to do so I opened the sac and cleared it away from the tiny dark muzzle. The mare's contractions stopped: my heart almost stopped too. Before I could decide what to do she pushed again and the shoulders appeared, followed quickly by the body, hips, and hind legs of a large, dark filly. By this time the foal was breathing and starting to lift her head and move her front legs.

This entire process, from the time I first checked on her until the foal was delivered, took thirty minutes! Within another twenty minutes the foal, after several unsuccessful attempts, had managed to get to her feet, find the mare's udder and was having her first meal. To me, the beautiful perfection of what I had seen renewed my faith in an omnipotent being.

This young woman had observed the *second stage* of labor in a normal, uncomplicated parturition.

Actually, there are three stages of labor in the normal foaling process:

Stage I: Internal or invisible preparations for parturition, ending in "the breaking of the water";

Stage II: Parturition or the birth of the foal;

Stage III: Passage of the placental membranes or afterbirth, involution of the uterus, repair, and with it return of the reproductive tract to a normal, healthy state.

Stage I

HOW TO RECOGNIZE THE FIRST STAGE OF LABOR

External appearance immediately prior to entering Stage I:

Well-sprung ribs and sprung abdomen
Flaccid and atonic musculature
Unsteady gait
Full tense and warm udder (P.M.)
With or without milk on teat ends

Entering the first stage of labor:

Suddenly flat-sided (stand in back of mare and look forward)
Stand on side and view prominent drop of abdomen near pelvis
Profound relaxation of vulva and tail

Additional external changes:

Full warm udder—wax, colostrum, full extended teats dripping milk
with no dimple visible
Broken out—sweating
Restlessness
Frequent defecation
Walking and digging
Quietly eating

Internal changes—silent and insidious:

Movement of foal from transverse position to longitudinal or in the
birth canal
Ready for delivery and pushed up into birth canal with intact placental
tissue through dilated cervix

Additional internal changes:

Heart rate increases 20 to 30 beats per minute (establish normal chart
two weeks prior)
Body temperature decreases 2 to 3 degrees

All of these above changes indicate imminent parturition. Do not leave
your mare's side.

In other species the first stage of labor is clearly visible, with symptoms
of abdominal straining and strenuous muscular activity. It is quite different in the case of brood mares. There is no external evidence of the
internal changes that are taking place during the first stage of a mare's
labor.

Because of this quite normal absence of any external abdominal muscular activity, the mare can slip through the first stage of labor undetected
by the untrained or inexperienced person.

But unless the first stage of labor is recognized, it is not possible to
determine the status of the mare. It is *most important* that this stage not
be missed because once labor (the second stage) has commenced there is
no provision for delay as exists in other species. Interruption or cessation
of the process can result in the loss of the foal and present a danger to
the mare.

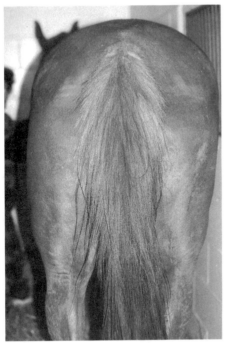

First stage of labor: dramatic abdominal drop; slab-sided. The foal is no longer in a transverse position.

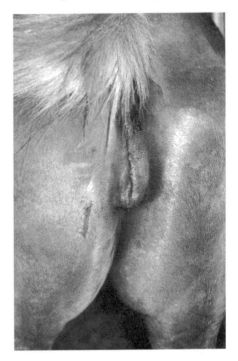

Progressive vulvar relaxation. Note udder increases in size and is lower between the hind legs. Also the first stage of labor.

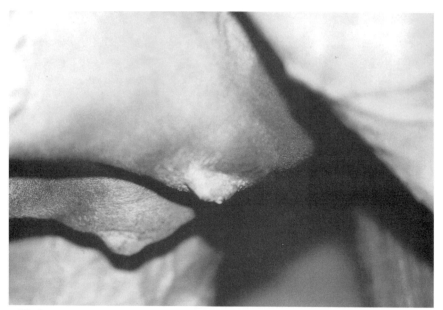

Milk droplet on teat (white), not wax. Dipples still evident. Do not leave the mare when these signs are present. The mare in this photograph delivered 7 hours after the picture was taken.

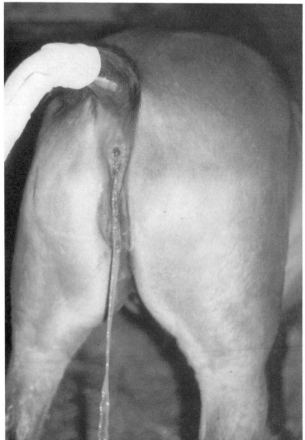

Mare breaking water. She should drop down immediately and begin contractions. She has passed through Stage I and is entering Stage II (delivery).

Restlessness, stall-walking, switching the tail, and kicking at the abdomen are the most common signs of stage one. Sweating over the shoulders, flanks, and chest is quite a reliable signal; it may occur with or without the restlessness.

Such behavior can simulate colic, so it requires very close observation to differentiate between colic and the start of labor. If the mare looks at her sides, gets up and goes down for short periods, snatches grain or hay while still walking, perhaps defecates frequently, and passes small amounts of urine, you can be quite sure that the first stage of labor is well into progress.

Elevation of the tail, with flicking movements, is a direct reflection of internal pressures created by the advancing fetus. (NOTE: Do not confuse up and down flicking movements with normal side to side tail swishing. I have learned that this characteristic "squirrellike" up and downward flicking of a mare's tail occurs *only* when abortion or delivery is imminent! Please take careful note of this unique equine behavior.) The gradual relaxation of the tail musculature (ideally, well developed) and surrounding area, coupled with a sudden, profound relaxation of the vulva, are signs that parturition is imminent.

The mare's udder should be dripping, even streaming, milk. Note, however, that mares vary from the extreme of no udder at all to a full flow that has saturated their hind legs for days preceding delivery.

Even though the mare may show several of the above indications that parturition is near, there exists no evidence of straining to show what is happening inside the mare during this first stage.

Nonetheless, two major changes are taking place:

First, the uterine wall, which is composed of circular and longitudinal fibers, contracts and moves the fetus from its eleventh-month, lopsided location in the one horn and body of the uterus to the centrally located position in preparation for delivery.

At this time the foal is ideally presented in a dorsosacral position; that is, the spinal axis of the foal is in a parallel plane with the spinal axis of the dam, with both forelegs preceding the head.

The *second* internal change, happening simultaneously with the first, is the gradual dilation and softening of the cervix, which permits the departure of the fetus from the uterus to, and through, the dilated canal. All these internal changes take place with an intact placenta and without disrupting a quiet, external abdominal picture.

A mare may "break out," become restless, defecate frequently while walking about the stall, or even eat, and then abruptly get down and, with a sudden rush of water, present through the vulvar lips a grayish-white sac with a foot inside.

This mare has just slipped through the first stage of labor with total absence of muscular activity or visible contractions, and we are suddenly facing the second stage.

The length of time of the first stage can vary from a short interval to the extreme of twenty-four hours and still not interfere with the production of a live foal. No danger exists for the fetus during this period if the placenta is intact and providing oxygen and nutrients. Simultaneously, the hormonal effects upon the mare's system continue to cause relaxation of musculature, gradual cervical softening and opening, and positioning of the foal for delivery.

There is still no danger should cessation of the normal process develop, *unless* the water bag has broken or premature separation of the placenta causes the foal's oxygen support to cease.

The foal may be compared with an astronaut or a deep-sea diver. As long as its support systems are intact and functioning, it can survive in its own safe sac. But the built-in margin of safety is not great and premature or off-schedule interruptions immediately create a potentially precarious situation.

If the attendant is able to recognize the first stage of labor, he or she should scrub the mare's perineal region meticulously and bandage her tail from the dock to just below the bone of the tail. Incorporate the remaining loose hairs by folding them up over the bandaged area and continue bandaging until all hairs are covered. A 3-inch sterile gauze bandage is ideal, for it is disposable; however, a freshly laundered leg bandage is acceptable.

The bandage protects the tail hairs from contamination and prevents interference of the tail with delivery. The bandaged tail is out of the way of the mother, the foal, and the attendant.

The bandage, which should be removed after the afterbirth is passed, prevents the tail from becoming soaked in feces, urine, and placental fluids and thus, hopefully, eliminates an undesirable source of irritation, contamination, and potential infection.

A last-minute check of the stall for any offending areas or dangerous projections (nails, board edges, tubs, or buckets) is a sound preventive measure. The attendant now has the difficult task of quietly leaving the stall, to wait patiently and observe.

Stage II

The start of the second stage of labor is easily recognized by the rupture of the placental membranes, which releases a large volume of fetal fluid. This is referred to as "the water bag breaking."

As many mares break this membrane while standing as do those who go down to a resting position.

From the moment the water bag breaks until the foal is completely delivered and respiration has started, *time is precious and very short*. Once this second stage is started, strict, alert watchfulness is essential. Delivery will progress relentlessly until completed.

At this point, let me make it clear that there is a double-sac arrangement that has been protecting the foal throughout its fetal life. The foal lives in its intimate amniotic sac, which floats throughout gestation in a surrounding insulation of fetal fluid, fully contained within an outer, heavy, supportive second sac—the allantois chorion. This in turn is attached to the endometrium or one-cell thick inner lining of the uterus.

When the cervix is fully dilated, the fetus enters the birth canal and is moved along by powerful uterine contractions to that point at which the foal's foot, still encased in the amniotic sac, ruptures the outer sac—the allantois chorion or placenta. It is this rupture that produces the great escape of fluid.

This water, in reality the amniotic fluid, not only lubricates the mare's reproductive tract but provides vital moisture and the lubrication necessary for easy delivery of the foal. The foal is actually delivered in its own protective, slippery, water-filled membrane—the amniotic sac.

After the great rush of water, usually several gallons in volume if properly released, the mare should lie down. She will usually remain up on her sternum, in a doglike position, for a short period before rolling over on her side. She then assumes a position with all four legs extended stiffly in a manner peculiar to mares and also (interestingly enough) to sows.

This position is an indication that she is down to serious business. A laterally recumbent position is helpful because her body weight complements the uterine contractions as well as the dynamic abdominal contractions.

Her closed glottis makes possible positive pressure to reinforce the diaphragmatic action, thus helping to push out the fetus effectively in a rapid, explosive fashion.

Occasionally a mare will remain on her feet, walking around the stall after the second stage of labor is under way. She may rise, then go down again, with the foal's forefeet (and even the head) already presented.

This is frightening to see, but with a quiet mare it is a waiting game. Stay out of the stall and, if given a chance, the mare will probably go down and deliver normally. If the mare insists upon staying on her feet or becomes violent—placing the foal in jeopardy—then it becomes necessary to enter the stall to protect the foal.

If, while she is standing or walking, powerful abdominal contractions are visible, it is clear that the mare intends to foal standing and help is definitely required. Ideally, one should have two or more persons present under these circumstances. One person should be at the mare's head to prevent her from walking, and one or more are usually required to deliver the foal and to prevent it from dropping to the ground, prematurely rupturing the cord or possibly sustaining injury to its head, neck, or spine.

However, if everything is proceeding normally, the delivery will go along unassisted. The attendant should stay quietly out of the mare's view and allow her to go down. It is quite evident that all the preparations and as much knowledge as can be gathered should be available, with skilled personnel standing in the wings—all ready to act if needed. When the mare is down, it is permissible for the attendant to enter the stall unobtrusively to check on her position. If she has chosen a poor location—too close to the stall wall for safe delivery—she should be forced to rise and, hopefully, reposition herself correctly. If necessary, grasp her legs and pull her clear of any obstructions.

At this juncture, if you see a grayish-white sac enclosing a forefoot beginning to appear through the vulvar lips, you can assume that the delivery is progressing normally. However, the attendant should be acutely aware that *just before or simultaneous with* the rupture of the placental membranes is the moment when a foot, encased in the amniotic sac, can become lodged in the roof of the vagina and the floor of the rectum.

If, after two or three nonproductive contractions, the sac is not visible and a profound bulge of the rectum can be seen appearing with the contractions, an immediate exploratory examination must be made.

The attendant should rapidly scrub hands and arms; then, with fingers cupped, his hand should enter the vulvar lips and locate the elevated leading foot. After he is sure that the foot is lodged, he should quickly rupture the sac, introduce his cupped hand into the sac, and place his palm over the sharp little foot to serve as a shield for the roof of the vagina.

Surprisingly, the foot will easily align itself, which allows the process of delivery to resume.

The mare's reproductive future may be preserved by this simple but essential act. If the foal's foot position is not corrected, the tremendously powerful forces of delivery behind it will inadvertently injure the reproductive tract and sometimes destroy perineal tissue from the point of penetration outward, resulting in a rectovaginal tear.

If for any other reason the sac does not appear after several unproductive efforts on the part of the mare, you are well advised to summon help immediately; any delay may cost the life of the mare, the foal, or both.

Instantly, after calling for assistance, force the mare to rise and keep her walking until help arrives. By this action the fetus is allowed to gravitate back down into the abdomen and may be repositioned in the large, roomy uterus. This is the *only* known way to delay the delivery process safely until your veterinarian arrives.

Getting the mare up on her feet prevents the loss of valuable fluids from the placenta that are essential to a lubricated, satisfactory delivery; it also prevents her powerful contractions from wedging the foal into an irretrievably dangerous position.

Walking a large mare with a questionable malpresentation, be it major or minor in degree, can inflict no harm because the heavy mare will eventually drop down anyway, in spite of all human efforts. Perhaps one can avert a condition that could become irreversible if the delivery process were allowed to proceed without interruption.

The walking might just provide the time necessary for veterinary assistance to arrive. When there is any doubt, the safest procedure is to insist that the mare stay on her feet as long as possible.

Usually, forceful abdominal contractions will continue at intermittent intervals throughout the second stage of labor. It is normal to observe two to four powerful contractions interrupted by short rest periods of perhaps 10 to 30 seconds. When the grayish sac appears, subsequent to or concurrent with the onrush of water, one forefoot will be found enclosed in the sac, 6 to 8 inches in advance of the second forefoot. Shortly after, the muzzle will follow, lying on or to the side of the forelegs. The angulation created by this position permits one elbow and shoulder to precede the other through the birth canal, thereby reducing the circumference of the foal's shoulder mass.

The average mare will bear down with continuing contractions so as to expel the foal until the head and neck appear; then her efforts cease and she rests for a short period. She is usually exhausted by this time because, although only the head and neck are visible, the shoulders have actually just cleared the pelvic canal.

After her short rest she will generally finish delivering the chest, abdomen, hips, and hind legs with relative ease.

The time required from the start of the second stage of labor to completion of delivery can extend from 20 to 60 minutes and still be within normal range.

If all is well, the prudent attendant may quietly crouch behind the mare as she lies on her side. Entering the stall too soon may distract the mare and cause her to rise, disrupting the foaling process. However, entering the stall too late may delay recognition of problems.

When the front feet and legs are well in sight, the slippery and surprisingly tough membrane should be opened and turned back away from the foal. Scissors will be helpful, for this sac is difficult to tear open with your bare hands. By sliding a scrubbed hand inside the slippery, well-lubricated sac, the attendant will immediately feel the foal's legs: all this while the amniotic sac is protecting the mare's birth canal from irritation, trauma, and possible infection. One forefoot should be encountered instantly, closely followed by the second forefoot, then the muzzle. The forefeet can be grasped if one is very careful to maintain the one-in-advance-of-the-other position in order not to alter the single-shoulder presentation. Traction may be applied during, *and only during,* the mare's contractions. Between contractions *just adequate manual traction* should be maintained to preserve the forward progress that has been achieved. This reduces the degree of fatigue for the mare and shortens the delivery time—which benefits the foal as well as the mare.

When applying traction, care should be taken to maintain the foal's legs, head, and neck on a plane parallel to the mare's vertebral column until the shoulders have cleared the pelvic canal. This has occurred when the forefeet, knees, head, and neck are visible through the vulvar lips. At this time traction, be it ever so gentle, should be directed slightly toward the mare's hocks; obviously this will make passage of the contours easier, as the foal's abdomen, hips, and hind legs are passed.

Excessive traction *should be avoided at all cost.* It is unlikely that the strength of one person could be harmful to either mare or foal; however, the combined strength of two or more untrained, enthusiastic helpers could inflict irreparable damage to both the mare's genital tract and the vulnerable foal.

Do not hurry the mare's delivery. Permit her to deliver at her own rate, so long as the foal continues to advance with each contraction. Traction applied, other than concurrently with the mare's contractions, could provoke too rapid a delivery. Nature will normally allow adequate time and proper relaxation of the reproductive tract to permit passage of the foal into its new external environment.

As pointed out earlier, the mare usually ceases and rests for a short

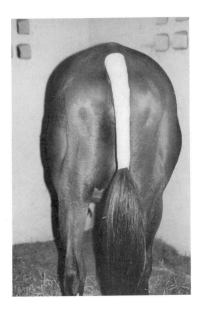

Parturition. A normal delivery.

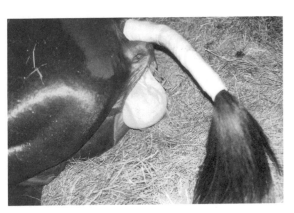

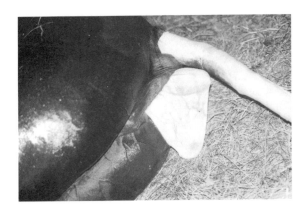

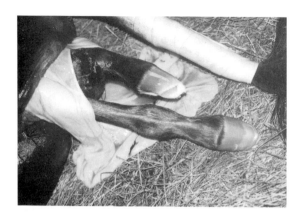

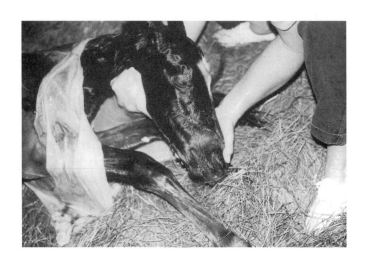

while after the head and neck have appeared. The attendant should do nothing to interrupt this brief rest period. A quiet environment is essential. Any distraction could disturb the matron when she most deserves privacy.

This momentary pause in the delivery process permits the watchful attendant quietly to cope with the membranes that should be cleared away from the head of the new foal—especially those from the nostrils. It is not unusual to see bluish-white oral and nasal mucosa at this point in delivery; there is no reason for alarm at the sight of a blue tongue extending from the foal's mouth.

If after one or two minutes the mare does not resume active labor, gentle traction exerted on the foal's front legs will stimulate delivery. The shoulders, thorax, abdomen, hips, and hind legs, contained within the amniotic sac, will appear.

Initiation of the foal's respiration is stimulated by reflex. A normal foal will be breathing by the time its hind feet arrive in the world. But if this has not been accomplished by that time, every effort should be made to clear the nasal passages of fluids and accumulated excretions.

Merely allowing the head to drop to the side of the forelegs during delivery (nose downward, but free of the bedding) seems to aid in the escape of nasal fluids, reduces the chance of pulmonary fluid retention, and enhances oxygenation with the expansion of the lung tissue.

Very careful use of a small rubber bulb for aspiration of the nasal passages may be helpful. A small oxygen unit for use in aiding the start of respiration is commonly found in large equine nurseries. However, a word of caution: this modern practice *absolutely* requires trained personnel because improper or continued use of oxygen can be very harmful to foals.

As the newborn arrives onto the bedding, the remaining amniotic sac should be removed from the hind legs, after which the foal's entire body and extremities should be rubbed dry immediately with the towels you have ready. Vigorous toweling stimulates both respiration and circulation, and creates warmth as it absorbs the moisture from the foal's sometimes heavy coat. Such care reduces some of the initial stress on the foal and helps to make its introduction into the world a little less traumatic.

The horse has an unusually long umbilical cord compared with other species; this provides continued communication with the mother's endometrium for several minutes after delivery of the foal into its strange, new environment.

An intact cord is essential to the foal's life during a normal delivery and is absolutely imperative during a delayed delivery. *It is of utmost importance to prevent premature rupture of the umbilical cord,* for the intact cord provides continued maternal support to the foal, even though it is now outside the protective uterus.

A precious bonus of about 1 pint of oxygenated and enriched blood is still waiting to pass from the maternal placenta into the foal's circulatory system. If the cord ruptures or fails to function, this added uterine-blood transfusion remains in the placenta, serving no purpose at all. Eventually it is lost in the bedding.

Everyone should pray that the mare will remain down, resting quietly, and allow the attendant to curl her leggy foal close to her hindquarters in order to avoid breaking the cord before the end of the umbilical pulsations.

The attendant should support the foal against the mother with one hand and gently hold the cord with the other hand to check the strong pulsations, which usually continue for a minute or a minute and a half after delivery.

When the pulsations cease, the foal should be allowed to kick away from the mare, finally rupturing the cord as nature intended. The umbilical cord should not be severed other than by natural means. If you are in any doubt about this, take no action until you have consulted with your veterinarian.

The navel antiseptic in your medicine box should be applied as soon as the cord breaks. Make *very sure* that the navel stump is well saturated before it touches any bedding or contaminants.

For generations horse people have had to endure the fear that a nervous matron may suddenly jump to her feet immediately postpartum and prematurely break the cord. In her determination to find her newborn, in spite of her total exhaustion, on weakened hind legs and with staggering gait, such a mare presents a real hazard to herself and her foal. By such violent actions the cord is prematurely broken, or the foal may be forcibly lifted up and, sometimes, pulled into the path of her unsteady hind legs.

Today there is a trend to inject a tranquilizer, under veterinary supervision, of course, at the onset of the second stage of labor in order to prevent injury to the mare or foal. This type of tranquilizer can be used without fear of any depressant effects on the contractions or the overall delivery process. It is obviously beneficial, self-explanatory, and especially comforting to the owner of the mare.

The normal postpartum mare will remain down for a minimum of a few minutes to a maximum of an hour. It is not unusual for the comfortably resting mare to remain down even though her new foal is on its feet and almost ready to nurse. But protracted time down is cause for concern and your veterinarian should be called.

If the mare chooses to remain down after the cord has been broken, the foal can then be slid around to her head so that she may inspect, lick, and become acquainted with her newborn, while still enjoying a well-earned rest.

As the mare regains her feet, your first concern should be for the safety of the foal. The attendant should protect it until the large, weakened matron has had time to regain her stability and awareness, and until she can locate and recognize the damp creature that is her new baby.

When the mare is back on her feet, with the foaling membranes trailing behind her, it is essential that the attendant tie a respectable knot in the slippery amnion. Tie it so that the sac is elevated above both the bedding and the mare's feet, permitting its own weight and pressure to remain on the still-attached maternal placenta.

This is not always as easy as it sounds, but it is vitally important to prevent the mare's hind feet from accidentally stepping on the amniotic sac, which would create enough undue pressure to result in severe injury to and bleeding in the uterine lining and cervical canal. Such trauma to the reproductive tract could cause scar-tissue formation, with subsequent inability to regenerate normal tissue, and possible resultant infertility.

I must stress the importance of this simple attention as an invaluable service to preserve the mare's reproductive future.

As the membranes slowly peel away from the maternal endometrium and descend into full view, it often is necessary to retie the knot in order to maintain its proper height.

In the case of a first foal out of a maiden mare, the attendant should be careful to avoid having wet, placental membranes hanging over the hocks of the nervous new mother; such an unfamiliar sensation might cause her to kick at whoever attempts to gather up the translucent amniotic sac in order to tie it securely above hock level.

DELAY

It is well for you to know that whatever triggers the second stage of labor into action can sometimes misfire, resulting in the loss of foals through cessation of the labor process. Many foals literally die in the birth canal for want of an active, timely delivery. Failure of continuity of the process can also adversely affect the mare—the delay in delivery time as well as the weight on her pelvis for a prolonged period may result in some degree of ataxia, or muscle incoordination, or paresis, which is partial paralysis.

Inefficiency in the second stage of labor occurs more frequently in maiden mares, less often in *multipara* mares. In the maiden mare, uterine inertia is primarily the result of hormone deficiency; while in older mares who have had many pregnancies a reduced amount of uterine muscle tone is a handicap, as is fatigue.

Very old mares should be watched carefully for this interruption in the delivery sequence, for they are prone to uterine inertia. If, for any cause, labor is delayed for any period of time, serious problems are indicated and your veterinarian should be summoned instantly.

The larger breeding farms that produce more than 100 foals each season handle all routine foalings with their own personnel. But it is truly an unusual year if I am not called upon at least six or seven times to attend an unusual situation within this number of foals, or handle life-or-death emergencies with their foaling mares.

Ninety-five percent of mares will deliver unassisted, if everything goes according to nature's plan. This truly seems miraculous when one considers the complexity of parturition, the explosive nature of delivery, and the overall narrow margin of safety.

To the lay person the remaining 5 percent of mares who may be in trouble might seem insignificant, but the seriousness of the situations represented by this small percentage of deliveries shows clearly the formidable physical and mental demands made upon practicing veterinarians by critical complications. Reduction of this 5 percent figure is a major goal in the professional life of the practitioner.

Oddly, the percentages favor the owner who raises only a few foals each year, though he or she is not exempt from problems.

Just recently I was called late in the evening by a young couple who had just pulled a dead foal from their mare. They explained that the mare had lost a great deal of blood and was unable to get to her feet.

When I reached their well-tended and attractive little barn, their faces—white with fatigue and concern—somewhat prepared me for what was to follow.

The mare was down in a stall that was literally covered with blood and a beautiful dead foal lay beside her.

Startled by my appearance, the mare lifted her head and made a feeble but unsuccessful attempt to rise. After administering an injection to the mare to make her more comfortable, and running intravenous fluids and medications into her for hours, the mare was finally able to stand.

According to the young couple, the foal had been presented normally with both forefeet in advance of the muzzle. At this point the mare had begun to throw herself around the stall and her contractions ceased. I examined the mare and the true tragedy was revealed. The forefeet had been deflected and the foal emerged through a rectovaginal rent that had been torn beside the rectum.

In their anxiety the owners were not aware of the location of the foal and with their combined strength had forced the foal through the unnatural opening, only to find that the foal had died during their frantic efforts, which had undoubtedly enlarged the tear.

After extensive repairs the mare was able to conceive late in the following year. These young people were fortunate; they could have lost their mare as well as the foal or, at best, have had a mare no longer able to reproduce.

Representing the other side of the coin, a friend and client has bred an occasional mare and has had perhaps a dozen or so foals without incident over a period of twenty years. She will inform you unequivocally that, based on *her* years of experience, mares require only superficial supervision during foaling.

Stage III

As the foal enters the world, the dam reaches the third stage of labor. A profound physiological process has now been started in the mare, from which her reproductive system may not be completely free or totally regenerated for a month or longer.

This third stage of labor can be divided into visible evidence and invisible physiological changes.

The visible aspect is the expulsion of the fetal membranes. The average healthy mare expels the placental membranes with the gray, allantoic surface of the placenta outermost.

When a mare regains her feet, immediately postpartum, the fetal membranes will be very much in evidence—hanging through the lips of the vulva. A heavy, gray membrane, interlaced with white veins, will be uppermost, with the glistening, slippery amnion lower and, most likely, trailing in the straw. The gray, upper membrane is the allantois chorion (or maternal placenta) turned inside out by the direct pull of the attached umbilical cord—much the way a person would peel off a sock. The foal is delivered *in advance* of the placenta and *within* its inner amniotic sac. At this point, the heavy placenta's smooth gray surface assumes a drapelike contour and is expelled, following the amnion and the cord.

At this point it is perfectly normal for the dark reddish area of the placenta to be visible sometimes as the under surface of the now inside-out placenta. This angry red area represents the part most intimately identified with the uterine surface, where all gas and nutrient interchanges have been occurring while the fetus was *in utero*.

Early or premature placental separation will result in presentation of the dark, reddish maternal chorion surface outermost and the smooth, gray allantois surface innermost. In such cases—when a premature total separation of the membrane from the endometrium occurs prior to its expulsion—this angry red placenta is outermost.

These placental membranes, or afterbirth, should be expelled naturally within a short time by the normal mare. The average time involved in separation and passing varies from the normal 5 to 45 minutes. If a mare has not "cleaned" or passed the afterbirth within two hours after delivery, the afterbirth is considered to be retained, indicating a pathologic disorder. Then it is essential to summon your veterinarian, who will examine and properly treat your mare to help her in the release of the afterbirth.

It is considered a cardinal sin to apply or permit manual traction to aid in the expulsion of the mare's afterbirth. It is well-documented that, in contrast to all other domesticated animals, the nature and type of placentation in the equine cannot withstand or endure separation brought about by any means other than that of strictly physiologic release. Manual traction is *strongly opposed* by equine authorities because it will certainly result in untold damage to the endometrium—directly affecting future fertility.

In those infrequent cases during delivery when the amniotic sac is detached from the umbilical cord and the still-attached placenta by the struggling foal, the natural gentle traction provided by the weight of the sac is absent and this can delay the normal separation and passing of the placenta.

If this should occur, pick up the amniotic tissue, gather it at its center, and tie it with baling twine to the broken umbilical cord extending through the vulvar lips. Nature's traction is thus reestablished. If the cord is not present, the amniotic sac can be tied to any part of the placenta that is available—producing almost the same result.

When the membranes have totally passed, they should be placed in a tightly covered container to protect them from curious dogs and cats until a professional inspection can be conducted. The veterinarian will carefully spread the placenta out on the ground to determine its completeness and consistency. Size, weight, and color will be checked, and from these an overall impression of health or disease can be determined easily.

Immediately after the placental membranes have been passed by the mare, the uninitiated may be puzzled by the appearance of a brown, free-floating object from within the placental tissues that looks like a "spare"

Afterbirth was tied, but the mare is slowly releasing the allantois chorion. As it slips, it should be retied to prevent the mare from inadvertently stepping on it, causing irreparable damage to the uterine lining.

Complete placenta—no hippomanes.

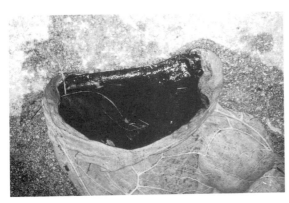

Aperture in the body of the placenta, through which the foal emerged. The dark red surface is intimately attached to the endometrium (inner surface of the uterus).

Nonpregnant horn of the placenta. It is recognized by its wrinkles and smaller circumference. This horn is more likely to be fragmented and thus retained postpartum.

Pregnant horn of the placenta. It is large and smooth and seldom, if ever, retained.

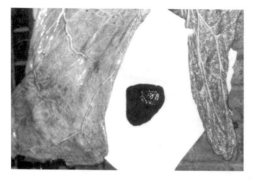

A free-floating body (acellular), the hippomanes (placed on a white paper towel), is found in 90 percent of all afterbirth membranes. Function unknown.

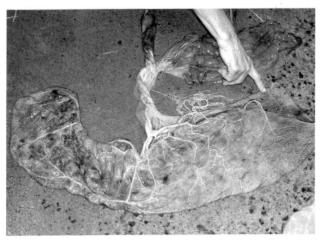

Incomplete placenta. A portion of the afterbirth is still attached inside of the mare. If this is not recognized, the mare will founder and die of blood poisoning (septicemia).

Multiple fertilized ova, each with its own umbilical cord, found commonly in mares' placentas. Most mares deliver one healthy foal. Some inner regulatory mechanism of selection must arrest these fertilized ova.

part. This substance, called hippomanes, resembles a liverlike sponge with its irregular shape, amorphous mass, and rubberish consistency. It ranges in size from 4 to 6 inches in length and 3 to 4 inches in width, and is 1 to 1½ inches thick.

The function of this mass in the placental tissues has remained a mystery, for its presence and significance are unexplained. Basically it is fibrin in nature, with no clearly defined cellular structure. The hippomanes is thought by some scientists to be associated with progesterone production and thus with maintenance of pregnancy.

An expelled placenta mirrors the uterus by the presence of a distinct body with a large rent where the foal emerged and two distinct horns. The large, smooth *pregnant* horn of the placenta is distinguishable from the smaller, deeply ridged, and multisacculated nonpregnant (nongravid) horn.

To any experienced practitioner, the placenta reveals the genital health of the mare and her chances of regaining fertility. Thus, the practitioner is alerted not only to immediate postpartum needs of the mare, but also to any needs of the neonatal or newborn foal. The whole complex story can be interpreted swiftly by an experienced eye.

In the postpartum period the defenses of the uterus are at their lowest ebb; consequently, any indication for or justification of human intervention immediately postpartum must outweigh the dangers of such examination.

At this moment, the huge, empty, thin-walled, pendulous uterus contains a strong negative pressure, or vacuum, created by the expulsion of the fetus, the fetal fluids, and membranes.

When the mare arises after foaling, the downward pull of the trailing membranes opens the vulva and normally admits a large volume of air. The additional insult of a uterine examination allows another inrush of microbe-filled air to fully inflate, contaminate, and possibly infect an otherwise healthy mare. Even in knowledgeable, competent hands the need must be extremely urgent to risk anyone examining a mare's reproductive tract before the *eighth* postpartum day.

There are only four exceptions to this hard and fast rule:

1. An obviously sick septicemic foal;

2. Dystocia or difficult delivery;

3. Intrauterine infection—profuse vulvar discharge;

4. Incomplete placenta (failure to clean completely).

GENERALIZED TREATMENT FOR ANY BROOD
MARE IN ABOVE CASES

1. Recognition of sick or septicemic foal; weak, undersized, scours, eating or not eating, febrile or afebrile.

Immediately examine placenta for color, size, weight, and completeness. Veterinarian then should flush matron with 1 pint of Zonite in 1 gallon of sterile water, using a Foley catheter to assess color of back flow and repeat daily as indicated for three days. Betadine solution serves well in some cases. Wait until the eighth or ninth day to take cervical or uterine cultures.

2. Dystocia or difficult delivery: see chapter on dystocia.

Gynecologic examination and treat as above. Delay any required suturing or surgical repair until the eighth or ninth day.

3. Intrauterine infection manifested by profuse vulvar discharge.

Gynecologic evaluation and treatment as above.

4. Incomplete placenta—prudent examination will reveal missing part or parts. *Never permit manual removal.* Place antibiotic boluses deep into the stretched uterus for three days. Support daily with injectable antibiotics and keep a daily temperature chart. By the end of third day, the fragment should be freely accessible in the body of the uterus. No traction is ever needed!

Should any of these conditions exist, competent veterinary treatment is required.

The tip of the nonpregnant placental horn is the most likely fragment to be found attached in the nonpregnant uterine horn. If attached fragments are discovered and permitted to remain in position, and if appropriate local medication is infused into the uterine horn, along with systemic support, these fragments then are usually found floating free in the body of the uterus within twenty-four hours. *Traction of any kind should not be undertaken to free these fragments.*

The physiologic release of placental fragments by means of medication then makes possible simple manual removal from the uterine body. Note that this manual removal of the offending fragment is absolutely essential or it will remain in the body of the uterus and cause serious consequences.

Laminitis (common founder) or septicemia (blood poisoning) and, perhaps, death can result from the retention of the attached or floating fragment.

When observing a questionable mare, any attendant is well advised to immediately begin a twice daily temperature reading and chart recording.

My experience has revealed that a dramatic spike in body temperature

(103°–105°F) is the first true symptom of septicemia (blood poisoning) resulting from a retained placental fragment.

The average mare with a retained placental fragment usually appears asymptomatic—that is, symptomless. Her relatively normal appetite and attitude are misleading until the sudden onset of symptoms appears about 24 to 48 hours postpartum. The alarming part is that once symptoms develop they are difficult, if not impossible, to reverse, in spite of treatment. But it is not impossible to arrest them; therefore I stress the importance of a knowledgeable, conscientious examination of a shed placenta—that same discarded placenta that you carefully collected and secured in a clean container to await the arrival of your veterinarian.

No two placentas are ever exactly alike, so it requires wide experience to interpret the messages revealed by this close scrutiny.

The invisible aspect of the third stage of labor involves the internal changes that occur immediately after birth. Subsequent expulsion of discharged exudates and dynamic fluid exchanges are aided by muscle fibers under hormonal control to bring about the ultimate involution—reduction in size—of the uterus following delivery.

The rate of involution and the subsequent efficiency of the uterus differs from mare to mare. Some mares return to breeding soundness by their foal heat, which may vary from the eighth to the twelfth postpartum day. (Old-timers insisted upon the ninth day, without consulting the mare.) Other mares continue to exhibit a poor degree of uterine involution on their second heat, which varies from the twenty-seventh to the thirty-second postpartum day. Clearly the ability of the uterus to return to its nongravid size, so that it is healthy and capable of supporting a new pregnancy, depends on various factors. They include:

1. Good physical condition, reflecting adequate prenatal care;

2. A normal, smooth delivery, free of complications;

3. A reproductive tract free from trauma and intrauterine infection;

4. Prompt, proper, and complete postpartum care;

5. An individual mare's innate hardiness, including her ability to regenerate and recover adequately;

6. The age of the mare and number of her previous pregnancies;

7. Genetic or familial fertility.

These factors will determine the mare's ability to involute, repair, and regenerate her reproductive tract.

The quantity and quality of her milk production is also a direct reflection of the health of a mare's uterus, and her ability to provide nourishment for her foal can be affected by any combination of those seven factors—especially by the quality of her prenatal care.

There are three interrelated actions that can cause the apparent coliclike symptoms by some mares, either immediately postpartum or as much as several hours after delivery:

1. The gradual peeling away of the fetal membranes from the maternal endometrium as these membranes are passed;

2. The profound physiologic changes occurring as the uterus begins to return to a nongravid condition;

3. The strong uterine contractions, creating postpartum pain induced by action of the pituitary gland.

These contractions aid in the expulsion of the placental membranes. After the membranes are expelled, they will continue in varying degrees, depending upon the individual mare's makeup. Continuing action of the contractions brings about cleansing of the large empty uterus of exudates and fluids. Contractions also cause blanching and constriction of open capillaries in the maternal endometrium, thus effectively preventing hemorrhage or excessive blood loss.

The sucking of the foal is also an adjunct; it indirectly stimulates contractions that are responsible for the return to uterine health.

Circulatory changes brought about by dilation and constriction, under hormonal influences, comprise a major part of the postpartum physiologic phenomenon.

We have touched only lightly on an intricate and complex process, although there is sufficient material known at this time for an entire book to be written on the intrauterine chemistry of the mare.

The postpartum pain suffered by the dam is usually shown by her rolling, kicking, straining, tail switching, and occasional breaking out into sweated areas—all of these signs simulating colic. Often more pain is exhibited by individual mares during the third stage of labor than during the two previous stages. Such reactions present an obvious hazard to the mare, her foal, and their attendant. Unfortunately, they occur in the immediate postpartum period when the neonatal foal is least able to protect itself. This is the time to bring your vial of Dipyrone from the refrigerator and hastily inject 40cc IM and repeat in ½ hour if needed. Combine with 2–4 ounces of an oral colic mixture prepared in advance by your veterinarian.

Each of the three stages of labor presents certain periods that are critical to the survival of the foal and the safety of the mare. It is vitally important that impending dangers be recognized. During the first stage, it is difficult for even the most experienced foaling attendants to identify an interruption of progress in time to act appropriately. Throughout labor, as in the first phase, mishaps occur that the best of attendants later recall with deepest regret, vowing to sharpen their powers of observation in the future. There is no discredit in being panicked enough to call for professional help.

What *is* unforgivable is for someone to stand by and watch while events take place that too often are disastrously irreversible.

One dark, sleepy morning about 4 o'clock I was suddenly roused from bed to attend a foaling mare. After receiving directions to the farm, I hurried to my car and drove the five-mile distance. It seemed to take an eternity.

A young man met me with a small dim flashlight as I approached the lane to the farm. He informed me that the lane was impassable and that I must follow him on foot for the remaining distance to the barn. Surprised, I snatched my black bag and a pail with some cotton, and started the trek behind the pale yellow light. I had to scurry over rough terrain to keep up with the worried young man and the fast-disappearing light. No lights could be seen ahead at the barn and I was then told that no electricity was available.

I followed the tiny gleam of light into the barn: as my eyes gradually adjusted to the darkness, I finally was able to see a large, heavy-structured mare standing almost motionless in the stall.

With outstretched hands I located and felt her distressed body, which was covered with dried sweat, with warm and cold patches discernable on her hide. I knew that we were in for real trouble.

As I approached her hindquarters and proceeded to examine the quiet mare, one hind leg suddenly lashed out in pain. A strand of amniotic tissue was dangling from beneath her heavy wet tail. This immediately signaled the seriousness of the situation.

I scrupulously but swiftly scrubbed my hands and arms and asked that proper restraint be applied to the mare so that I could examine her thoroughly in safety. Exploration of the mare's vaginal vault revealed a large foal properly presented with its head and forefeet at the vaginal vestibule. The foal was extremely dehydrated and obviously dead.

Heartsick, I began to deliver a large, fully developed colt in the usual manner, but with great care; it was most important to be sure that the mare's reproductive tract would not suffer any permanent damage.

The agitated young man began to tell his story as I carefully removed the dead foal. About 1:00 A.M. he had found the restless mare steaming slightly and covered with sweat. Shortly afterward he saw her expel a small quantity of fluid, drop down in the straw and, after a few feeble muscular contractions, regain her feet. The mare had stood, shifting her weight in an uncomfortable manner, and small amounts of fluid were occasionally expelled. Her pain was evident, but not profound. She became quieter and her coat eventually dried out about 3:00 A.M.

Devoted and conscientious, the attendant remained quietly at her side watching every movement until he finally sensed that all was not well. Where was the foal? Leaving the mare, he ran for a half mile to the nearest phone and put in his call for help.

Reconstructing what had happened, I could tell that the mare had obviously started to deliver in a normal manner, but suddenly, after breaking her water bag, was unable to muster enough uterine tone and abdominal muscular contractions to expel the large foal. The foal was properly positioned and ready for entrance into the outside world—yet missed it by only a few short inches. Either hormonal failure, exhaustion, or a combination of each can be the cause of cessation of labor—usually resulting in a dead foal.

A delay in labor from any cause is perilous and results in reduced amounts of oxygen and nutrients for the foal. In this case, the amniotic fluids had escaped much earlier, making delivery difficult because lubrication and moisture were lacking and harmful tissue changes were taking place.

An alert and knowledgeable attendant should recognize any interruption in the delivery process and immediately summon help. Some older, learned brood mare owners are perfectly competent and capable of cautiously slipping a scrubbed hand between the vulvar lips of the mare to discover the location of the forefeet and the head. If the foal is properly presented, a simple tug on the forefeet can, in some cases, stimulate and reestablish active labor.

This young horseman had spent his entire life on a farm, attending dogs, cats, sheep, goats, and cows—all of which he had watched through gestation and assisted when they were delivering.

Unfortunately this was his first foaling.

The young man had assumed that the mare's situation could be equated with all the animals he had previously watched during parturition. He had all too naïvely witnessed a critical (and disastrous) example of the unique, irreversible functioning of a brood mare in desperate trouble.

An early, hasty call might have saved the foal. Thank God I could save the mare.

Horses are herbivores with a special type of placenta, totally unlike ruminants and their rugged placentas. Never confuse these facts.

Also, the carnivore and omnivore (hogs and humans) placentas are highly efficient, so therefore quite dissimilar when compared with the equine.

5

Dystocia and Its Various Forms

Dystocia is defined as a difficult or delayed birth. While I do not intend to offer a "crash course" on veterinary obstetrics, I do intend to alert and teach the average caring horseperson how to recognize trouble during parturition and then know how to handle the emergency situation should it arise during delivery.

No one wants to stand by and watch a tragedy develop. By reading this chapter *carefully* and by learning what can be done by memorizing a few basic principals, you may not only save your foal but you may also be of assistance to someone else's foal that's in trouble. Veterinarians cannot always be present, so in lieu of professional assistance or until it can arrive—*read, memorize*, and then with some degree of confidence, go into action.

I know it has been said that a little learning is dangerous, but at the risk of sounding corny—a little knowledge can save a foal and a little more knowledge can save a generation of horses and horsemen.

Educate Yourself and Be Prepared!

I would like to devote the next few pages to all of the unlucky and unfortunate mares, foals and their owners. All have sacrificed and some have suffered greatly, especially those mares who have lost their lives while trying to give birth alone, along with the ones that perished while attended by unknowledgeable, well-meaning people. It is tragic that they suffered when an appropriately timed tug on a foot, or repositioning of a leg may have made the difference.

I find it inexcusable for a matron to be unattended during her time of greatest need. Most of the time Nature, with a little attention, does just fine, but on occasion she slips up, and the equine matron pays the price, often with her life or questionable reproductive future, not to mention the foal's life. On many sad mornings I have been summoned and arrived only to see an exhausted matron with a large fetus inside the birth canal, the nose inches from the precious breaths of life. It is avoidable tragedies such as these that have prompted me to write this book.

People stand by and watch this unnecessary situation occur. If only they had done their homework. Reading, learning, and watching for the "red alert" signals would enable them to get into action and perhaps save the future of the mare and foal.

It has been my experience that the "buffer zone" for error is very narrow or almost nonexistent. If all goes well it looks easy, but a dystocia can strike instantaneously.

The word *dystocia* strikes fear in the hearts of all brood mare owners. Those that have experienced it will never forget the sickening feeling when delivery is suddenly delayed and minutes separate life from death. This is the moment when all your knowledge comes intact and your mind is prepared for any judgment. *DO NOT BE TIMID!*

The Placenta

The mare's placenta is classified as "diffuse" with thousands of tiny villi that project into the uterine lining. It is last on the list of efficiency in its attachment to the maternal uterus. It is also last on the list of durability for the safety and nourishment of the fetus. The uterus and placental attachment belonging to the horse is considered primitive in relation to all other domestic animals, human beings included. Unlike other species, the equine placenta tends to peel away from the walls of the uterus at the slightest provocation—hormonal, infection, or trauma.

It will in some cases begin to fall away in separate loose pockets, and through its feeble and weak attachment, it may precede the birth of the foal, hence placenta previa. Although it occurs in other species, the serious implications in the mare are great. These detached areas serve no protective purpose during birth and compromise the foal's oxygen supply. Placenta previa can also cause physical blockage, thus delaying foaling. A race appears to exist between the foal's arrival into the outside world and oxygen depletion.

The foal, however, is blessed with an unusually long umbilical cord. In some cases this helps maintain the oxygen source to the foal should delivery be delayed or if there is any compromise in placental function.

To further complicate the issue, the foal has characteristics of its own that can add to delayed delivery: the foal's size, shape, and extreme flexibility, not to mention his short body, long slender neck, and disproportionately long limbs. All this predisposes the incidence of malpositioning.

Unfortunately there are those cases where a foal is so large that adjustments are impossible. One can only pray that alignment is precise and Nature is on your side.

How to Recognize Dystocia

There are two major causes of dystocia:

1. Uterine and placental malfunction;

2. Malposition of the fetus.

The three stages of labor in the normal act of parturition have previously been described. I would like to be as accurate about dystocia, but the fact remains there is no known method to predetermine an impending dystocia. However, the ability to recognize stage I labor (active and silent, refer to stage I) is the best red-alert signal for impending trouble when initiating stage II.

The key to success with any impending parturition is proper preparation. This statement will never ring more true than with the onset of stage II (actual delivery time) when a possible dystocia comes into focus. It is indeed too late then to make arrangements. Most mares become intractable with progressive pain and frustration. Prompt, skilled attention is required immediately.

There are many serious and sometimes irreversible cases of dystocia that can be handled only by medical professionals or the very rare and exceptionally well-advised horseman.

Once a mare is bred, you have eleven months to prepare for the big event. During this gestation period you have ample time to map out a course of action with your veterinarian should a tragedy develop. Valid reading material is invaluable when referral is necessary. Discussions with your veterinarian add confidence during this special time.

I intend to detail only the so-called easily correctable problems. Perhaps this will help you save time by recognizing a serious situation quickly and reacting efficiently. Before we embark on the many forms of dystocia, I feel it necessary to elaborate on preparation.

Advance Preparation for an Emergency Dystocia

Especially in the absence of a veterinarian, you first will want to apply a sterile tail bandage and meticulously scrub the mare's entire perineal region.

Then have ready:

- Several pails of clean hot water.
- Smooth slippery antiseptic for use in the pails—Dairmol, Novalson, or any surgical scrub. Avoid alcohol or iodine bases.
- Several rolls of sterile cotton.
- Many laundered and neatly stacked towels.
- Autoclaved obstetrical chains or smooth braided ½-inch ropes, 5 or 6 feet long with a braided loop on one end. Six ropes are usually sufficient.
- Large can of lard (unadulterated) or 1 gallon of heavy grade mineral oil for lubrication purposes.

In dystocia cases most of the natural uterine fluids meant for lubrication have inadvertently escaped prior to assistance arriving on the scene. If caught early and the mare is forced to stay on her feet and walk, then the precious uterine fluids meant for protection during foaling would remain in her abdomen, along with the foal, which would otherwise be lodged into perhaps an irretrievable position.

In advance of an upcoming foaling season, your veterinarian may, upon request, prepare and dispense a syringe and needle with an appropriate sedative just in case he or she cannot be there. The label should be dated and detailed and should be kept in the refrigerator—for *emergency use only!*

The prudent use of the sedative may enable you to explore the mare's vaginal vault, locate the foal and perhaps even determine why she cannot move the foal along.

If you have learned to recognize the signs of stage I as previously described, it will give you a time advantage. Do not leave the mare's side. Most mares' water bags rupture with a rushing sound simultaneously with recumbency—however some mares remain standing. While standing, the amount and the force with which the amniotic fluid is released can, in some instances, be confused and interpreted as simple urination. Be careful not to make this error, as she could be in stage II with no fetal movement—that stage of action and parturition. *Now is the time to watch for foal movement!* If no fetal signs appear, the mare could be suffering with uterine inertia. *Keen observation is vital now.*

Uterine Inertia

Uterine inertia is sneaky and not easily recognized. The mare's water bag does in fact rupture and she takes on the form of a foaling mare. Soon however, the weak intermittent contractions cease and the mare may even resume eating and walking around as though all were normal. This situation can be lethal as the foal's lifeline could or could not be functional.

This is the moment that a well-advised horseman will meticulously scrub and slide a cupped hand inside the mare, determine an aligned foal, and then give a tug on one foot. This small gesture can in fact prompt the mare to resume rhythmic contractions.

There are those rare cases however when a mare needs more than a simple tug to start contractions. Some mares make you do it all alone, giving little or no help and with no contractions. These foals must be manually pulled, ever so gently, into the world, as the mare seems not to care. Some even remain standing. While delivering a foal standing, it is necessary to support the entire weight by holding the foal up near the birth canal to prevent the premature rupture of the umbilical cord.

If the cord remains intact until pulsations cease, the foal will receive an additional 500cc or one pint of extra blood. Otherwise, this blood would be lost in the placental tissue.

Malposition of the Foal

Although uterine inertia can be insidious, make no mistake that the malposition of the foal has its own "devilment." Uterine inertia has a deadly calm stillness. The malpositioned foal can be its own hell to the mare, causing her to react quickly and violently because of the pain.

Recognition of stage I labor brings forth stage II. Begin looking for the grayish-white smooth sac located between the lips of the vulva. Immediately after the water bag ruptures is the time action should take place—the sac should be seen. This sac should encase a tiny foot soon to be followed by another tiny foot with the foal's muzzle nestled either on the top of the legs or alongside. *If* this sac does not appear after two or three powerful contractions and there is no sign of a foal—then this is a *dystocia. Do not wait! Immediately* force the mare to her feet and begin walking her.

Allowing the mare to remain down in a recumbent position, straining with her huge abdominal muscles, could cause the malpositioned foal to become hopelessly locked in the birth canal. Drive the mare to her feet. In some instances a whip must be used—better a few welts than a dead mare!

Once the mare is on her feet, the foal can then slip back into the large, presently stretched uterus. Gravity at this time is on the mare's and the foal's side. Curiously, there have been many cases reported that after walking the mare, foals were apparently repositioned and subsequently delivered without additional aid. This borders on a miracle, but is nonetheless true.

Last but not least, the forced walking prevents loss of precious amniotic fluid so necessary for lubrication. This lubrication is vital to the genital tract and the foal during its excursion through the bony pelvis and birth canal.

In lieu of professional guidance or assistance, a qualified and informed person is a needed asset. His or her newly read or acquired information regarding difficult births and his or her honed skills as a horseperson play a valuable part in mare understanding and restraint.

By this time, meticulous (but rapid) scrubbing from the shoulders down to the hands in one of the aforementioned surgical preparations should almost be completed. When scrubbing, put extra effort on both hands and clean under each fingernail. (Fingernails should have been filed down in advance of her due date.) Everything should be preassembled as time is of the essence. The anxious mare will only tolerate her pain for a short period. Pain is always progressive in severity, never less.

Sedation, especially IV sedation, would indeed be a luxury at this tense period. However, the prudent and humane intermittent use of a twitch can at times give the operator an opportunity to explore and truly assess how serious the blockage or dystocia is.

Even though you may know your mare, be careful—pain can be an unpredictable force and she may lose her normal restraint. I have found that most mares are in such pain that they seem to be unable to kick backward while being forced to walk—but do not count on it.

When you attempt to explore her birth canal, she should ideally be walking in a large circle. This will definitely benefit both the mare and you as the operator. At this time, slip your cone-shaped, clean, lubricated hand in between the lips of the vulva, being careful to place the palm side of your hand next to the hairy, wet foal. Keep the slippery amniotic membranes to the outside of your hand. Keeping the smooth membranes away from your hands and fingers enables you to better distinguish and identify the foal's anatomical parts. Do not panic—a mass of many-layered membranes, often prematurely ruptured, can confuse even the most experienced person. While continuing to walk behind your mare, persistently but cautiously slide your hand forward respectfully and steadily between contractions. Never force penetration during a strong contraction. Wait and make progress while the mare is briefly resting between large contractions.

One man's strength can do harm during repulsion (or pushing the foal backward into the uterus) if applied with great anxiety. Vital tissue, especially the thin membranes that cover the poorly protected bony pelvis, are vulnerable to damage with the slightest trauma. Below is a list of malpresentations that will be explained in detail shortly.

- One foot or leg deflected backward.
- Both fourlimbs deflected backward.
- Head and neck of foal tucked under the pelvic rim.
- Head and neck deflected tightly to one side.
- Both forelegs over the top of the foal's head and neck.
- Upside-down foal.
- Hip lock.
- Hind foot advancing with the body mass and forequarters.
- Breech presentation.

The list is formidable, but be assured that with reading and memorization of basic principals and their reasons, any intelligent and "lucky" farm manager can, in the absence of qualified professionals, attempt to prevent a mare and foal from perishing.

Anything that delays parturition should be considered dangerous and should immediately be treated with the greatest possible skill, haste, and respect for the mare. Even the most seemingly minor aberration or poor position, if not quickly corrected, can result in the death of the mare or foal or both.

Before discussing the major causes and treatments of dystocia, a word of caution! *Ill-advised or misplaced assistance or traction can do more harm than good.* Yes, a strong person can pull a foal from a mare, but the well-intentioned act could be tragic. Most of the time the damage is hidden and not recognized until the veterinarian examines your mare for the next breeding season. *Under no circumstances should a foal be physically pulled from a mare.* She is not a cow!

When traction is necessary, it is vital that the foal be aligned properly. Also, it is important to remember that the floor of the mare's bony canal is the most vulnerable area for stress and sustained weight. I cannot overemphasize the importance of aligning the foal before it enters the canal. It seems uncanny that most dystocias make it to this point and then, if anything goes awry, cessation of progress appears directly over this area. Vital nerves traverse this unprotected area that also add to consequences of a protracted period of dead weight and no normal movement.

The bony pelvic canal is a rectangular-shaped rigid aperture through which all foals must traverse in order to enter the world. If repositioning of the foal is required, however, the foal then must be pushed back out of this narrow inflexible canal and back down into the large uterus. Thus repositioning and necessary adjustments can occur.

When the mare is forced to her feet to walk, the foal automatically slips downward into the large uterus. Oftentimes this is a great advantage. The forelegs tend to slip backward with the body, thus allowing your hand to locate the head and jaw of the foal. Cup your hand under the muzzle and elevate the head into a proper position (the upperside of the forelegs). Steadily guide the forelegs and watch the mare then deliver with relative ease. The old saying: "Proper alignment, easy foaling."

Malpresentations

FOOT OR LEG DEFLECTED BACKWARD

One of the most common causes of a delayed delivery occurs when one of the foal's legs is deflected backward, while the other leg and the head are attempting to make progress. This can be recognized by a hand inspection. Usually one foot can be located with a muzzle nearby.

Have a helper walk the distressed mare, and follow as closely as possible and apply a sterile loop around the available pastern. This rope serves for identification and stabilization. (All horse people, but especially equine obstetricians, should be blessed with long arms and even ones that can stretch when necessary.) Now with great strength and agility, begin with one arm to *push* the looped leg and head backward, down into the stretched uterus. At this time, the other arm should enter the vagina and

First Stage of labor. It is nothing short of a miracle how the term fetus, during Stage I, manages to depart its long-term intrauterine location and align itself within the birth canal. The foal's disproportionately long, slender neck and lengthy, flexible limbs attached to a short torso can only represent a disadvantage. Compared with other species, much can go awry.

These drawings depict three essential position changes required to align the foal in preparation for a successful delivery through the rigid birth canal.

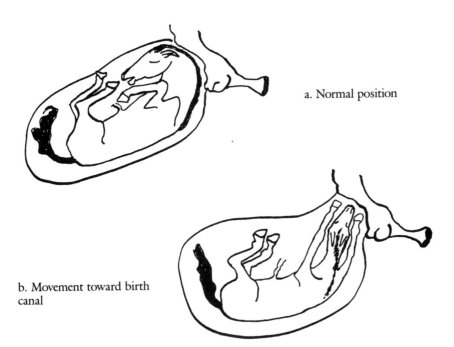

a. Normal position

b. Movement toward birth canal

c. Almost ready

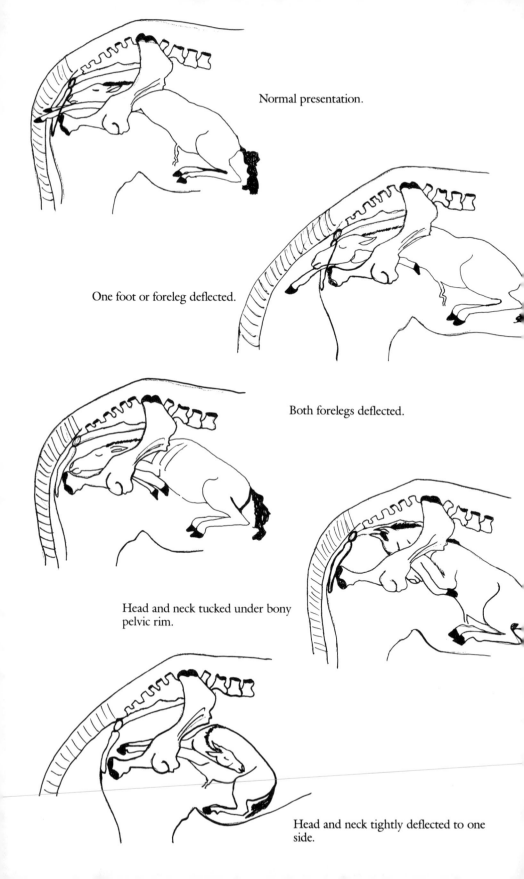

Normal presentation.

One foot or foreleg deflected.

Both forelegs deflected.

Head and neck tucked under bony pelvic rim.

Head and neck tightly deflected to one side.

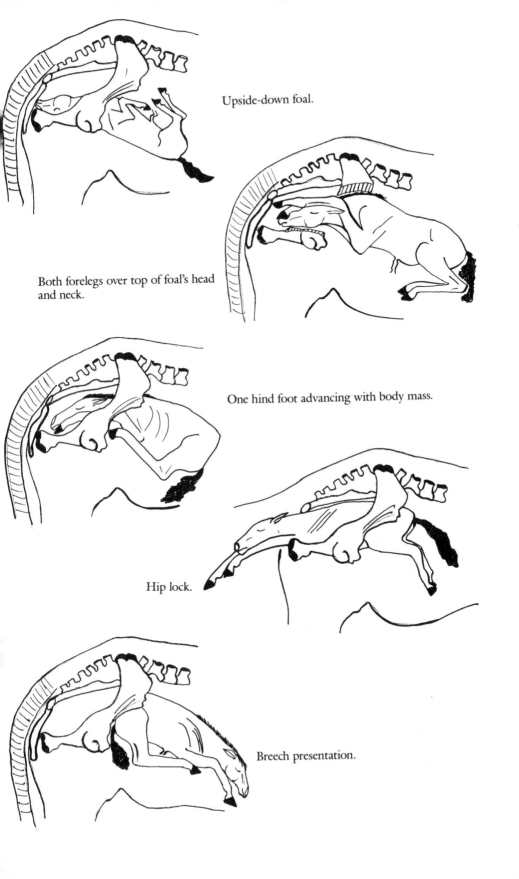

Upside-down foal.

Both forelegs over top of foal's head and neck.

One hind foot advancing with body mass.

Hip lock.

Breech presentation.

search backward for the flexed or locked member. Keep walking and praying that the mare will not decide to kick. *Caution*—when you locate the flexed limb, *grasp it above the knee and elevate it as high as the area will permit*. Simultaneously slip the palm of your other hand underneath the flexed foot. As you elevate with all of your remaining strength, there may be adequate room to slip your hand with palm upward, so that the foot will ease into your palm. As the foot seems to free and fall into your hand, your palm can sustain all stress and prevent puncture of the mare's vital tissues, preserving her future fertility. Under no circumstances should traction be applied until all sharp and heavy structures are aligned and protected manually.

Now slip a little loop of sterile rope over the second pastern and begin slight traction in rhythm with the mare's contractions. By this time the mare most likely will become recumbent and begin serious contractions in order to deliver in as normal a style as possible. Although she is now able to move the foal with each contraction, continue to keep one foreleg slightly in advance of the second leg until you can establish that the shoulders have cleared the cervix, and then a foal is born!

FORELIMBS DEFLECTED BACKWARD

The second most common cause of dystocia in the brood mare occurs when both forelimbs are flexed backward and lodged under the pelvic rim. Usually the complete head of the foal will be presented outside under the tail of the mare. This can be startling, but remember to force the mare to her feet and begin walking her in a circle. Walking in a circle aids the operator, who must follow her every move. Scrub as previously recommended.

The head is very wet and the blue tongue only adds to everyone's anxiety. Be determined. With the mare walking, begin the herculean task. Push the entire head back through the vaginal canal and into the uterus, all the time searching for the forelegs. All backward tractions or pushing should be carefully synchronized between any powerful contractions so the mare won't be injured.

With your hand, carefully follow the foal's head and neck down to the shoulder until you feel a forearm. This method assures you that it is indeed a foreleg before you attach a loop and begin traction. Imagine the damage that could be sustained if the loop was applied to a hind foot! Upon proper identification, apply the loop of soft, strong autoclaved rope, which should be carried around your arm or wrist ready for use.

Secure the loop around the pastern, just above the coronary band and hold on to the rope outside. Repeat the procedure on the opposite limb, again ascertaining that it is a forelimb, and then apply the safety loop. Now align the large head and pull the legs ahead of the foal's head. Be careful at this point to advance only one foreleg at a time; the other foreleg follows closely but never evenly, as the large shoulders must pass through the canal at a slight angle, thus reducing the overall circumference of the shoulders. Remember the bony canal is unrelenting, so hold the ropes snugly. Give and take with mild traction, checking your alignment, and with a little luck a foal is born. Remember the secret to a smooth delivery is in the alignment.

HEAD UNDER THE PELVIC RIM

The third most common cause of dystocia occurs when a foal's head is tucked under the pelvic rim. For some unknown reason it leaves its usual location on top or on one side of the forelegs. When it drops between the forelegs before reaching over the pelvic rim, it can easily drop below the ledge. To recognize this problem, both forelegs can be presented with no evidence of a muzzle, when suddenly all forward motion ceases. After two or three powerful contractions, with the legs remaining in the same position and no muzzle yet in sight, you should quickly scrub and get the mare on her feet and begin walking. Closer observation will show the foal's slender neck arching upward in the cervical canal almost like a cobra. This increases with each powerful contraction while the muzzle continues to become more embedded with each push.

To correct this situation, one must explore the vaginal vault. This is done by sliding a clean, lubricated hand along one of the foal's legs until you discover the lodged chin or muzzle. Now grasp both forelegs and begin to push them steadily backward. This repulsion is done between contractions, of course. Be careful and patient until you reach the point where you can slip your hand between the foal's chin and the hard bony pelvis. With the foal's chin in the palm of your hand, continue carrying it forward while intermittently applying traction to each foreleg. Again I remind you to give and take, while watching the alignment, one leg slightly in front of the other.

Once a foal is repositioned, it always amazes me how rapidly the mare senses that all is well and quickly gets down to business and delivers her foal almost uneventfully.

HEAD AND NECK DEFLECTED TO ONE SIDE

The head and neck turned to one side is another malposition not commonly encountered, but one that is equally serious. In this instance the foal's forelegs appear straight and somewhat ready but nothing more happens. The delay is abrupt and indicates a blockage. Experienced horse people sense immediately that something is wrong. Get the mare on her feet and begin walking. Slide your meticulously scrubbed, well-lubricated hand along one leg on either side. You will feel a mass of tissue on one side only. This is a deflected head and neck turned onto its side and tightly squeezed backward against its rib cage, causing a complete block and cessation of movement, in spite of continued unsuccessful contractions. The massive neck occludes the birth canal, making it literally stuck into this position. Without assistance, this mare and foal would die. Ideally someone in attendance with some training, and in lieu of professional help, will go into action and aid this suffering mare.

If the mare is not already on her feet, get her up immediately and begin walking her. Apply the little autoclaved ropes with the loops around each visible pastern. This will at least insure that you have two of the foal's legs. Then slide your scrubbed, lubricated hand into the birth canal, keeping your palm next to the wet hairy foal and the outside of your hand next to the slippery membranes. Keep the membranes clearly out of your way as they can easily become entangled within your hands and fingers, causing confusion and unnecessary delay.

With concerted strength, begin to apply great backward pressure on the deflected neck while someone else simultaneously applies backward traction on each of the looped visible legs. At this tense moment, your helpers must remain quiet and listen to your commands, reacting accordingly.

Sometimes the neck is so large and so tightly lodged in a flexed position that your hand can hardly make its way through and under the mass of tissue to finally reach the foal's jaw. (I remember once praying that my arm would be long enough!) Adequate lubrication can be a blessing, especially if some of the natural amniotic fluids have escaped. If you can, slide your arm under and downward with the loop woven in your fingers, ready for action, when you finally reach the foal's mouth. When you can determine the foal's jaw, apply the loop of rope in a slip-knot style around only the lower jaw of the foal. Be certain to check that the loop is snugly on the interdental space of the lower jaw, avoiding the tongue, as this area will not injure during traction. The interdental space on a foal is just behind the front (incisors) and just before the normally hidden molars.

There are no teeth present in this prescribed area and it is ideal for traction purposes.

At this moment, complete cooperation is needed by all involved. Instruct your helper to resume backward traction of the forelegs in between contractions while you hold on to the rope securing the lower jaw. When the backward repulsion of the entire foal body finally allows adequate space to slightly move the head of the foal, then instruct your helper to maintain the foal in that position. Once you feel that the foal has been retracted sufficiently, deftly apply traction on the head and jaw. Be patient, as it is exciting to feel the head begin to turn slightly, but the level of the shoulders must be maintained at the body of the uterus or just at the level of the cervical canal. Once the head is straightened and in alignment with all other limbs, then gently apply slight traction in rhythm with the mare's perhaps weakened contractions. She will soon pick up the pace and go on and deliver, once everything is in alignment.

BOTH FORELEGS OVER THE TOP OF THE FOAL'S HEAD

This type of dystocia has a "red alert signal" all its own. Both forelegs are evenly presented and slightly apart with no signs of a foal's muzzle present. Quick observation tells you that the foal's head is missing from its normal perch and immediate action is needed.

Scrub meticulously and quickly. Your helper should have the mare on her feet and walking. While the mare walks, slide your clean, well-lubricated hand inside along the foal's leg, constantly trying to locate the foal's head.

When you finally locate the head, you are in the position to prevent the chin or jaw from lodging into the pelvic rim, stopping a dystocia previously described.

UPSIDE-DOWN FOAL

Recognition of this form of dystocia is not at all difficult. Both forefeet are presented with soles upward, revealing many soft tissue layers on the bottom of the foal's feet. This sight, while unexpected, is unnerving even to the most seasoned horse person.

With all four limbs pointing upward, it would seem safer to turn the forelegs in a twisting manner and attempt to turn the foal onto its stomach or the natural delivery position. However the dangers of free loose legs combined with an untimely powerful contraction by the mare could sustain great trauma, lacerations, or even puncture the vaginal or uterine wall.

I prefer for safety's sake to grasp the straight-up legs and apply downward traction toward the body mass and then, if the foal is in alignment, follow through the canal, continuing to hold the limbs downward until the shoulders clear the canal. Then with well-lubricated hands and arms, reach backward and grasp both hind legs, applying all of your reserve strength to hold the hind legs backward into extension. Continue to hold the hind legs backward until the foal slips out into the world.

One can easily imagine the damage that one loose extended hind leg pointing straight upward inside of the birth canal could inflict on any mare, especially during a strong contraction.

If a veterinarian is fortunate enough to determine this problem early, while the foal is still in the uterus, it may be feasible to rotate and reposition the foal for its excursion. Then the matron will finish the job efficiently.

HIP LOCK

Hip lock is another form of dystocia that develops insidiously and takes everyone by surprise. Just when you think all is well and your mare is foaling fine, all motion ceases abruptly. The foal has cleared the shoulders through the pelvic canal and then all forward motion stops.

Do not panic! Think. Where should the foal's hips be at this moment? The foal's head, forelegs, and thorax (rib cage) are quite visible. A hip lock must be the answer! Quickly scrub.

Immediately grasp each foreleg and cross them, one onto the other in a twisting manner. Simultaneously apply a backward pressure on both forelegs. If this combined action does not promptly produce relief, then quickly but deliberately switch arms and legs, thereby reversing the twisting action. With all of your strength, continue to push the entire forequarters of the foal backward toward the uterus. The release is quite abrupt when it suddenly frees itself. It is a great relief to the mare and she delivers quickly.

HIND FOOT ADVANCING WITH THE BODY MASS AND FOREQUARTERS

This type of dystocia was not recorded in earlier veterinary literature. Just recently it has begun to be recognized and considered as a potentially dangerous dystocia. If uncorrected and forceful traction is insisted upon, this displaced foot can and will tear the mare's vaginal floor, causing her death or damaging her reproductive tract permanently.

The delivery seems to start out quite well, with forelegs, head, and neck presented during each contraction. Then suddenly, just as the shoulders begin to crowd through the tight pelvic canal, a sudden unmistakable stoppage of motion or total blockage appears. All movement of the foal ceases in spite of the mare's powerful persistent contractions. A blockage is a feeling and/or sound which, once experienced, will never be forgotten. Any seasoned brood mare man or woman will turn pale and agree.

Meticulously scrub as previously described and deftly slide your well-lubricated cone-shaped hand in on either side of the foal's not yet visible shoulders. Pause and then wait for the mare's contraction to cease, as any movement of your hand seems to stimulate effort on her part. Then carefully continue to slide your hand down over the ribs and abdomen of the foal. At this point your hand might just touch a little semisolid wet foot where it does not belong. In some cases, it is to be found just in front of the incorrectly forward-flexed stifle, causing the complete blockage of the foal. Consequently, this out of position hind foot has increased the entire circumference of the body mass, making forward or backward movement of the foal impossible.

If the foot cannot be located, then continue to slide your (now numb and bloodless) hand farther downward and slightly underneath the foal's abdomen, precisely on the rim of the bony pelvis. If you find the foot at this most undesirable location, it will have wedged itself (through persistent contractions) forward and downward with the foal's added weight pressing on top of the vulnerable pelvis and its unprotected nerves.

If you do not yet find the foot, retract your hand and arm and hastily, yet respectfully, repeat the same procedure on the opposite side of the foal. You are searching for the cause of a sudden blockage and all symptoms indicate a hind foot forcing its own delivery. This foot is totally out of its prescribed location, deep down into the uterus with its partner foot ready to follow the body of the foal in complete extension.

When you locate this rugged foot, be careful and not overly anxious. Be cautious, as an untimely contraction could easily fracture your hand or arm. *Warning: Do not under any circumstances push this foot backward!*

If you have helpers, instruct them to be alert at this time so as to react to your requests quickly. Slide your well-lubricated hand backward *behind the lodged foot* and grasp the pastern or ankle, then through brute strength attempt to elevate the foot from its mooring. Simultaneously have a helper push the foal backward with great strength and mustered force. When you feel the slightest release or movement, deftly slide your hand from the pastern area toward the foot and with the palm upward catch the foot as it frees from the pelvic tissues or from under the body of the foal. If it all works in the manner in which I have described, no harm will have been done to either the mare or the foal. The mare will startle you with the speed with which she will efficiently complete her parturition.

BREECH PRESENTATION

This is the last malpresentation that I will discuss because all others are in the category of professional veterinary obstetrics.

If you have never witnessed a breech presentation, it can indeed be a frightening sight. You can also become easily confused and excited when the foal is beginning to deliver. It is the experienced veterinarian or farm manager who recognizes the early and peculiar symptoms and springs into action.

Not unlike all other deliveries, once the water bag has ruptured, progressive motion is a must! Breech deliveries notoriously suffer delays more often than any other form of delivery.

To recognize a breech birth, you will see two feet and legs presented *even in length and both are turned downward*, not just slightly twisted, but downward. Scrub. Slide your clean, well-lubricated hand along the two legs. Follow them to the next joint and try to determine whether the joint above the ankle is a knee or hock!

A hock joint in complete extension can simulate a knee and has been known to cause consternation even among professionals. Chestnuts are located above the knee and below the hock, but in a water-soaked foal they are indistinguishable. Then slide your hand further backward, constantly feeling for a displaced head, but keep your hand on the surface of the leg. At this time your hand should feel a small hairy and very wet tail. Now you absolutely know that this is a breech.

Although the foal can be either right side up or on its back, it is definitely better for both the mare and foal if it's on its stomach. This position seems closer to Nature's way and aides in its alignment for delivery. If on its back and the foal is small in relation to the mare's pelvic size, a heroic attempt to twist and rotate the foal could be tried but is ill-advised in the absence of professional assistance.

Apply slight traction on each leg evenly. This encourages the matron to continue with her timely and rhythmic contractions.

I repeat: Although a breech is opposite from the normal, the one and only factor to emphasize is the maintenance of forward motion. While in the breech position, undue compression on the foal's navel cord as it passes through the tight birth canal and over the bony rim can, if delayed, compromise the oxygen flow to the foal. The brood mare characteristically takes a breather and then resumes contractions. Watch that the brief rest does not occur when the umbilicus is resting on the pelvic rim, just prior to delivery of the large shoulders and thorax (rib cage).

Because of the breech position, the chances of the rest period occurring at this most unwanted location is greatly enhanced. Combined with the damaging or added pressure or weight on the cord is the hazard of undue weight and pressure on large unprotected nerves emerging up over the rim of the pelvis. With only a thin membrane covering the bony rim, any delay of motion or any sustained weight can present a threat to the mare and the foal. Remember: Attempt to keep the foal moving, but be gentle at all times. A simple "tug" on a foot or leg can initiate contractions.

The large and infamous obturator nerve is the most commonly affected in breech births. This nerve is responsible for the mare's ability to support her hind limbs upright. If the nerve is only slightly bruised, the mare will usually rise and cope somewhat with the instability. Watch carefully for the safety of your foal at this time. Sustained and protracted pressure on the nerve or the adjacent area can cause partial (paresis) or actual paralysis.

Extreme caution is advised if this condition is suspected. Be aware and watch for instability when the matron decides to rise. This situation could become extremely dangerous if the mare becomes excited and somewhat intractable. A sedative of choice is ideal and useful to have on hand for just such an occasion. By all means, guard the innocent foal, and removing it from the stall is even better. Be certain to keep the foal within the mare's sight at all times.

The unsteadiness could continue from one hour to several days, so be well advised to build a straw bale stock support around her. Most mares cope with this temporary arrangement and settle pretty well with some sedation. Be sure to allow room for the nursing foal.

With each foaling the damage sustained on the nerve tissue progresses and ultimately the mare will be unable to regain her feet after some future foaling. Remember, any slow delivery or stoppage of movement is ominous and reason for concern, but even more so during the breech delivery.

Summary

1. Walk the mare. Keep walking;
2. Push the foal back into the abdomen, then attempt to make adjustments;

3. If the mare is already down and unable to rise, elevate the hind-quarters and lower the head and neck;

4. Use sterile lubricants;

5. Apply traction in synchrony with contractions;

6. Mild traction may be allowed to help maintain the mare's progress between contractions;

7. Ideally you have prepared for such a situation: Education, sedation, ropes, and a veterinarian on call, even talking you through the procedures on the telephone.

When to Get Professional Help

The following list of presentations require immediate emergency professional assistance or, ideally, immediate hospitalization:

- Contracted foal
  locked joints; fetotomy or embryotomy performed at farm; caesarean section performed at hospital.

- Twisted twins
  blocked at cervical entrance or exit.

- Transverse fetal position
  palpable transverse spine; palpable abdomen with umbilical cord; caesarean section recommended.

- Ruptured uterus
  diagnosed by the palpable presence of intestines inside the vagina; euthanasia recommended.

- Twisted uterus
  hospitalization.

- Monstrosity foal
  incomplete development; genetic malfunction.

Dystocia is defined as difficult birth. I define it as unadulterated pain! Veterinary obstetricians and gynecologists all have drugs and equipment to relieve a dystocia—pain.

When a dystocia occurs on the farm far away from a modern equine hospital, fortunately veterinarians have two barbarous procedures that can save the life of the mare when the foal has already perished: an embryotomy and a fetotomy. These procedures consist of dismembering the dead fetus and systematically removing sections at a time, so as to preserve the mare's future reproductive system. It is a herculean task, requiring hours of skilled dedication, education, and strength. Add modern medicines, effective anesthetics, and an angel mare. The experience is sad and lonely!

Today is brighter, however. More modern equine hospitals are available to the mares in need. The infamous caesarean section is the ideal situation for both the mare and her foal. Inhalation of general anesthetics, with their improved safety margins, gives both patients a distinct advantage.

I am ashamed to say that as a child growing up on a Thoroughbred breeding farm, I witnessed forcible deliveries in mares and their foals. It was because of such acts that I was driven to learn a better way to cope with problem births. I know that Nature has rules of her own, but I also know that through modern medicine and education those rules can indeed be improved upon. I would like to think we have advanced from barbaric deliveries and unnecessary deaths to humane deliveries and life.

6

The Neonatal Foal and the Postpartum Mare

Now comes the period when the mare is recovering from the miraculous act of giving birth and the foal is adjusting to its brand-new world.

The neonatal foal stretches its legs and tests its muscles—helping its psychologic and physiologic forces to gather awareness, strength, and coordination. Many incomplete and sometimes traumatic attempts are endured by the wet, gangly, long-legged newborn before it achieves its balance.

It seems that once the foal has managed a standing posture—however briefly—each subsequent attempt is easier. The trial-and-error period usually begins within the first ten to twenty minutes of its life and can last as long as an hour.

During these few moments, the average foal will rise, fall and rest, then try again and again. Some individual foals, unfortunately, sustain injuries during these floundering efforts. Flakes of straw, taken from the bale, can be stacked around all four walls of the stall to provide additional protection for the young one. The careful attendant can prevent injuries during these early struggles by offering manual support to protect the foal from severe falls until it balances itself fairly well and its postural reflexes begin to establish themselves. Once its stability is fairly established, the foal can be guided toward its mother's mammary glands.

The mare's udder should already have been cleansed by rubbing it gently with a towel dipped in hot water and wrung thoroughly dry. Be certain that the towel *is* wrung dry and cooled so that the mare will not be burned.

Careful attention should be given to the space between the two mammary glands, for this is a prime location for accumulated dirt.

After this cleansing it is wise to expel a few streams of colostrum from each teat, then coat the teat generously with the "advance" milk. This diminishes the bacteria present and induces milk flow in the mare.

In addition, the practice of preparing the udder in this manner has been very helpful with nervous maidens, older disagreeable mares, and for those mares that have unusually large firm udders by preventing a sometimes painful "bag," thus avoiding a reflex kick by the mare to a hungry foal.

An angry mare's squeal, accompanied by tail switching and lashing out behind, will rapidly convince most owners of the value of those few minutes spent preparing her udder. Even more important to remember is the fact that both anal and vulvar discharges from the mare drain down and over the udder because of the mare's physical conformation. It is reasonable to assume that abundant and harmful pathogens are only too available for the foal to ingest.

So, cleansing the udder is an essential postpartum procedure.

But all efforts may be valueless if one has to cope with an unreasonable mare who will not allow her foal to approach the udder to nurse.

Now is the time for your veterinarian to administer an appropriate tranquilizer. Sometimes, just standing by the mare's side to reassure her and quiet her is all that's necessary. Judicious use of a twitch or holding the mare's front leg up until the foal nurses also can be helpful. Fortunately, after the foal has nursed, even the most difficult mare usually succumbs to the appeal of her new baby.

If the attendant thinks he now can look forward to a long uninterrupted sleep he is due for a disappointment. *The first twenty-four hours postpartum is the period of highest mortality for both mare and foal.* Vigilance and continuous observation are of utmost importance, for this is the time when foaling complications and congenital maladies are most often manifested.

Once the normal foal locates the teats and actually takes in six to eight swallows of colostrum, the experienced owner enjoys a real sense of satisfaction: a major step in the struggle for survival has been taken.

The newborn will probably fall exhausted in the straw after its brief meal and rest momentarily, only to stir quickly and struggle to repeat its previous achievements. Gentle help from the attendant at this time will shorten the foal's search for a second meal.

Your foal is now ready for 1,500 international units of tetanus antitoxin and 5 to 6cc of injectable Pen-Strep preparation (penicillin and dihydro-streptomycin), plus a warm, old-fashioned soapy enema. *Avoid* the use of commercial preparations.

There is a current trend among veterinary practitioners not to inject the tetanus antitoxin because they feel there is no need to protect the newborn foal since immunity has been scientifically proven to be available in the colostrum from the mare. However, too many variables exist that could jeopardize the foal's life if this simple protection is not provided. Because of an individual mare's peculiarity, there is always the possibility that *that* particular mare might not produce antibodies in her colostrum in spite of having received her toxoid vaccination. There is also the possibility that the mare streams milk days—or even weeks—before delivery and may no longer be producing this valuable protection at adequate levels; hence a deficit may exist for her foal.

In addition, the known natural habitat for the tetanus spore is the feces of the horse. A newborn foal with an open navel (the best-known medium for growth of spores) may struggle for hours in the manure-laden straw before finally reaching its feet and successfully drinking the mare's colostrum.

It seems reasonable, in view of all the circumstances and the unique birth environment of the foal, to inject a preformed passive immunity to preclude any doubt of the foal's protection. The insurance that results from injection of the antitoxin will not in any way inhibit the ingested antibodies if they are present in the mare's milk.

In my twenty years of practice the routine injection of tetanus antitoxin to thousands of foals has yet to produce an unfavorable reaction, and of the thousands of foals injected not one has been lost from tetanus.

The intramuscular injection of 5 to 6cc of Pen-Strep should be repeated daily for a total of three days. These injections afford protection for the foal whose open navel is a dangerous portal for the entry of harmful bacteria into the foal's entire system, as well as protection against bacteria ingested or inhaled during those first few days of life when *no* foal can afford the slightest additional stress. The proper use of an antibiotic can be considered an asset and an adjunct to the mare's nutritious "first" milk that is so heavily laden with antibodies.

Constant observation and daily examination of the navel stump for the first ten days is essential until it appears dry and ultimately shrinks, finally to disappear.

This is the course followed by the normal navel. Retreatment and cauterization is occasionally required if moisture is present or if the cord stump is unusually large. Some new foals require several treatments, whereas others need only the initial treatment at birth.

Navel tissue is elastic, so that it retracts readily when naturally separated and properly cauterized. But its recoil property may seal in bacteria and produce a medium conducive to bacterial growth. Therefore, the importance of a daily examination cannot be overemphasized.

The navel cord should never be transected, severed, cut, ligated, or subjected to any other human intervention: nature's course of separating the foal from the fetal tissues should *not* be interfered with.

The enema should be properly prepared and must be administered with proper equipment—preferably a pint enema bag or can with a soft rubber tube. The tube should *never* be inserted into the rectum deeper than 4 to 5 inches.

Care should be taken, during administration of the enema, to allow for the escape or backflow pressure of fluids from the anus, and to protect the rectal mucosa from irritation.

After exercise and ingestion of some colostrum, most foals will defecate and clear the rectum of meconium, a semisolid accumulation in the intestinal tract developed during intrauterine life. Meconium varies in consistency and can produce varying degrees of constipation in some foals.

In the absence of a suitable enema, many foals suddenly become visibly uncomfortable. With a tail elevated and switching, accompanied by visible straining, the foal simulates colic. This syndrome usually indicates the need for removal of accumulated, firm fecal balls from the rectum by an enema. Then, that accomplished, the foal will nap comfortably.

A routine enema is a good practice for every foal, whether defecation has been observed or not. It not only stimulates peristalsis and helps to evacuate the posterior bowel, but also allows for movement in the anterior bowel. Don't be trapped into complacency by evidence of fecal passage, for the presence of fecal material, even following an enema, does not prevent subsequent constipation. Impacted meconium can manifest itself at a later time—usually twenty-four to thirty-six hours after birth, and in spite of one or more fecal passages.

At this time, the new mother also needs consideration. A fresh pail of *tepid* water, a generous portion of legume hay, and a carefully prepared warm bran mash will help her relax and assume her new role.

Wet straw or any offensive material should be removed from the stall; a generous amount of fresh, dry bedding should be added for the comfort of the mare and her newborn. Avoid bedding that is too deep or too heavy, for it can impede the new foal's uncertain locomotion.

Delay the use of any additional, strong disinfectant on or around the stall floor for at least twenty-four hours to prevent inhalation or contact with the foal's skin, navel, or mucous membranes.

The previously alerted veterinarian should have arrived by now and carefully scrutinized both mare and foal, received answers to routine questions concerning the actual foaling, carefully examined and assessed the condition of the placenta. All information applicable to future care should be recorded accurately and included in the individual foal's veterinary record.

Both mare and foal should receive a complete physical; a routine blood test will give your veterinarian a more complete picture and a baseline from which to follow your new foal's progress.

A direct proportion exists between the early detection of illness (or recognition of deviations from the normal) and the institution of treatment, with a predictable prognosis. So I cannot overstress the importance of frequent critical inspections of newborn foals for the first twenty-four to thirty-six hours of life.

Although the mare provides no intrauterine antibodies to the foal during embryonic life, they are abundantly available from the colostrum or first milk. Alone among all other mammals, the horse has *no in utero maternal antibody source* for the foal.

Such absence of antibody placental transfer is well documented. The placenta is incapable of transporting the large molecular antibodies. Therefore the baby is unprotected by preformed antibodies when it arrives in the world, and its open navel is too readily invaded by hostile microorganisms.

It establishes its breathing pattern by reflex action and struggles to its feet despite the great disadvantage of disproportioned limbs. The time lapse before the normal foal nurses may vary from fifteen minutes to an extreme of three hours—the foal still may survive.

The unattended foal is lucky if it arrives in the world with adequate stamina and perserverance, a cooperative mother, and adequate consumption of colostrum before its energy sources from intrauterine life are depleted. Unfortunately, it seems to be a race against time for the vulnerable, totally unprotected baby, who must ingest the richly laden colostrum for any chance of survival.

This single source of protection is available from the mammary glands for a limited period of time only—forty-eight to seventy-two hours. Thereafter mare's milk, without the beneficial antibodies, replaces the colostrum and provides only natural, normal nourishment.

An added hazard for the neonate is the brief term that the foal's duodenum will permit passage of the large molecular antibodies from the colostrum passage through the intestinal tract into the circulatory system. This time of selective absorption has been documented as the first forty-eight hours of the foal's life. *Hence, the critical early need for colostrum is of paramount importance.*

Nature has provided all these necessary ingredients for the new arrival—protective antibodies, an abundance of glucose, together with the essential laxative ingredient—yet a stopwatch schedule for survival exists that is often difficult for some weaker foals to manage, especially those unattended or those under the care of an attendant who is unaware of the life-or-death urgency of this strict time schedule.

The foal arrives in a stall teeming with hostile and nonhostile microorganisms, possessing absolutely no immunity—totally dependant upon reaching the precious colostrum from its mother, its only source of antibodies.

It must make many adjustments following its stormy, explosive, hasty delivery. Initiation of respiration by reflex action, clearing of the respiratory tract and lung tissue, accompanied by the establishment and regulation of body temperature, and the development of musculoskeletal tone—all must synchronize to enable the foal to struggle, fall, rise, and eventually walk.

The presence of the sucking reflex is a reassuring sight to the watching attendant. It will appear before, or shortly after, the foal is able to stand.

It seems to be an overwhelming task for the new foal not only to have to support its body weight in an upright position but also to learn to bend and flex its long slender neck in an effort to reach its mother's udder. It is fatiguing enough to struggle with four unwieldy legs, without coping with the problems of reaching and twisting its head and neck in the unusual position required for sucking.

In no other species do the young have to work so hard to nurse. The procedure can be extremely tiring for some foals. And the faltering hunt for the small and seemingly inadequate teats suspended from above is made even more difficult because of its inefficient vision.

Until the foal's vision develops sufficiently—usually between forty-eight to sixty hours after birth—the suckling must depend upon instinct, olfactory and auditory senses, and the all-important tactile hairs on its muzzle that guide it to its mother and help it locate the udder.

In contrast to a calf, the foal is provided with a relatively small, inaccessible source of nourishment. Yet fortunately, mare and foal are usually so proficient in the feeding process that human intervention seems to be an intrusion.

There is great variation, however, in the strength and vigor of healthy foals. Some foals arrive in the world with their heads held high—whinnying, alert, and able to get to their feet almost instantly. Others lie weakly in the straw, moving feebly, and require hours to gain their feet. These weak but otherwise healthy foals, literally only a few feet from the udder and salvation, will perish unless they receive aid.

There are two courses of action required to help the weak foal:

If the foal can support its head and neck, it can then be held upright in a position that enables it to reach the mare's teats. This requires a little patience but—provided a sucking reflex is present—the foal will be able to nurse successfully. After a short rest and another assist, the foal quite likely will improve its performance. With each successive meal the improvement in strength, coordination, and attitude is surprising.

Some of these weak foals seem to possess collapsible, telescoping legs and it is literally impossible to maintain them in an erect position long enough for them to obtain nourishment. Here is a case of not being able to take Muhammad to the mountain; so, by using a bottle, the mountain must be brought to Muhammad.

A standard infant's bottle with the holes in the nipple slightly enlarged serves very well as a temporary solution.

If the mare's udder is carefully cleansed with a warm moist towel, she will let her milk down and it will not be difficult to milk her in order to obtain the required *maximum* of 4 ounces of colostrum for the first feeding.

I have learned to look upon mare's milk as a magic substance, for I have watched so many of these weak foals get up unassisted, find the udder and teats, and actually nurse in a natural way *after* receiving one or two feedings from a bottle at half-hour intervals. In my experience, helping these foals by bottle feeding strengthens the instinct to nurse from the mare; in no way does it inhibit this spontaneous action, even though hard-headed horse people often do not believe it works.

Several factors are responsible for milk letdown in the mare. In the preparturient mare, who shows great mammary development and milk production well in advance of delivery, pituitary action is the known primary cause. However, it is strongly suspected that unidentified intrauterine changes, resulting in additional hormonal elaboration, are also involved. Such a mare has usually prepared herself for delivery in a completely competent manner, but her mammary build-up may be excessive.

In the postparturient mare the same hormonal influences from the pituitary gland and the uterus are present, together with a normally active foal whose presence (and, perhaps, the existence of the fetal membranes) plays a major role. The mare's olfactory and auditory senses are stimulated: an instinctive maternal response to the foal is immediate.

Once the foal is on its feet, there is a surge in hormonal response. The insistent search for nourishment and intermittent contact with her mammary tissue, together with the profound effect of its blind sucking, combine to effect the vitally important milk letdown.

Successful uterine involution, with cleansing of the placental membranes and resultant uterine health, influences milk availability directly.

Any time I am called to see a mare with a small udder and reduced milk flow, I immediately examine the uterus for its general condition and assess her for hormonal inefficiency. In nine out of ten mares, a reduced milk-flow problem derives from an unhealthy uterus.

Be grateful for a live foal and a seemingly well mare. But this is only the beginning . . .

The Newborn

You have a foal standing and nursing; now you might think you can snatch some well-earned sleep. On the contrary, a wise horseperson knows that he or she could leave a contented mare and her newborn for a quick breakfast only to return to a far different situation. From the early illusion of overall well-being, many attendants or owners are shocked by the dramatic changes that can occur during that brief absence. Suddenly, they must place an urgent call to summon emergency medical help.

If the eleven months of prenatal time, care, and vigilance have been worth the owner's physical and emotional strain, obviously he or she must persevere in order to assure the mare and foal of continuous and careful observation for the first twenty-four hours after birth.

This is the critical period, since most serious complications of congenital or intrauterine origin show themselves at this time. Early detection and immediate attention will often be the decisive factor in the race for survival. It can be disastrous to leave a "normal" mare and foal, only to return and discover an irreversible condition because of a brief time lapse.

Not long ago an experienced farm manager waited with and watched a pregnant mare through a long night: the efficient mare delivered a vigorous colt around 5:00 A.M. He continued to observe the mare and her foal. Within a short time he was pleased to see the foal stand and nurse, and the mare's fetal membranes "clean."

With a great sense of satisfaction he watched the pair a few moments longer, then walked down the aisle of the brood mare barn to his office, put a pot of coffee on to perk, and sat down for a short nap.

Soon the buzzer signaled that coffee was ready. A mug of strong hot coffee revived him. He walked back to the new arrival's stall for a last look before leaving the barn to the stableman who would soon be reporting for work.

The foal was down and resting, but something about his appearance made the manager enter the stall for a closer inspection. When he ran his hands over the new colt, he was horrified by the change that had taken place. The foal was limp, weak, and unable to rise.

In less than an hour I was at the foal's side. I found him in critical condition and started emergency treatment instantly. Fortunately this story had a happy ending—the foal survived.

The problem had not developed until after the foal was born. He came into the world with a concealed systemic infection and once independent of the "support system" of the mare he was unable to cope. Interestingly enough, this mare had a history of having lost her foal the year before in a mysterious manner.

Newborn foals lack the hardy innate defense mechanisms found in most other mammals. Their systemic resilience (or the ability to rebound from environmental stress) is weak or not sufficiently developed, and in the absence of prompt, vigorous emergency efforts by a veterinarian, foals of this sort may deteriorate quickly—perhaps die. Early recognition of any departure from the normal, plus prompt medical attention, seems to provide the only hope for most acute, predetermined maladies of intrauterine (or congenital) origin.

The delighted owner who has just watched a new foal nursing, napping, urinating, and defecating regularly has good reason to feel assured that all is well, but should continue the bleary-eyed watch for indications of impending trouble.

Short but regular meals, short but frequent naps, short excursions around its huge mother—all present a picture of a normal exuberant foal.

The apprehensive owner may well ask, "How does one recognize an impending problem?"

There are five criteria by which one may know that all is well: probably the most important is the act of nursing. The other four, not necessarily in order of importance are: short regular napping, physical activity, frequent urination, and regular defecation.

When a young foal is afflicted with any problem, regardless of its etiology, the first symptom is depression coupled with weakness. Nursing does not decrease in frequency; however, it appears that the amount consumed at each feeding is reduced, resulting in a slow build-up of milk in the udder. This build-up of milk in the semifilled mammary glands is usually indicated early by simple drops of milk on the teat ends. In a very short while the mare's udder will be large, firm, and even painful, with occasional streams of precious colostrum lost forever in the straw.

If a foal decreases its milk consumption ever so slightly, the resulting degree of physical deterioration seems grossly disproportionate to the small decrease of nourishment. Anyone in attendance should take and record the foal's temperature immediately. Watchful observance of its activities and attitude is essential from this moment on.

When questioning your foal's condition, *the first rule* is to examine the mare's udder. It takes a profuse milk producer to supply more than a hardy, vigorous foal demands. Condition of the udder, therefore, is an important clue to your foal's physical condition.

All healthy foals keep the mammary gland drained of milk at all times.

This demand gives the mare's udder the appearance of a flat, soft gland, dark in color and shiny in texture. A simple, reliable sign that a foal is not up to par is visible evidence of milk hanging on the mare's teats, once the nursing pattern is established. This ominous symptom is positive proof that the baby is not nursing. Streaming of milk from a full, tense udder that is unusually light in color shows further progression of an already existing condition.

The udder acts as both tattletale and stopwatch, and assuredly indicates a sick or depressed foal, regardless of cause. Its size and texture, and the amount of milk flow, indicate the period of time involved and, very probably, when the last meal was consumed.

When your baby foal appears with a "milky nose," that is, with milk all over its nose—from below the eyes, down over the top of its nose to the muzzle—whether wet or dry, it is a clear sign of systemic weakness.

Most weak foals are unable to cope with the mare's normal milk stream and their tentative approach to the udder results in a strong release of milk from both teats, which sprays over the foal's face. However, this is seen most often happening to a foal that has been ill and is recovering rather than to one who is *becoming* ill.

The second rule to follow is careful attention to the napping pattern. Short frequent naps are essential to the newborn's progress, growth, and general well-being. These naps, combined with frequent nursing, usually occur when the baby's stomach is full. I have never seen a healthy foal nap with an empty stomach.

While the foal is resting, the condition of the navel should be reassessed. Size, length, and evidence of incomplete retraction of soft tissue ends, as well as signs of any swelling or slight bleeding, should be given careful consideration. *The average size of a navel cord is comparable to the circum-*

ference of a man's finger and should be no longer than 3 inches at most; normally, the umbilical stump is about 1½ inches in length.

If any moisture is present on the cord end, or if any of the other variations are visible, I recommend prompt retreatment or recauterization.

For the resting foal any slight noise, interruption, or irritation should elicit immediate response; the normal foal will be alert and on its feet quickly.

Respirations should be even, steady, and not too rapid. The normal range varies from twenty-five to forty a minute. Evidence of shallow breathing, panting, or disruption in rhythm should be noted and reported. This symptom, in combination with any other deviation, warrants veterinary inspection. In these young foals any departure from normal, no matter how unimportant it may seem, requires professional observation.

To repeat: brief rest periods, sandwiched between milk meals and combined with some physical activity, is the normal neonatal's schedule.

For the first few hours physical activity usually amounts to an exploration of the dam's huge body, investigation of her far side and, perhaps, a quick inspection of the stall area. This is *the third rule* to be observed strictly.

The importance of a safe and solid stall for the newborn is now clearly evident. If that effort has been made, the owner or caretaker may relax and enjoy this new arrival without fear of unnecessary injury. The foal's curiosity appears to grow by the hour, and the inquisitive creature undoubtedly will explore every square inch of its new world within the first few hours. Any unprotected or dangerous spot will surely be discovered early by the venturesome foal.

In fact, mothers even seem to be more content in a solid, secure stall.

Years ago several members of my family purchased a pregnant brood mare from a very experienced horseman. When they went to inspect her, the big good-looking mare was alone in her stall, even though it was early spring and much too soon to have weaned her previous foal.

The conscientious seller of the mare explained why the mare had no foal by her side. It was his practice, when the young foals started eating from their mother's feed tubs, to tie the mare by her tub with a rope shank and feed the youngsters in a separate tub.

Because young foals always eat more slowly than their mothers, this prevented the mares from eating their grain and then nudging the babies aside in order to finish up the extra portion.

One night the rope shank accidentally was left in the mare's stall with one end securely tied and the other dangling free. Somehow, during the night, the foal had tangled the loose end of the rope around his neck and strangled. It was one of those terrible things that couldn't happen—but did!

More recently, one of my young patients, only a few days old, managed to jam his halter ring into the hook of the handle of a large, plastic water pail. The pail was hung high but not high enough. At dawn he was found unharmed, perplexedly wearing the huge pail attached to his halter.

Of course, there was no way to learn how long this empty pail had been such an encumbrance or how many possibilities of serious injury this poised young creature had managed to escape without turning a hair. Apprehensive caretakers held the foal secure; since there was no way to detach the pail, the halter was then carefully removed. Once the halter was off, it was found to be impossible to separate the pail from the halter—even with the efforts of two men armed with pliers!

So, a reminder: *Be certain that all obstructions are removed or elevated to a level above the baby's extended head and neck.*

Water pails, feed tubs, hay racks, and—above all—screw eyes and nails are the most common dangers. Close in all holes and spaces between boards, and secure a solid door or stall screen with *no open space underneath.*

If you have ever seen a foal's body, either dead or with mortal injuries, hopelessly wedged beneath the bottom of a door or screen, the dreadful sight is never forgotten.

Unfortunately, it is not uncommon for foals left peacefully sleeping in the evening to be found in the morning seriously injured or dead because of an improperly prepared stall.

The fourth rule when watching over the essential physiologic functions is a careful eye on urination or voiding. New foals urinate frequently and the volume of urine is usually small. The urine of the newborn should be almost watery clear and should flow evenly with no evidence of straining. (With increasing age the urine will increase in volume and assume a characteristic turbid appearance.)

In the case of colts, note should be taken whether or not the penis extends from the prepuce during urination. If the penis remains retracted, the urine dribbles from the prepuce. This condition will not permit the navel to dry, causes irritation to the prepuce, and provides an ideal environment for bacterial growth. A wet navel is an ominous signal and presents a threat to the life of the foal.

The fifth rule concerns defecation, or the discharge of excrement from the rectum. It occurs less frequently than urination and is not as easily observed and evaluated. Only in the absence of straining or signs of discomfort in the foal can it be assumed that the gastrointestinal tract is functioning normally.

Carrying the tail elevated and arched, with occasional straining, is positive evidence of mild constipation. This should not be confused with attempts to urinate. Here is a signal for an immediate enema. If this condition progresses in spite of treatment, the foal will roll on its back and stretch its head and neck in a characteristic upside-down position, indicating impaction of meconium or well-developed constipation.

Behavior of this kind by the foal should serve as a danger signal: the foal requires immediate and appropriate attention.

Remember always that neonatal foals have little resistance to infection, disease, or stress. They seem to dehydrate quickly and then deteriorate if allowed to depart from the normal behavior pattern—nurse, nap, back to nurse, urinate, nap, nurse again, perhaps defecate, nap, and nurse.

The slightest alteration of this pattern requires prompt checking of the foal's body temperature by careful use of a rectal thermometer.

A foal's normal body temperature is 101.0° F; any elevation is significant. However, a subnormal temperature is even more significant and requires hasty action. Remembering the very narrow margin of safety present in most foals today, it appears foolhardy to delay a call for assistance when in any doubt. A short ten years ago foals were lost that today are being treated successfully because of advances in medical knowledge, techniques, new drugs and procedures. Early recognition followed by prompt treatment very often produces miraculous results.

Now that your foal has been safely established in his or her new world, we should turn to consideration of the needs of the healthy postpartum mare.

Your mare should be put on a daily evening program of a large warm bran mash for the first postpartum week. The mash provides essential gastrointestinal bulk, aids in lactation, is high in protein, and supplies a mild laxative.

Immediately after delivery of their foals, some mares suffer from what I describe as "postpartum blues." Sluggish intestines and sore abdominal muscles are the aftermath of the strenuous demands made during parturition. As a result the mare may be reluctant to defecate. I strongly suggest tubing your mare with one gallon of heavy grade white mineral oil.

This syndrome is seen more often in horses than in any other species for the brood mare possesses an unusually large, heavy musculature that is physiologically overworked and stressed by her characteristic explosive delivery. Reduced appetite, reduced water intake, and diminished milk supply for the foal are all signs of the postpartum blues and can immediately affect the health and progress of the foal.

To recognize the onset, watch for signs of depression in the mare, reluctance to move, and reduced amount of fecal material—hence an unusually clean, dry stall eighteen to twenty-four hours postpartum.

Your mare can be made more comfortable by veterinary assistance and can better tolerate her foal's demands, lactate more efficiently, and carry on her important job if her gastrointestinal tract is functioning properly.

I'd like to offer a suggestion in the last month of gestation for prevention of these "blues." Experience has dictated that the balance between proper exercise and appropriate diet prevents gastrointestinal complications associated with delivery.

Along with an abundance of exercise daily in the paddock or pasture, the importance of the dietary change mentioned earlier—the eleven-month daily bran mash—is again stressed for the all-important last month of gestation. Incorporation of a daily large moist, fluffy bran into your mare's diet will have supplied much-needed bulk, warmth, and protein.

The postpartum mare should be fed abundant legume hay, have a salt block in her feed tub, and free choice of water at all times.

It is to be expected and perfectly normal for matrons to have a very wet and dirty stall in the mornings and for them to consume unbelievable amounts of grain, hay, and water. The absence of such a typical "brood mare stall" should alert one to the possibility of some gastrointestinal problem.

In spite of the constant production of waste materials, a real effort should be made to keep a clean, sanitary, and well-bedded dry stall for the sake of the foal.

The foal and the mare should be kept in their stall until the third postpartum day. By this time the foal has the advantages of increased strength, improved musculoskeletal coordination and, most important, has developed some visual efficiency.

Turning Out

The first turning-out day has always been a highly controversial subject. Some horsemen prefer turning the pair out into their private paddock on the second postpartum day. However, experience, together with statistical information, has taught us that it is better to wait until the third day—weather permitting. The beneficial effects on the mare of early exposure to sun and exercise are in direct conflict with the well-being of the foal. Waiting for the third day is advantageous for the foal and presents only a slight disadvantage to the mare.

Exercise enhances uterine health by promoting drainage and discharges, thereby inducing more efficient uterine involution. This in turn leads to a shorter rehabilitation period and helps the matron to regain her important reproductive capabilities. Appetite, lactation, and all physiologic processes are increased by outdoor exercise; however, most mares do not suffer because they have been deprived of this one day's confinement.

A peculiar complication results from the fact that although the mare and the foal at this time have different, conflicting requirements, the two are interdependent and inseparable. Yet the needs of the foal seem to outweigh slightly the needs of the mare; the foal *is* the end product for which we all strove mightily and its safety should be placed first.

Geographic location, season of the year, and weather conditions will all influence greatly the amount and length of exercise periods. It is easy to envision the growth and developmental advantages provided a foal that has the advantage of moderate temperatures with sunbaths and lush grass, in contrast to a foal that is confined by low temperatures, short hours of sunlight, no grass, and unfavorable footing. There are also foals who have the advantage of fine pastures and an abundance of sun, but must endure high temperatures, humidity, and annoying insects. All these factors play a part in the growth rate and weight gain of the foal.

Now comes the turn-out day. It is an exciting moment for the owner to see the mare escort her newborn to the big world outside their stall; and it is an exciting time for the mare and foal as well.

This momentous occasion requires careful planning. Wait until the third day. One hopes that the sun will be out, the temperature ideal, no falling barometer, and the footing safe. (If the weather is bad, wait until it improves.)

The first outing should not exceed 15 minutes. Lengthen the period of outdoor exercise each successive day by 5- to 10-minute increments.

Do, please, arrange for a minimum of three people to assist in launching the foal's introduction to sun, fresh air, and footing different from that to which it has been accustomed.

The most capable person in the group should cradle the foal in his arms, with one arm around the chest and the other arm firmly encompassing its hindquarters.

The second person should lead the mare ahead of the foal at a pace that allows the pair to make progress and yet remain comfortably close, so as not to panic either the mare or the foal.

It is unforgivable to attempt to lead the foal by a halter as you would an older horse: *any force* applied to the foal can cause serious, perhaps permanent damage.

The third person is a bonus and can open and close doors and gates to make the exit to the paddock and return to the barn a smoother, easier operation.

At the entrance to the paddock, which has previously been prepared (see page 21), the mare should be led through the gate and immediately turned to face it. While the foal-handler holds the baby securely at the gate, the mare can then be released and permitted to wheel, kick, and run a short distance. She will usually return within seconds to check on the location of her baby. At this time the foal can be released to run with its mother with some degree of safety.

By following this procedure you may have prevented the mare from thoughtlessly kicking her baby in a split second of exuberance. Such accidents have occurred many times in the presence of horrified owners, who then have to endure the memory of such tragedies. Please remember that the mare can and does lose sight of the little one at her side if both are launched simultaneously, for she will surely give way to stored-up energy after her unaccustomed confinement.

When the animated mare quickly returns looking for her foal, and you have turned the foal loose, then observe the pair moving off together. A prettier sight is hard to imagine.

Close the gate and continue to watch, allowing the pair to enjoy their first freedom for a few minutes.

Do not allow the foal to tire to the point that it must actually lie down on the ground for the first few times outside.

At the end of a week's seclusion in the private paddock, the mare will have regained her strength from the ordeal of parturition and the foal will have gained musculoskeletal and visual competence, qualifying the two for admittance into the brood mare and foal band.

They will become a part of a society in which they will be called upon to fend for themselves. It is amusing to see the careful appraisal they undergo when first turned out with other mares and older foals before they are accepted as part of the group.

As we discussed earlier, it is essential to remember that the first ten days of life are the most critical for the newborn, for the conditions indicating any problems will show themselves during this period. Here, then, is a real challenge for the discerning owner, trained attendant, or professional horseman. These are the days in which to detect early variations from the norm and thus reduce the often critical time lapse before treatment can be instituted.

The truest index, next to keen sharp eyes and careful daily observation of the mare's udder, is the prudent use of a rectal thermometer. Any fluctuations from the normal body temperature of the foal—101° F—are to be noted. Lower readings in the morning and *slight* elevations in the evening are not unusual or significant *if they remain within one-fifth (or two-tenths) of a degree plus or minus 101°.*

Newborn babies of all species require a specific normal body temperature in order to initiate, develop, and maintain the basic physiologic processes necessary for life to continue. Life processes depend greatly upon constancy of body temperature, which in some individuals can be affected by the temperature of the environment and general habitat.

Exposure to temperature extremes can directly reduce normal physiologic function. The young foal's system will not function efficiently with either too high or too low a body temperature.

Any slight elevation is significant if accompanied by clinical signs such as depression, inappetence, irregular or rapid respiration, or a change in the character of the feces.

However, a subnormal temperature should cause you greater concern than a slight elevation. A temperature below 101° indicates the presence of an infection—usually of intrauterine origin, through navel tissue, or some other condition of more serious nature. *A minimal fluctuation of 1 degree plus or minus is significant enough for your veterinarian to be advised.* And every effort should be made to establish the best possible environment while waiting for your veterinarian to arrive.

Keep the foal as warm as possible in a clean, comfortable stall. Frequent temperature readings are important information when your veterinarian arrives.

Upon arrival, the veterinarian will want to see the afterbirth, take a blood count, and check the foal's immune status. This can be done with a portable zinc sulfate test.

Depending upon the test outcome and the overall condition of the foal, the doctor may suggest that a pint of hyperimmune serum be given intravenously right there in the stall. The blood count will also direct the veterinarian as to the seriousness of the situation.

These screening tests are our first line of defense with the neonatal foal.

Strong outward signs of septicemia (blood poison) are manifested by weakness, increased respirations, increased down time, and decreased nursing.

When you walk into your mare's stall and see milk streaming from her udder, you know that your foal is sick, even without looking at him.

In some cases, during the first three days a foal will look bright, nurse, and yet show a subnormal temperature. In the absence of other symptoms, without early recognition and establishment of appropriate medical measures, these foals are often lost.

Again, time and timing is of the essence.

The Postpartum Mare

It may seem that the foal has occupied the bulk of our attention in this chapter.

Now, a few facts about the mare should be discussed. But before we move to the happy subject of the healthy, trouble-free mare, some comments must be made about death in postpartum mares.

Death in the postpartum mare is probably caused more often than is recognized by internal hemorrhage—either intrauterine or from the large vessels within the uterine ligaments. Postpartum hemorrhage is usually seen in mares who are older than fifteen and possess unknown fibrosed, calcified arterial walls with areas of degeneration.

The actual hemorrhage is caused by the rupture of an artery or large blood vessel at the weakened site. The force and stretching prior to, during, and after delivery traumatizes an already pathologic vessel. It then ruptures and hemorrhage results.

If the bleeding is intrauterine, and the vessels involved are few in number or small in size, the surrounding tissue can contain the escaping blood—forming a blood blister—and thus create an opposing force that may help to control the hemorrhage. Any bleeding of the broad ligaments is more serious.

When the blood escapes into loose tissue, or if a large vessel is involved, naturally there is greater blood loss. If the blood escapes into the abdominal cavity, with no pressure present to contain the flow, death occurs before the condition can be diagnosed.

Internal hemorrhage may develop immediately after foaling or within the first twelve hours. Consistent symptoms include a low-grade abdominal discomfort, ceaseless pawing, then sweating and a definite anxious expression. The site and size of the vessels predetermine the fate of the mare. Not all mares that hemorrhage die. Treatment is not too successful, but in borderline cases it can make the difference between life or death.

Eventually, when the mare is in a black sweat, cold to the touch, and her expression stary or glassy, it is best to remove the foal from her stall. She will be unaware of its presence as she approaches death.

A second cause of death in the postpartum mare occurring within twenty-four hours is rupture of the uterus. Sustained during delivery, peritonitis develops, and death follows quickly.

Let us turn to the trouble-free mare.

Assuming that she "cleaned" her afterbirth promptly, is lactating sufficiently to meet the demands of her hungry foal, is eating hungrily, and is comfortable and alert, she fits perfectly the picture of a normal, healthy postpartum mare.

About the fifth postpartum day it is not unusual to see a thick chocolate-colored vulvar discharge. This is not an indication of disease or infection; it is a perfectly normal part of the important physiologic "clean-up" of the mare's uterus and reproductive tract.

Exercise is important too and the only known way to augment the flow of this discharge. If the mare could be persuaded to walk on her hind legs for extended periods of time—especially during the postpartum period—then nature's method of providing natural drainage would be in effect, and uterine health would be established rapidly and efficiently.

Exercise also helps in improving tissue and muscle tone—all of which aids in accomplishing uterine involution.

By the seventh postpartum day at the earliest or the eighth day at the latest, whether you expect to breed your mare back or not, she should receive a complete gynecologic examination by a veterinarian.

Any intervention before this time is absolutely contraindicated except in the presence of symptoms that spell danger.

By the seventh day varying degrees of regeneration have occurred and the mare is at the precise physiologic stage that reveals the greatest amount of information in order to arrive at an accurate evaluation of her gynecologic health. Such an examination will also tell vividly the story of what occurred during parturition.

At this time any needed corrections can be made, treatment administered, and her fertility status can then be determined.

7

The Foal to Its Weaning

The precocious foal's progress is astounding. Its ability to run, buck, scratch an ear with a hind foot, nibble a few strands of hay with its mother, and even push her aside at the feed tub in order to snatch a few mouthfuls of grain are usually accomplished within the first few days of life.

I have seen foals only hours old kick and play in their stalls. Some exceptional and hungry youngsters get down on their knees to nurse from their resting dams or impatiently paw at their tired mothers—demanding that the mares get to their feet so that they can more conveniently suckle from the more conventional position.

The mare and foal should be outdoors in their private paddock for progressively longer periods each day until they join the brood mare band, but it is necessary to remember that although the new foal appears to be mentally and physically advanced, it still requires careful supervision and protection. Its defense mechanisms are still at low ebb and an additional risk is its high susceptibility to environmental stresses.

For at least the first few weeks a young foal should never be turned out in any kind of falling weather or during extremes of temperature. The foal should not be permitted to become fatigued, wet, chilled, or overheated at any time during its early life.

It is much better to put the mare and foal out for two short periods each day rather than for one longer period that might be physically dangerous.

A quiet rest period in the security of the stall or any protected environment between exercise periods permits the foal its choice of activity —to nap, rest, nurse, or nibble at hay in the safety of its shelter.

Now is the time to fit a halter properly on the new foal. This is a much easier and safer operation with two people present rather than attempting the task alone.

One person should cradle the foal front and rear while the second person quietly places the halter on its head. *The halter should be adjusted so that it is snug but not tight.* After the halter is adjusted, if one finger can be placed comfortably under the straps at every point, the fit is correct.

A halter that is too loose is a dangerous invitation for the foal to place its foot through a gap while down resting, or allows room for the halter to become caught up in stall equipment—pails, latches, snaps, screw eyes, or even shrubbery if the foal explores while turned out in pasture.

The ideal foal halter should be fully adjustable in three critical areas— the noseband, the head stall, and the throat latch. It should be made of stitched leather with small, lightweight metal fittings. It will require frequent adjustments as the foal grows, but at the first fitting undoubtedly there will be an excess of dangling leather that should be securely taped to the halter for safety's sake. Do not trim off the excess, for you are sure to need all of it to accommodate the rapid head growth of the young foal.

Leather is the material of choice, even though there are nylon halters available for foals. Leather's advantage lies in its stretchability—even to breaking point. In an emergency situation, nylon is too indestructible unless equipped with a safety release.

The small light foal halter placed on the foal is his or her first exposure to discipline. He will rapidly become used to wearing it. A young foal's halter is not to be used to lead or restrain him at this stage; it should be considered as the first of many steps used to teach the foal to accept what humans expect of him.

Even though the foal is wearing a halter, he should be held and led as he was on his first day in the private paddock until he becomes too large to cradle. Then he must be gently and considerately *taught* to lead.

A foal should never be pulled forcefully by his head or allowed to pull against the halter. Any outside force is transmitted to the cervical spine and irreparable damage may be inflicted unknowingly that may not become visible until the foal is a weanling, yearling, or even later.

The young equine's unusually long neck, relative to its body size, is the most vulnerable target area for stress forces. One school of opinion is convinced that young horses that suddenly develop a degree of ataxia (or muscular uncoordination) must have suffered some traumatic confrontation while being led or held by their heads at a very early age.

It is foolhardly, therefore, *ever* to permit anyone to use force or to pit his or her strength or weight against the foal's tender, flexible neck.

Some foals for various reasons start drinking water from their mothers' pails, a paddock trough, or a stream at an early age. Every effort should be made to prevent a foal from drinking water because this will decrease its milk intake, or it may even stop nursing if its fluid requirements are satisfied by water.

The effect upon the foal's gastrointestinal tract is not only undesirable but critical.

Intractable, debilitating diarrhea will soon develop in foals that substitute water for milk. Unless the source of water is removed and the foal promptly treated, the severe weakening fluid imbalance, and resulting dehydration from lowered resistance, will open the door to the ever-present and always-ready pathogenic bacteria.

These foals are always depressed, show either elevated or subnormal temperatures, and become progressively less interested in nursing, with a steady unmistakable deterioration of their physical condition. As added insult, when the mare's udder becomes enlarged and tender, she grows uncooperative and will move away from the already weakened foal, who is now not interested enough to persist in nursing attempts.

All foals' natural environments include availability and free access to water. But it is the rare individual or sick foal who will be seen drinking water; even more serious is the foal that drinks and is *not* seen.

Careful watching may be required to catch some of these purging, wet-tailed foals at the water pail, but the telltale results in the form of a fetid, watery diarrhea are undeniable evidence.

Soiled, wet-bottomed foals always appear miserably uncomfortable and will eventually lose all their perineal hair if that area is allowed to dry and mat. A bland soap-and-water scrub daily during the attack of diarrhea will alleviate the physical discomfort, decrease the itch, and reduce the amount of subsequent hair loss.

Until the foal reaches the age of four months be alert to this dangerous water-drinking syndrome. *When such a condition is recognized, remove the water source. Then your veterinarian should be consulted.* The foal should be kept at stall rest or under shelter until it is completely free of symptoms and is again nursing normally. The water pail in the stall must be raised to a level that makes it impossible for the foal to drink water until it is fully recovered.

The presence of diarrhea from any cause, other than the normal occurrence during the mare's foal heat and subsequent cycles, is significant and requires attention. Diagnosis and treatment in order to avert the danger of rapid dehydration and its serious consequences are mandatory.

An insidious deficiency exists in *all mares' milk* that involves not its quantity but its quality. Both heavy- and light-milkers exhibit a deficit of two trace minerals essential to the health and growth of the foal. Abundant lactation is deceptive, for that fact alone is not an indication of the presence of adequate nutrients.

Research has proved that hay and grain must be consumed by the foal from the first three to five days after birth to compensate for the deficiency in milk quality. If hay and grain are available and the foal remains disinterested in spite of its mother's example, it is imperative to teach the foal to eat by repeatedly placing small amounts of grain in its mouth.

About 48 to 72 hours after birth, when colostrum is no longer produced, the normal milk then in the udder is representative of what will be present until the foal is weaned. Lactation peaks at about six weeks. Both the quantity and the quality of the mare's milk gradually decreases after this time.

So it is not mere coincidence that every foal will look its best at about six weeks of age, then gradually decline in overall "thriftiness" and anticipated growth rate unless additional nourishment is provided from another source.

The two vital trace minerals mare's milk lacks are copper and iron. Both are essential for the formation of red blood cells.

Blood studies performed on neonatal foals usually reveal relatively satisfactory or normal values. About the fifth or sixth day following birth there exists, unfortunately, a constant finding of unnecessary anemia, which mirrors the trace-mineral deficit and creates stress and susceptibility to infection. A reduced number of red blood cells and a lowered hemoglobin content are found in otherwise clinically normal foals. This potentially damaging anemia is spontaneously corrected as soon as good-quality hay and grain are offered to and consumed by the foal.

In light of our current knowledge, research clearly indicates that our stalwart maternal source of nutrition is, in fact, substandard. This is a difficult finding for older horsemen to accept: they do resent any deviation from the adage that "Nature knows best" and are *very* reluctant to adjust to any changes in feeding practices. But it is time to bow to the facts now known and to grow our foals as they can be, should be, and deserve to be grown.

In my opinion, the only value of mare's milk, after the decline following the sixth-week peak, is to aid in washing down the hay and grain that the foal eats.

This seemingly impertinent, but not disrespectful, attack upon motherhood's efficiency should shock many from traditional complacency and, I trust, convert many more of us to accept newer and better feeding methods.

Creep Feeding

As soon as the foal shows an interest in its mother's feed tub, provision should be made for it to have grain available *always*. The mare's voracious appetite, her size, and the fact that she eats more rapidly than her foal makes it difficult, if not impossible, for the foal to have the amount of feed that it wants and needs.

Most foals eat a few mouthfuls of grain, then nurse, then go back to the tub for a few more mouthfuls. Some mares will patiently allow their young to share the eagerly anticipated ration of grain; but there are many others who, with pinned ears and a well-timed nip, refuse to allow their foals to eat.

Of all the solutions to this problem I think "creep feeding" is the simplest, safest, and most satisfactory method.

A creep is easy to construct in any stall, is inexpensive, and can be temporary. All that is required is a round smooth fence rail of sufficient length to fit diagonally across one corner of the stall.

The foal's feed tub is hung at about the level of its nose in a convenient corner of the stall and the rail positioned so that the foal can easily walk under to reach its tub, *but far enough out from the corner and positioned so that the mare's long neck cannot extend to the foal's tub.*

Some of the enthusiastic reports I've had from owners credit huge amounts of grain consumed by the foal, whereas later it has been found that the ingenious mare, with her seemingly endlessly elastic neck, happily consumed her baby's supply. Her range is unbelievable!

As I stated before, grain should be available for the foal *at all times,* so that it has free access to any quantity it wishes to consume. A small amount of concentrate (grain) should be placed in the tub. As soon as it is eaten, it should be replaced. You will be able to determine very quickly ap-

A foal hours old.

Normal mare and foal.

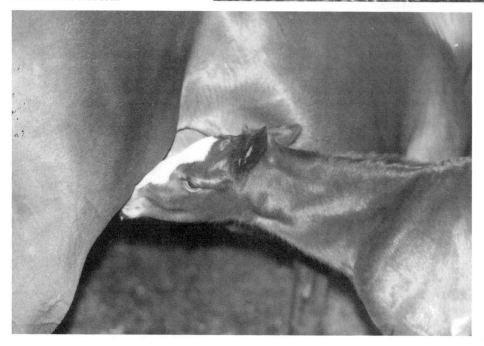

Septicemic foal.

Isoerythrolosis (incompatability during gestation). Note barrier separating the foal from the mare, thus preventing the foal from nursing. Lab tests determine when the mare's milk is safe for the foal to ingest (usually 60 to 72 hours postnatal).

proximately how much to put in the tub and how often, so that the feed remains fresh, clean, yet constant.

Do not expect a foal to find stale, sour, fly-covered, or dirty grain palatable.

Some breeds do not, but Thoroughbred foals start eating small amounts of grain by the time they are three or four days old. And it is not unusual for a foal to consume *6 or more quarts* of concentrate daily at six weeks.

Foals that are creep-fed usually surpass in both size and condition those that share their mothers' tub because their substantial nutritional needs are satisfied.

To repeat: it is essential to provide free acess to high-quality legume hay and good heavy concentrates at all times. Foals must have this in order to achieve their inherent, genetic growth potential. As well, we have found that young horses raised on constant creep feeding are not subject to gastrointestinal upsets or feed founder, as are other animals on an erratic diet schedule.

A "field creep" is more expensive and more complicated to build, but if the climate in which you intend to raise your foal permits the mare and foal to be turned out for lengthy periods of time, it is a definite asset.

Erect one with a solid partition toward the north and construct it in such a manner as to protect the selected hay and grain from falling weather—moisture, warmth, and reduced amounts of oxygen are conducive to mold propagation and the neurotoxin of botulism, both number-one deadly enemies of the equine population.

Secure a blueprint of an ideally thought-out "field creep" and proceed from there!

When erecting a field creep, take care to select a location where the mares usually meet and relax, so that the environment is conducive to rest and leisurely snacking. It is a rare foal who eats if its mother has wandered away.

A special mare that I have attended for the past five years for each of her four foals is a perfect example of a mare that does not produce a sufficient quantity of milk for optimal growth of her babies.

This magnificent big mare—with tiny mammary glands—is extremely fertile and is almost always the first mare on the farm to foal. Her newborns are slightly smaller than average and, even though the mare is a patient and tolerant mother, the quality and quantity of her milk does not meet the needs of her young.

By spring much younger foals have outstripped hers. Because no provision is made for a separate feed tub for the foal on this particular farm, it is not until weaning time that the early arrival has an opportunity to eat without competition.

At this farm weaning is started as soon as the earliest foals are six months old, so this mare's foals are usually weaned in June or July. By the September 1 deadline, when all unweaned foals are separated from their dams regardless of size or age, our older but smaller foal has just begun to catch up with its rivals because of its eight- to ten-week start of noncompetitive eating.

It is not until the following spring, however, that discrepancies appear to have been fully compensated for and her yearling begins to approach its genetic potential. What a different story it would be if this lovely mare's foals were only creep-fed!

Feet

Care of the foal's feet during the first few months of life is simple but important. Some foals require attention as early as the third week, while others may not need any attention during this period.

The rate of foot growth and wear varies with the genetic makeup of the individual animal, climatic conditions, terrain, diet, and other environmental influences.

When the foal walks or trots, it should "break over" the toe in a straight line as the foot is brought forward. A pointed toe makes correct placement of the foot difficult if not impossible; then the foal will break over on the inside of the foot (causing a toed-out gait) or on the outside of the foot (causing a toed-in gait). These undesirable pressures upon the longitudinal axis of the long pliant legs and joint planes almost inevitably cause irreversible damage.

The foal's feet should be inspected frequently for evidence of points developing at the tips of the toes. When you see *any* interruption in the rounded contour of the toe, a few strokes of a blacksmith's rasp is all that is needed to restore the proper rounded shape.

It is not necessary for a blacksmith to round off the slight tip that may develop at the front of the foot. In fact, many foals are more tractable when in familiar hands.

The sole of the foot should not be touched or "dressed."

Deviations of legs and feet that cause uneven and unequal wear of the foot wall are usually self-perpetuating. *Corrective trimming and shoeing to eliminate defects, therefore, are exacting procedures requiring a farrier and your veterinarian's prescription and supervision.*

Vaccinations

The foal fortunate enough to ingest colostrum as nature intended has the advantage of available passive immunity by means of preformed antibodies. Unfortunately, the *in vivo* life of antibodies it receives from its dam lasts no longer than three weeks. Sad to say, these antibodies have broken down long before the foal's defense mechanism machinery begins to function in a dependable manner.

It is not until the foal is four months old that its reticuloendotheal system will respond to specific stimuli and form antibodies appropriate to specific challenges. This lag period represents a period of extreme susceptibility—hence, of danger to the young foal. I always feel a sense of relief when foals are finally vaccinated at sixteen weeks and are then able to develop their own active immunities.

The protection afforded by proper use of vaccinations for foals can be very gratifying, *but their improper use can be devastating.*

Any recognized need for protection against infection or disease during this lag period should be administered in the form of appropriate preformed antibodies that provide immediately available passive protection.

If the foal is vaccinated before its defense mechanism is capable of adequate response, it is questionable whether immunity is provided. Even though no adverse clinical effects have been recorded after improper use of vaccines, one then speculates as to whether the foal has been protected adequately. But, after the first sixteen weeks, with a proper vaccination program, one can be fairly confident of the establishment of ample protection.

Vaccinations recommended at this time are tetanus toxoid, influenza and rhinopneumonitis vaccine. At a later date additional vaccines are indicated and available at the discretion of your veterinarian, who undoubtedly will suggest the use of bivalent Encephalomyelitis vaccine and Strep-equi bacterin—all at the proper time.

Tetanus, Influenza and Rhinopneumonitis

When your foal has reached the proper age, an initial vaccination of tetanus toxoid rhino influenza vaccine may be administered concurrently, although they should be given at *separate injection sites.*

The initial vaccinations are followed by a booster in four weeks; then a yearly booster injection is all that is necessary.

Influenza and rhino vaccines are killed-viral injectable preparations that are safe, reliable, and confer relatively secure protection against the ever-present "pesky" respiratory infections. Their use is popular for horses of all ages, but they are a very important part of the immunization program for continuing health of your foal.

Since this vaccine has been widely and regularly used, I have observed a dramatic reduction in the incidence of sick horses—especially in populations where there is exposure to other horses who have been near shows, competitions, sales, or any other situation involving large numbers of previously "unintroduced" animals.

Before your foal receives its tetanus vaccination, it should be given a thorough physical examination for the presence of hidden lacerations or puncture wounds. Tetanus spores usually remain inactive until ideal tissue conditions exist: reduced available oxygen, warmth, and moisture. Particular danger lurks in any deep wounds containing dirt and partially closed up by matted hair; these could have been present for an unknown period of time. A thorough examination of the feet and lower legs is of utmost importance because of their proximity to the tetanus-spore-laden manure. If any questionable wound is discovered, the foal should not be vaccinated, but should receive a dose of tetanus *antitoxin* instead. The vaccination should be deferred for three weeks.

After the use of tetanus toxoid in a healthy foal, free of wounds in which active or inactive tetanus spores could exist, there is a period of vulnerability—immediately postinjection—that lasts for five days before the foal produces needed specific protective antibodies. *If a deep, contaminated wound is present in any young foal, the use of vaccine is contraindicated.*

Even with the great prevalence of tetanus spores in the soil of a horse's world, in my many years of practice I have known only two foals to develop and die of that dreadful (and untreatable) disease. Both were between three and six months old—the time that antibodies from their mothers' milk had been dissipated and the needed vaccine had not been injected. One foal had stepped on a concealed nail and the other had sustained a puncture wound that was hidden by its heavy foal coat.

Neither injury was detected until the symptoms of pain and gross infection, with heat, had drawn attention to their injuries.

Tetanus is preventable but not curable.

I can accept a loss from a disease or condition for which we have neither vaccine nor specific drugs, but it is unthinkable for foals to lose their lives because of neglect or poor barn management.

Well I remember a distinguished old veterinarian in his nineties who had been a very good friend during my teens telling me stories of horses lost from lockjaw during the early years of his practice.

He told of puncture wounds, especially of the foot, that presented terrible exercises in futility as he fought uselessly to save lives. He tried desperately to culture the organism. Armed only with turpentine and iodine, he attempted to burn and destroy the causative agent.

He was overwhelmingly grateful when the tetanus vaccine was finally developed and available, and he could treat wounds and infections without the haunting specter of lockjaw.

Today I feel the same gratitude when I am able to provide solid protection against this dreaded disease by a simple injection. My friend was so impressed by tetanus toxoid that I wish he could see the wonderful progress made in equine immunology during the past twenty years, let alone the monumental advances in chemotherapy.

Encephalomyelitis

Eastern or Western Encephalomyelitis—the deadly sleeping sickness—is caused by neurotrophic virus affecting the world's horse population.

There is a very effective bivalent vaccine against these fatal diseases that attack the nervous system. It is administered once a year in two doses ten days apart. The recommended time for this vaccination (variable in different geographic locations) depends upon the vector (specific mosquitoes and blood-sucking insects) present in your geographic location.

In 1971 a neurotrophic virus invaded the United States and was responsible for many deaths. Called VEE, this virus orginated in Venezuela and as early as 1940 authorities were aware of its devastation and slow spread. It traveled through Central America and Mexico, finally reaching the Texas border in 1971.

The panic that occurred when the disease began killing horses on U.S. soil broke down the last barriers of resistance to legislation, and drug companies were permitted to produce a specific vaccine.

Almost 3 million horses were vaccinated at government expense in 1971. Many additional horses were vaccinated during the year at their owners' expense, and the outbreak was quelled.

Because the vaccine is irritating to muscle tissue and usually causes postinjection depression and dullness (with resultant transient fever in some cases), the safety of the vaccine has been questioned by some eminent pathologists at the University of Kentucky. In general, equine practitioners do not recommend the use of this vaccine unless they are faced with the danger of exposure.

Studies from 1940 to the present time indicate a continuing threat because of the cyclic character of the encephalitis viruses that endanger unprotected horses each year. Horse owners have become complacent since 1972 and tend to ignore the ever-present hazard of a spontaneous outbreak.

Fortunately, you are able to protect your horses from these neurotrophic viruses.

It seems unbelievable that human deaths and severe disabilities from these same viruses are recorded each year, but no vaccine has been produced yet for mankind.

Rhinopneumonitis

Another serious disease to be reckoned with is the two-pronged *Rhinopneumonitis* virus.

In young horses it is seen as an upper respiratory infection, characterized by fever, serous nasal discharge, and reduced white-cell count. The duration of the illness is relatively short and the recovery is usually complete and uneventful. In older horses the symptoms are very much the same, but less severe as some immunity has been developed.

The insidious attribute of rhinopneumonitis is that the mildest case (or even exposure of a pregnant mare to this virulent virus) can cause abortion.

The rhinopneumonitis virus causes upper respiratory problems in young horses and death in the unborn foal. The diabolical rhinopneumonitis virus has a great affinity for the allantois chorion of the placental tissues. It attacks exactly the spot where the placenta attaches to the maternal uterus. The outcome: spontaneous abortion or, depending upon the stage of gestation, a slow, insidious development of pockets of placental separation will ultimately cause abortion.

As the placenta grows and develops, this virus becomes more hazardous to the pregnant mare. Vaccinations begin in the fifth month of gestation and are repeated in the seventh and ninth months. This schedule seems to confer a fair immunity to the brood mare.

The young foal begins his first rhinopneumonitis vaccination at fourteen to sixteen weeks of age. I strongly suggest monthly boosters if your young horse is stabled in a highly populated equine area.

A pregnant mare so exposed from the sixth month of gestation to full term can abort at any subsequent date without demonstrating symptoms of the disease. If abortion does occur, the only blessing is that the mare will be immune to the disease for one full year.

Young horses (unless vaccinated) serve as a reservoir for this destructive virus. To allow any unvaccinated horse of any age to come into contact with a mare pregnant past her fifth month must be considered the height of stupidity.

Streptococcus equi

Young horses have no defense against bacterial invasion, especially the streptococcal diseases. Almost every young foal suffers through a period of fever, muco-purulent nasal discharge, and swollen glands to develop its own antibodies.

Streptococcus equi is the causative agent of strangles and can make a foal very uncomfortable because of sore and swollen glands around the head, eyes, and jaw. This disease is highly contagious and will spread rapidly through a barn, affecting even older horses if they have reduced immunity.

Strep-equi bacterin is not a new product, but it is a very useful one when an outbreak threatens. It is irritating to muscle tissue and sometimes results in a sore injection site because its compatibility with certain individual horses is unpredictable.

Caution:

1. Do *not* follow label directions!

2. Administer (only) one third of all recommended dosages.

3. Scrub the injection site meticulously and use *only* the rump muscles (gluteal).

However, with prudent use and careful dosage, this bacterin can be safe and effective and has a valid place in the protection program for your foal.

Reactions to Vaccines

Prior to any vaccination, a physical examination by your veterinarian can prevent the occurrence of a reaction from an ill-timed vaccination, which causes discomfort to the foal and embarrassment to the doctor, if an animal is injected during the incubation stage of a disease. A thermometer and a stethoscope, along with a little history of possible exposure, will help your veterinarian make the decision as to whether it is wise to vaccinate at this time or to defer treatment.

Currently there are trivalent and quadravalent vaccines being produced by reputable drug companies that advertise their effectiveness, convenience, and economy in horse journals. I am not yet convinced as to the safety of vaccines in combination—especially the live or attenuated viral preparations.

Perhaps time will prove the efficacy of their use and, above all, their safety for the patient. Convenience and economy *are* important; but it is my philosophy not to abandon a tried-and-true method in favor of a get-it-done-quick approach that reportedly has been responsible for several serious reactions.

Reactions from any vaccine can vary from a simple swelling and soreness of the site of the injection—accompanied by dullness, depression, and even slight fever—to the extreme of an anaphylactic response, indicating the red alert of serious trouble.

Warning signals of this reaction include anxiety, restlessness, increased respirations, sweating and—sometimes—severe hives with associated swelling. An anaphylactic response requires *immediate* veterinary assistance, for it may progress to a point that interferes with breathing and oxygen intake.

Anticipated reactions can be prevented by a preinjection physical examination, combined with the use of *reliable and refined drugs* from a reputable drug company.

Let me caution you that shortcuts, indiscriminate use of seemingly harmless drugs or vaccines, untrained hands, and the judgment of an inexperienced person can and do represent a hazard to the foal's health and well-being.

Don't be tempted to buy your own stable drugs and vaccines from mail-order lists, from dusty shelves at tack shops, or at auctions in order to save a few pennies. Proper refrigeration, storage, and shelf life all control the effectiveness and value of the drug in question.

The few pennies saved are negligible when one considers the potential dangers of questionable drugs. Unfortunately, labels can be changed easily—misrepresenting the origin, date of manufacture, and expiration of use.

We seem to receive exactly what we pay for, and pennies saved unwisely can be very expensive for both you and your foal.

Parasite Control

The single most important service you can render your foal is the establishment of a modern, sophisticated parasite-control program, and your scrupulous attention to it.

An infestation of internal parasites (or endoparasitism) presents a serious challenge to every foal from the age of six weeks throughout the rest of its life.

Internal parasites represent the greatest continuous danger to your foal's overall health, growth rate, efficiency, and resistance to disease.

If parasites go unrecognized, and therefore untreated, they can cause a variety of pathologic effects upon horses of any age, but the changes are especially severe in foals.

Pathologic tissue changes that occur as the result of parasitism at an early age are usually irreversible and can, conceivably, exist for years—continuously and adversely affecting a horse. Your recognition of this need for prompt action to combat the overwhelming, rapid multiplication of endoparasites is essential for the prevention of irreparable damage to the foal's lungs, circulatory system, and gastrointestinal tract.

Parasitism in a foal is usually exhibited by "unthriftiness," a pot belly, rough coat, and a ribby appearance.

An underweight, depressed foal with teary eyes, runny nose, and a cough that resists medical treatment is a textbook description of a parasite-ridden foal.

Do not mistake this condition for a "cold." For years I have been called on to treat foals fitting this clinical description: the young patients have a normal temperature and a poor appetite.

While the concerned owner stands by watching my methodical examination, he or she may expect me to announce that the foal is, at the very least, a victim of pneumonia. If, with stethoscope in my ears, I announce that I can hear the worms crawling around in the foal's lungs, their eyes widen and a peculiar blank expression appears on their faces. When I state my intention to "tube" the foal in order to eliminate the offending parasites, their expression changes to one of horror: they envisage extensive chemotherapy, intravenous fluids, and, perhaps, oxygen therapy. They seem more than slightly convinced that I am, at best, not going to help the foal and, at worst, literally going to kill their pride and joy.

Tube-worming never quite produces an instantaneous cure, but the results are rapid and always gratifying. Within a few days the annoying cough disappears, the foal's appetite returns to normal, and he or she is active, clear-eyed, and playful.

The somewhat puzzled owner has yet to be convinced that the worm medicine was not an unorthodox cure for pneumonia! Needless to say, foals in my care are wormed regularly on a rigidly maintained schedule.

Tube-worming is a simple yet thorough treatment and is truly imperative to the health—even the life—of the foal.

A stomach tube is introduced gently through the horse's nostril and passed down the esophagus into the stomach. In experienced hands the tube is neither dangerous nor uncomfortable for the horse since the medicine is deposited directly into the stomach. By bypassing the taste buds, the olfactory senses, and the sensitive mucous membranes with the tube, there is no drug irritation and the full volume of medicine is delivered in an effective, concentrated dose. This makes it possible for the medication to reach all parts of the stomach and to pass into the intestines without an admixture of interfering grain.

There is no known method of deworming a horse that is superior to the stomach tube. For a time—with the advent of the automobile and consequent reduction of the horse population—the skill of tubing the horse for removal of endoparasites became a lost art. Now, fortunately, use of the stomach tube has regained its important position as an essential part of modern equine veterinary practice because of the renewed interest in horses for sport and pleasure.

The chore of tubing the horse lost its popularity to the convenience of powders, drenches, and boluses—all of which, supposedly easier and quicker, are relatively ineffective. Ninety-five percent of well-fed and well-loved horses will reject worming powders in their feed. Although they are advertised as a panacea and reported to be highly palatable, it would be extremely helpful if the horse could read this convincing information!

Drenches are unsatisfactory, no matter how skillfully administered. The person giving the drench usually winds up with more of the medicine in his hair, down his arms, and on his outside than the horse receives in its insides.

From my earliest attempts to administer a drench to the present time, the outstanding characteristic of drenching a horse is the instant need for a shampoo to remove the medicine from my own hair!

Boluses can also be an effective worm medicine or *anthelmintic,* as it is termed, but they require more skill in their use than the other two methods. Inaccurate administration can cause rupture of the bolus, with subsequent release of irritating drugs on the tender oral mucosa.

In attempting to use worm powders, drenches, and boluses I have rarely discovered a cooperative patient, so I end up knowing that the animal received less than the required dose or that the medicine's effectiveness was greatly diluted by the large amounts of feed used to mask the drug in order to induce the suspicious horse to "take his medicine."

Every foal should be first wormed at six weeks. This first worming is directed primarily toward the destruction of ascarids, or round worms (*Parascaris equorum*), for they are unquestionably the worst enemy of a young foal's pulmonary system and gastrointestinal tract.

Worming should be repeated every month thereafter, including treatment for both ascarids and strongyles (bloodworms).

There are, essentially, three members of the bloodworm group that should immediately alert the horse owner. They are identified as *Strongylus vulgaris, Strongylus edentatus,* and *Strongylus equinus.*

Bloodworms create a devastating effect upon the foal's intestines, liver, and vital circulatory system; they appear at this stage of the young horse's life and must be stopped before they can migrate into the blood vessels.

Bot worms should be included as one of the troublesome parasites commonly affecting horses. There are three prevalent species in the United States: *Gastrophilus nasalis, Gastrophilus intestinalis,* and *Gastrophilus haemorrhoidalis.*

This parasite is unique in that the bot fly deposits her sticky embryonated egg on the horse's hairs—preferably inside the legs or on the hairs around the mouth. Inadvertently the legs are licked by the horse's tongue and the eggs are swallowed. The larvae then attach themselves to the stomach lining and remain so attached for months.

In my opinion, bot larvae are undoubtedly responsible for more acute gastritis, stomach disorders, and other forms of colic than are any other known causes.

Be suspicious of bot infestation when discomfort suddenly develops immediately after the horse begins to eat grain and just as the food reaches the stomach. *This sudden behavior can be diagnostic.*

Bot worming is most satisfactorily carried out in late fall, after the first few killing frosts. Bot flies are the source of infestation, so it would seem foolish to bot worm before a hard frost eliminates the fly—then worm —leaving the host free of bots until midsummer, when the bot fly reappears.

Although there are literally hundreds of worm species, I have touched only upon those that are most common and most troublesome. Your veterinarian can, if necessary, identify other offenders and treat your horse appropriately.

Every foal requires an accurate, well-time parasite-control program, which should be followed faithfully. The schedule can best be prescribed by your veterinarian: who can better determine your foal's needs?

The Effects of Parasitism

Failure to meet a prescribed schedule can weaken your program and allow massive reproduction of parasites to cause tissue damage that future wormings cannot correct. The use of worm medicine can only remove the parasites from the foal, not reverse harmful tissue changes.

Early in my practice I visited a small, weak, rough-coated foal with a bloated abdomen. The dejected foal was standing beside his mother, who also appeared thin and neglected. Tearing eyes, running nose, an intermittent cough, slight fever, and slight lung congestion led me to think of parasitism as a possible underlying cause. I treated the foal for the respiratory infection and took a fecal sample home with me.

When I prepared the sample and looked at it through the microscope it was almost unbelievable: the *entire* slide field was densely packed with ascarid ova! Even in college, where I thought I had seen the heaviest infestations possible, nothing like this was ever demonstrated.

Before I had a chance to return to treat the foal the next day for the overwhelming infestation, he had died. The owner's disinterest was upsetting and puzzling to me so I volunteered to do a postmortem examination to determine the cause of the foal's death. I was horrified to find the small intestine distended and literally filled with a twisted cable of large entwined ascarids. *There was no digested food at all in the intestines.*

In-depth discussions of parasitism in school had not prepared me for what I saw before me. And even though this was a terrible experience, it was an important lesson to me: I have been on the alert ever since that day. This one unfortunate foal has saved many other foals' lives.

True, this was an extreme case; but over the years I have seen varying effects of the ravage of parasitism, and in adult animals I often see the long-term damage inflicted by worms hosted during foalhood.

Where there are horses there are horse parasites: 100,000 worms per horse count is not an uncommon finding.

Farm and land management can aid greatly in controlling these harmful, debilitating parasites. Nevertheless, the use of chemicals or anthelmintics is essential to rid our animals adequately (although on a temporary basis) of these invaders.

It is disturbing to see a foal reach down immediately after worming to fill its mouth full of ascarid-contaminated straw. I usually turn away and rationalize that I have at least reduced the number present at that moment. *Reinfestation is a constant, never-ending fact.*

Parasites or worms are constantly with us. Commercial farms are well aware that management practices, together with the use of specific chemicals, must combine to combat the stubborn parasite as well as the modern-day parasite's ability to develop drug-resistant mutants.

Care should be taken to vary the drugs used, for an anthelmintic in repeated use allows resistant strains to develop quickly. These mutants remain in the foal's body—either in the intestines or by migrating through the blood vessels, lungs, and liver—to continue their damaging trail of invasion.

On large commercial horse farms with a concentrated horse population, the constant chore of repeated routine treatments—either oral drench, powders mixed with feed or, preferably, tube-worming—takes place every five or six weeks.

On a farm with fewer horses and foals, by contrast, medication every eight or ten weeks may be an adequate schedule.

The concentration of horse population increases the population of parasites in very direct proportion.

Pastures and paddocks never grazed over by horses are virtually horse-parasite free, while "horse-poor" land that has been densely populated and overgrazed creates the problem of constant reinfestation.

In such situations it is impossible to eradicate the parasite and it is a never-ending struggle to minimize the numbers of worms and their damaging effects.

Large farms are the worst offenders, for no matter how many acres of pasture are available, there seems to be little or no opportunity to rest or rotate the fields. Owners with one or two horses have a proportionately smaller problem.

The frequency of need to worm your foal will depend in part upon the environment in which it is raised. Some foals in less desirable surroundings will require monthly medication, while those living in near-ideal surroundings will need less frequent treatment.

A rule of thumb is 1 acre of pasture land per horse; this allows for ample grazing and a slower reinfestation rate.

The number, age, and type of horses, manner of stabling, geographic location, amount of pasture land, and degree of rotation practices are all vital components when establishing your parasite-control program.

Fecal samples gathered intermittently will provide insight into the competence of your program, and thereby direct your attention to the need for more or less wormings or a change in worm-medicine mixtures.

It is important that every member of your horse population be included in your worming schedule. Be certain that no one horse is neglected or felt to be unimportant, for this one will represent a weak link in the preventive program. This single individual—whether an old pony, a very young foal, or your favorite pleasure horse—can and will exude massive numbers of parasites, so nullifying all efforts to maintain a solid line of defense against the intestinal worm.

Any new horse should be isolated, immediately wormed, and kept in quarantine until its fecal examinations are shown to be negative.

Pasture contamination can also be controlled by rotation practices; by interference with the parasite life cycle by means of chain harrowing in order to break up and expose droppings to sunlight; and by annual soil testing for acid-base balance.

A classic case relevant here is the saga of a small farm with two brood mares in residence and only one foal the particular year. Over the previous two years, the 2 acres of land available for pasture and exercise were under continuous use and had become horse-poor (low in nutrition and parasite-ridden).

In spite of my suggestions during infrequent calls to the farm, the owners, who considered themselves intelligent and progressive, were blind to the fact that their small farm contained a built-in blueprint for tragedy.

Their five-month-old suckling foal was turned out in a small, worn-down paddock with little or no grass, and was chewing the fences to idle the time away.

Because the distance to the farm was great, I was called only when a critical problem arose. Their foal had been subjected to intensive antibiotic therapy, with all sorts of oral cough medicines for a constant cough and nasal discharge, without sign of improvement for an unbelievable two-month period. At their wits' end, they reluctantly called and I made the long trip.

My examination revealed a foal obviously being destroyed by parasites. I was stunned to learn that none of their horses had been wormed for over a year.

It is difficult to imagine the vast multitude of parasites unchecked in their reproductive cycle. The fact that a vulnerable foal had been subjected to this environment and confined within an acre together with millions of parasites is still appalling to remember.

The owners finally realized how unwise they had been: they had the foal and the other horses wormed immediately and made a firm promise to themselves to improve their pastures and abide by a rigid parasite-control program.

Although the foal responded well, showed weight gain, and apparently achieved good health, I am certain this youngster suffered damage from his long-standing heavy infestation by ascarids and strongyles and will be affected by faulty intestinal circulation and bouts of colic throughout his entire life.

I have been rewarded so often by the results of administering worm medicine to foals that appeared to be chronically ill (and under ineffective medication for an unidentified "respiratory infection") that when I see any sick foal for the first time, I must first rule out parasitism before arriving at any diagnosis.

Perhaps you can now understand my enthusiasm for the invaluable stomach tube.

Today's market makes available many types and kinds of worm medicines, which vary widely in safety, efficiency, and undesirable side effects. But, as is true of almost any research problem, the perfect drug has yet to be developed.

Discomfort, purging, uneasiness, and degrees of toxicity—sometimes lasting for several days—are all seen with the modern cholinesterase-inhibiting drugs. Your veterinarian is the best judge to select the drug of choice for your particular needs. During the last few years this group of drugs, highly capable of almost total worm removal, was developed and advertised with great fanfare in horse journals. Horse persons and veterinarians are looking forward to the day when a simple intramuscular injection of worm medicine will effectively deworm the horse.

In the past claims have been made for preparations that do just that. But beware, the price you pay for an untried or insufficiently tested product could very well be your horse's life. Thus, the parasites that lost the battle actually won the war.

I would rather see a few worms and not put my patient in jeopardy. This same group of drugs was also found to be incompatible and to react adversely with some of the commonly used phenothiazine-derived tranquilizers. These drugs are used in insecticides as well, and are responsible for the death of many of our birds. Chickens and pigeons that search through the droppings of treated horses to retrieve undigested grain are also killed.

This family of drugs is unsafe for use with horses, hence ecologically dangerous. In my opinion, its manufacture should be abolished.

In spite of our control methods, and because of the constant reinfestation caused by present-day standards of living, no horse is ever totally free of endoparasites. Anyone seriously involved with horses must battle to keep these potentially lethal parasites at the lowest possible level.

8

Weaning—a Controversial Challenge

Your foal has had all of his or her basic needs attended to and has had regular examinations to confirm the state of his progress and health. He has been vaccinated and his parasite-control program is well under way. He has been eating well (you know how much, if he has been creep-fed in his stall), and now it is time to consider weaning.

The ideal time the foal should be weaned depends upon the breed, the individual animal, and your particular situation. But on rare occasions the health and well-being of either mare or foal may dictate weaning at an unorthodox time.

Weaning signals a period of trauma—physical or mental, or both. The mare, the foal, and the owner are all involved to a greater or lesser degree—and your veterinarian is always involved.

Season after season I experience a rash of emergency calls to attend to accidents that occur during weaning. Many are serious in nature; some are absolutely unavoidable, while others could be prevented by careful advance planning.

Almost every weaning accident I have seen could have been avoided.

There are nearly as many methods of weaning as there are horse owners. It is interesting to realize that everyone thinks there is only one way to wean a foal—his way.

A very popular monthly horse journal still publishes a calendar that includes the phases of the moon best suited for weaning. Many old-timers swear by it. Now that biorhythmics have become suddenly popular, perhaps someone will work out a chart applicable to the mare and foal so that weaning can become easy and smooth for both.

I would like to suggest a few conditions that are essential before you embark upon any weaning procedure.

The foal should be in excellent health, with a good appetite. He should be as active, alert, curious, and vigorous as all normal foals are. Weaning should be timed so that the foal is not scheduled to be wormed or vaccinated just before or just after the date of separation from his mother.

The foal should be accustomed to being handled and used to being led while he is still with his dam. A good way to educate your foal is to break with the tradition of baby following mother. Gradually allow the foal the independence of becoming the leader to and from the pasture. Pause sometimes on the return trip from pasture and quietly lead the foal in a circle around his mother. If you take time before weaning to teach the foal to go where you ask him to go, at least one hazard is eliminated, or at worst minimized.

There are two methods of weaning: either gradually (which some people feel prolongs the agony of separation), or abruptly (which some people believe is cruel and provokes more dangerous situations). There is no one method that is infallible, otherwise it would be simple to spell out a step-by-step "how-to" technique.

Successful weaning requires perception and judgment. In anticipation of weaning time, look carefully at your mare and foal. Analyze, to the best of your ability, their needs, degree of dependence, and determine their innate attachment to one another. Include the temperament of each and their reactions to change in daily routine in this evaluation. Their response to a new and strange handler is also an index to their ability and readiness to adjust and accept the experience of weaning.

The actual calendar age of the foal is quite often secondary in importance to these clues.

A good weaning, whether gradual or abrupt, is one whereby the mother and her foal are ultimately permanently separated with gratifying results: a safe, contented baby and a relaxed, contented mother.

It is as important to care for the mare during and after the weaning process as it is to help the foal through the transition from dependence to independence.

You will find that most mares are relieved to be parted from their demanding and (especially in the case of big, strong colts) sometimes obnoxiously rough offspring, and are ready to welcome the separation in spite of a brief period of regret.

The mare's diet is the first concern. For the 48 hours immediately following separation the mare should be fed *no grain*; but *free access to hay* seems to keep mares quieter, while reduction of caloric intake will diminish milk production.

During the fifth or sixth month of lactation many mares seem to have a built-in control that reduces milk production in preparation for weaning so that, in the absence of the foal's demands, the average mare's udder readily reduces in size and milk production ceases without need for any special attention.

A good practice is to check the mare's udder each evening when she is brought in. Some mares are heavy milkers and may develop a full, enlarged, tight udder. Gentle milking (a few streams of milk) will relieve the excessive pressure that causes discomfort.

Remove *only* enough milk to relieve the tightness of the udder. If the mare is milked of even a few extra streams, milk production is restimulated. Rather than remedying the situation, you will have aggravated it and defeated the whole purpose of milking out.

Where is the shut-off point? Use your own judgment. Do not stimulate milk production; merely make the mare more comfortable.

One fall I received a call for help from a client who had weaned her only foal six weeks earlier and was unable to dry the mare up. In fact, the client plaintively reported that the mare was producing more instead of less milk. It was true that the client was concerned, but she was more than a little put out by the attention the mare still required.

I remembered having given her explicit directions on care of the mare's udder, so I was puzzled by the situation. As soon as possible I stopped in to investigate the mare's condition.

When I arrived at the barn, I saw that the owner's report was indeed true. The enlarged mammary gland was in full production, with unnaturally enlarged, swollen, and inflamed teats appearing more like those of a cow than the smaller teats normally found in a mare.

The obvious discomfort of the mare and the elongated teats were a direct result of the work of human hands. There was never a more conscientious woman than this client, who had overdone the milking to such an extent that she had not only encouraged further milk production but also had caused painful swelling and inflammation of the teats.

I have never seen irritated or swollen teats result from a foal's vigorous nursing, butting, nipping, or pulling at the dam's udder. The foal's little mouth, with tongue curled around the small, almost inaccessible teat (even when it is most demanding), is exquisitely gentle compared to the most careful human hand.

I always know that when, of necessity, a mare must be milked for even the briefest period she will end up with a very sore udder, in spite of the most gentle hands. (God made the mare's udder for the foal and the human hand will never conform to it as it does to the udder of the goat and the cow.)

No matter what method of weaning you decide will suit your mare and foal and your physical arrangements, the foal should be allowed to remain in its safe, secure, familiar stall and the mare asked to make the adjustment of moving to new quarters.

The same safety rules apply to the foal's weaning stall as those you followed in preparing the stall in which it was born. The walls and door should be solid, with no openings large enough for a little foot to slip through. All projections should be removed from the stall interior, and the tubs and pails hung at a level appropriate to the foal's height so that it is able to eat and drink with its head and neck in a normal, relaxed, comfortable position.

If you have an "only" foal and your stable does not include a "babysitter" of the proper size and temperament, perhaps you can arrange to borrow one from a friend or an acquaintance. An old foundered pony is an ideal sitter, for he will stand quietly while the foal romps and plays around him.

In any event, the sitter should be quiet, kind, and patient.

It is important that the foal becomes acquainted with his or her new friend *before* weaning. If the sitter is stabled next to the foal and turned out in an adjacent paddock, the foal becomes familiar with his appearance and his odor. The two can investigate each other and touch noses through a fence while the foal still has his mother with him for reassurance.

The Gradual Method

As I mentioned earlier, there are innumerable methods of weaning. One method that has worked well for many of my clients with only one or two foals is to wean gradually. Begin by separating the mare and foal for the evening meal. When the mare and foal are brought in for the night, the foal is taken to his familiar stall and the mare is placed in a stall next to the foal. If the feed tubs are hung so that the two will eat with their heads together, even though the stall wall intervenes, the pair will be very much aware of each other's proximity. After the foal has finished his grain, the mare is returned to the stall with her baby and the two are allowed to remain together for the rest of the night.

When the foal is settled and comfortable with this arrangement, the next step is to remove the mare from the stall in the morning. Feed the foal in his own stall and the mare in her new quarters in the adjacent stall.

This maneuver is not as simple to accomplish as it sounds, for the foal will be vividly aware that his mother is, in fact, leaving him. It is a much different situation from that of the mare and foal being led in together, but placed in separate stalls. This will be the first time the mare has been taken away from the foal, and you can be certain that he will insist upon following her.

It is wise to have a helper on hand the first few times the mare is led away from the foal. If one person walks into the young one's stall with feed bucket in hand, the mare can then be quickly and quietly moved to the next stall by the helper. When the foal realizes that his mother is going no further away than her new feed tub, he will relax and accept this separation just as he does the evening meal procedure.

The periods of time the mare and foal are separated should be lengthened gradually until they are together *only* when turned out. It is advisable not to leave them separated and unattended until you are certain that the foal has accepted the new arrangements. During the day (perhaps when the weather is unsuitable to turn them out), the mare and foal can be separated for a prolonged test period, but *only* while being kept safely under observation.

By now the foal should be well acquainted with his babysitter and ready to be turned out with his friend.

At this juncture the mare should be removed to a distant barn for the specific purpose of being out of sight and hearing of the foal.

If your property does not permit complete separation, an alternate plan is to leave the mare in and lead the foal to his regular paddock in which the sitter is already turned out and waiting.

A generous ration of choice hay placed before the mare in her stall will keep her occupied and quiet.

Even though there will be some calling back and forth, and restlessness for both, maintain your supervision while allowing both the mare and the foal time to adjust to this change of routine before you hit the panic button. If the foal's behavior is such that danger seems to exist, return the foal to the safety of his stall and try again tomorrow.

The majority of foals will settle down with the sitter, in spite of anxious questions from mother; soon mother will ignore the baby's calls.

There is a trend today to wean as early as possible, as opposed to the way of old-time horsemen who insisted that the mare and foal be kept together for six months—regardless of the condition of the mare or foal, and regardless of whether the mare is pregnant or barren, or whether she still has milk or has dried up.

The open-minded new breed of horsemen, not shackled to the old ways, have availed themselves of current information and today's new opinion of the limited value of mares' milk. To repeat a bit of our earlier discussion, the nutritional content of mares' milk is now highly questionable after the first six weeks of lactation. Creep feeding and provision of top-quality hay make up for this inadequacy to a great extent.

However, foals weaned at an early age seem to surpass those left with their mothers in spite of all efforts to supplement mares' milk.

How this new concept evolved, whether by design or accident, is unknown. Who courageously initiated the very early separation of mares and foals is also unknown, but the practice is growing rapidly. The results *are* known and are dramatically demonstrated by the superb physical appearance of such foals.

Years ago an orphan foal automatically was written off as a substandard horse, regardless of bloodlines. Professional horsemen had no interest in these foals whose future was predetermined by limited growth and poor development.

It is safe to assume, however, that because of the tragedy of losing mares and the necessity of hand-feeding orphan foals, new methods, milk substitutes, and special feeds have evolved—thus turning anticipated tragic losses into unexpected successes that are so outstanding that many people now welcome the trend toward early weaning. We may be witnessing the beginning of a rare change in the rigid, tradition-bound horse world.

Foals weaned early and sustained by freely available, highly nutritious grains, as well as leafy, green, properly cured legume hay, usually grow into outstanding physical specimens.

This conclusion has been drawn from comparative studies of all other foals in the same crops, with common environmental conditions. Even the most stubborn old horseman can be convinced if shown on the basis of fair comparison.

We know that early weaning is advantageous to both the mare and the foal. The mare is free of the nutritional demands of lactation. Her hormonal system is allowed to adjust from that of a milk producer to a balanced condition conductive to effective reproduction. And the nutrition and hormonal needs of the ensuing pregnancy are met more efficiently. Without the stress of her foal's constant demands, she returns easily to a contented state.

On large farms, the daily physical work of stabling, feeding, and pasturing is simplified by early separation.

If the mare is to be transported a distance to be bred, the foal can be spared the dangers and hardships of the trip and kept safely in familiar surroundings.

As a veterinarian concerned with equine reproduction, I find that the greatest advantage of early weaning—especially for those mares called "every other year mares"—is the return of the hormonal system to its natural state and subsequent increase of fertility.

The advantages to the foal are numerous. These foals eat more, grow better, and develop early independence. As a group, they seem to surpass foals of equal age in their ability to adjust, learn, and progress. They may eat or rest whenever they choose, in the absence of a competitive mother, which seems to be a factor in their unusual increase in growth and development.

Foals of equal age running and playing together seem to possess a better attitude: it seems to sharpen their ability to cope, compete, and become well adjusted. Rough play may result in a scrape or two, but this type of accident is relatively rare.

I have noticed that one-foal operations seem to produce more spoiled babies—either timid or overly aggressive, pushy foals. They do not seem to be as well prepared mentally to accept discipline or get along with other individuals of the same age group.

It seems obvious that foals should be treated like children in this respect—given decreased protective sheltering and increased exposure to freedom and other creatures of a comparable age. Supervision is vital, yet it should remain in the background. If possible, provide an environment in which youngsters can play hard but not become exhausted, eat in peace, and rest undisturbed. Then, stand back and watch them grow.

There are a few disadvantages to early weaning for the mare; for example, there is always the chance of mastitis developing if the mare's udder is not carefully watched. Regular inspection is necessary to avoid the incidence of painful congestion in the udder.

In addition, high-strung, nervous mares require care and consideration at weaning. A simple sedative can be of help to calm these mares.

It is a distinct advantage to wean foals early unless they show up with problems when they are given a thorough preweaning examination. Weak, sick, or underdeveloped foals should not be included in an early-weaning program.

If there is even a shadow of doubt, leave the foal with the mare. Any foal particularly dependent upon its mother, or unusually timid of nature, should not be weaned; further observation and a new evaluation should be made.

But, aside from a sick or overly dependent foal, there is no reason to deny foals the opportunity to grow into their full genetic potential.

Perhaps I can be thought of as narrow-minded, but I have to be thoroughly convinced before I am willing to change from the old tried-and-true methods. And since I am now a convert to the early-weaning approach, I would like to share with you some of the experiences that transformed my attitude. I had always felt that mothers and babies should be together as Nature intended; but when I see the outstanding results from programmed early weaning, it removes all doubt in my mind as to what is best for the mare and foal.

Perhaps you will join me as a proponent of this not-yet-popular discipline after reading of a few unusual experiences.

Years ago, a mare that was a patient of mine died three days after delivering a handsome liver-chestnut colt. I have unfortunately forgotten the details of how and why the mare died, but I remember precisely how discouraged and concerned I felt about the colt's chances for survival when I looked into the large stall that dwarfed the forlorn little orphan.

Fortunately the foal had been with his mother long enough to receive his priceless colostrum.

Remember that this was in the days before the development of mare's milk substitutes, and the best product at this time for feeding a foal was a milk preparation designed to be a milk-starter for calves. We diluted the formula with lime water and added Karo syrup to simulate mare's milk as closely as we could. Human baby bottles were filled with this formula. We enlarged the holes in the nipples slightly and the hungry little foal soon accepted this source of food.

Luckily one of the stablemen at the orphan colt's farm was thoughtful, patient, and caring. He took on the motherless colt as his responsibility and followed my instructions for regular, constant feedings to the letter.

Before long his charge was drinking the formula from a pail and eating grain and hay. A full pail of milk was hung in the stall constantly for the baby; the best hay and grain on the farm were always kept within his reach.

There were eight or ten other foals on the farm and after weaning they were all turned out together in a choice pasture. It had been a while since I had visited the farm, so when I was called in to treat an injured yearling I found myself looking with a critical professional eye at the weanlings pastured next to the lane. They looked all right to me, but were what I would consider just average.

I slowed my car down for a closer look and an outstanding young one caught my eye. I looked more closely and then recognized the orphan. He was larger than the other foals and his coat, sleek and shining, reflected his excellent condition. His strong, straight legs and well-rounded body were better muscled than those of his companions and he moved in a more deliberate and better-coordinated manner.

At the barn I was enthusiastic about the colt's development and praised the feeding program I thought had made his wonderful progress possible.

The owner shrugged my comments aside, saying that, after all, this colt was extremely well bred and was probably genetically superior. I remarked that his superiority seemed to reflect his nutritional state rather than his inherited characteristics, but because I had no proof I didn't pursue the discussion.

Over the years I have seen several other orphaned foals whose progress and physical condition indicated unusually good growth and development gain; in fact, I would say that they were superior to other members of the same crop.

More recently, special milk formulas and supplementary feeds have been carefully researched and produced specifically for foals. The impressive results are impossible to ignore.

One foal in particular was so outstanding that, even though there are other considerations to ponder in his history, I would like to tell his story.

Just a few years ago an exquisite, extremely well-bred, heavily insured matron that was about eight months into her gestation period slowly began to develop an inconsistent uncoordination in her hindquarters that shortly became very evident in her gait.

When I was certain of what I was seeing, I asked the owner to report the mare's condition to the insurance company. In order to abide by the conditions of the policy, as a veterinarian it is my responsibility to protect the owner's interests by reporting early any condition that might affect the animal's future health.

Surprised, I answered a series of calls within only a few hours from insurance underwriters apprehensive about the condition of the valuable matron. I was sure these calls did not reflect an interest in the lovely mare and her extremely well-bred unborn foal; rather, they showed concern about the amount of money involved.

My suspicions were confirmed the following morning when I arrived at the stable in which the mare resided to find an entourage of eight men in gray flannel suits staring into the dignified mare's stall. Soon, four veterinarians arrived and walked briskly down the aisle to the stall: two were from a nearby university and the other two were from an out-of-state school of veterinary medicine. The scene took on the appearance of a summit meeting of heads of state.

After I had my in-depth debriefing—as the farm veterinarian—I stood back and watched as the four veterinarians bustled around and examined every square inch of my patient.

The group emerged from the stall having concurred with my original diagnosis, but with their own, divergent opinions of how to manage the case. After discussing and observing the mare for several hours, the group came to the shocking conclusion that she and her unborn baby should be humanely destroyed.

I felt a terrible surge of righteous indignation at the injustice of what was proposed. This could not be!

While the mare's fate was being discussed outside her stall, the animal stood quietly and unconcernedly eating hay. She was obviously comfortable and contented in spite of her very evident pregnancy. The foal she was carrying represented a priceless genetic combination of the proven bloodlines of two outstanding racehorses and had limitless unknown potential. (It always seems to me that an unborn foal is like an unopened treasure chest with its contents yet to be discovered.)

Without hesitation or giving a thought to the ethics of what I was doing, I stepped forward, interrupting the other veterinarians and insurance company personnel, to summarize my observations during the past month of her care—including my comments on the current condition of the mare.

I emphatically and authoritatively reminded this august group of experts of the mare's pregnancy and the *two* lives they were discussing. The mare's appetite was excellent, she was completely free of pain or discomfort, and the size of the unborn foal indicated that it was within normal, acceptable range. Because it would be impossible to predict the rate of progression of the developing lack of coordination, why not allow the mare to live and continue her pregnancy to term? If she were observed carefully on a daily basis, it would be possible to let the mare herself make the decision; her actions and reactions would tell us when it would be inhumane to allow her to continue. (Mares do have their own way of telling one!)

The courage to take such a positive stand and suggest this approach wasn't based on my observation of just this one episode: I had been in Kentucky just the week before and had had a singular opportunity to discuss this frustrating entity as seen in the pregnant mare. In spite of all odds to the contrary, on this trip I had met the one practicing veterinary obstetrician experienced in ataxia, or partial loss of coordination in pregnant mares. We talked endlessly of his cases, their treatment, prognosis, and, fundamentally, his findings as to pregnancy termination—but, above all, of the mare's ability to deliver her foal successfully.

It was both encouraging and inspiring to realize that another veterinarian also considered the "right to life" of the fetus along with the "right not to suffer" of the mother. Bearing this principle in mind, I was mentally prepared to react quickly when this group's unpleasant, unexpected, and unfair decision was presented.

Their favorable response to my indignant plea was astonishing. In fact, their abrupt turnabout amazed me as much as had their original shocking decision.

I left the barn feeling victorious, only to hear later by telephone that the insurance-appointed veterinarian would be in charge of my favorite mare—empowered to make all decisions and report regularly from this date to the time of final decision. I had learned that when a claim is reported to an insurance company, the animal in question automatically becomes the property of that company until final disposition of the case is determined.

This mare had been in my care through seven previous pregnancies. I had delivered all of her foals and cared for them until they left the farm as young adults. It was a blow to give her up now. I always feel that somehow my patients belong partly to me; but rules are rules and personal feelings have to be disciplined.

No news is good news, as a rule, and I heard nothing about the grand old mare for a few weeks. One day I walked through the barn and tried to be casual as I glanced in her stall. Luckily her condition appeared to have stabilized; in fact, she appeared somewhat steadier on her feet. I felt a little left out, but I was pleased with the mare's attitude and condition.

Since I represented the farm, with eighty-some head under my care, I again tried to turn my thoughts from the insurance company's case.

As the last few weeks of the mare's pregnancy melted away, I would occasionally make an excuse to wander through the brood mare barn to glance toward her stall. Always I was pleased to see that all seemed fine. Her nearness to parturition—with her huge abdomen and milk supply ready—and her proper muscle relaxation brought me great pleasure, for the mare exemplified normalcy as she shaped up to foal. With crossed fingers I left the barn and went on my way.

Then came a crushing telephone call early one morning, demanding that I come quickly. My favorite mare had delivered a foal and had then been humanely destroyed by the insurance company's attending veterinarian.

I was devastated, but managed to dress and drive hastily to the barn.

In the stall—empty of her—I saw a large, handsome brown colt, wet and shivering. The alert foal looked everyone over carefully as if seeking reassurance from those of us who were present. A foal standing alone in a stall always looks so small, and is a grim reminder that all is not the way it is supposed to be.

This foal was so perfect in every way that he looked as though he had been ordered from some special catalogue. His small, erect ears were set perfectly on his classic head; the large, shining eyes were far apart, the muzzle small and soft. His straight legs were exactly right for his stocky, well-rounded, short-backed body, and the long, graceful neck—topped with a mane of soft, black curls—extended from the well-laid-back shoulders. He had strong quarters, with a sloping croup and an ideally placed wavy tail that matched his mane. It seemed as though each and every part had been carefully selected to construct the perfect horse. From his appearance a hidden treasure had indeed been found!

The exhausted farm manager finished rubbing the foal dry. He then told of the all-night episode ending in the birth of this beautiful foal and, sadly, the ultimate euthanasia of the mare.

What had happened? Couldn't the mare regain her feet after foaling? Yes, the mare was feeble but did—with great effort—regain her feet. The foal did nurse and obtained a few swallows of the priceless colostrum before the insurance-company veterinarian made and carried out the decision to destroy the mare.

The tired and disgusted farm manager knew how appalled I was, but gently reminded me that our friend the mare was and had been the property of the insurance company.

He pointed to the small but splendid example of a classic Thoroughbred, a combination of the most desirable genes, who stood looking at me and sniffing inquiringly at the antiseptic odor coming from my white coveralls. Proudly the manager informed me that the foal was to be my patient. An unexpected turn of events and an exciting challenge!

As soon as I heard this news not a second was lost in procuring supplies and equipment for my new charge. Baby bottles were sterilized, the holes in the nipples enlarged, and the bottles filled with a commercial colostrum substitute. The foal's demanding feeding program was scheduled and, with the farm manager's help, round-the-clock sitters were assigned.

After the routine care and injections that all neonatal foals receive and with a stomach comfortably full of warm milk, our new baby dropped in the deep straw of his stall, sighed contentedly, and went to sleep.

The farm manager took almost complete responsibility for the colt, abiding by the feeding program to the letter, knowing that for all baby foals there is a very narrow margin for error. He spent many late nights unselfishly giving of himself on the foal's behalf.

This beautiful colt learned to love him and he became the foal's substitute mother.

It was a moving sight to see the foal following him to and from the paddock, and to see the odd pair romping and playing together. This dedicated man would even stand in the exercise paddock and allow the colt to run and play around him, which was hazardous, for colts tend to kick and play hard with their friends.

A few years ago this colt would have been considered of little value because he was left orphan. He not only survived, but grew larger and stronger than all of his contemporary stablemates. He went on to the track and distinguished himself by winning many races; the last I heard of him, the Argentinians had purchased him and shipped him to their country to stand at stud. I feel privileged and enriched to have experienced this partly sad, yet wonderful series of events.

Had he been placed on the old formula, including cow's milk, lime water, and clear syrup as a sweetener (which proved adequate for survival, but appeared to be no more than just that), he would not have had much chance to achieve. Every foal that I saw raised on this formula survived, but all possessed the same physical characteristics: each appeared dwarfed or stunted in growth at weaning age, had reduced muscle tone and a pot belly. Because of their underdevelopment they were never even given an equal opportunity for the training and advancement offered their stablemates.

Today's story is very different. With milk substitutes and feeds precisely produced for foals, it is safe to say that it is now exceptional to find a hand-fed foal that does not surpass foals of equal age that remained with their mothers. I hope nonbelievers will be startled and even convinced by this evidence. To end with three questions:

Why are all orphan foals now superior physically?

What are we doing wrong?

Isn't it time for a change?

9

Pediatric Problems

Pediatrics is defined as that branch of medicine dealing with the care of infants and children and the treatment of their diseases.

Equine pediatrics deals with the foal through its first year of life.

Normal parturition and the uncomplicated delivery of a foal, together with its immediate neonatal period, have been discussed earlier in some detail. Fortunately, nature frequently prevails, and both dam and foal survive under almost any given set of circumstances, including environmental, hereditary, and congenital handicaps.

In many instances a foal may possess a built-in predisposition of hereditary origin and if exposed to specific circumstances of stress will develop a disorder, while another foal exposed to the same stress or environmental influence—without the predisposition—will be unaffected.

However, experience dictates that the chances for survival and for a long, healthy, vigorous life are greatly increased if a carefully planned health program is diligently followed.

In spite of the extensive body of knowledge available to us today, there still remain many areas of susceptibility that plague both the horse owner and the veterinarian. An enormous list of so-called incurable foal conditions still exists, but this is being slowly and methodically reduced by the efforts of a small group of dedicated researchers and practitioners (together with the support of some understanding owners), who refuse

146

to accept the failures represented by mediocrity of diagnosis, treatment, and follow-up.

Any deficiency in the physiologic functioning of the newborn is significant and will either be visible promptly or will show up in the form of future pathologic problems. Early recognition, due to the owner's or attendant's acute powers of observation and perception, often makes the difference between success or failure of medical or surgical treatment. When I contemplate foals cared for by perceptive people, I realize how fortunate these young ones are.

My staff had gathered in the clinic late one fall afternoon in expectation of an orthopedic surgery.

The horse had been meticulously "prepped." The anesthesiologist was on hand readying the anesthesia machine and the induction area. Both scrub and circulating nurses were busy arranging the various instrument packs and dressing packs needed for the operation.

I was about to inject the preoperative sedation when an urgent message was rushed to me: a foal was very sick, perhaps dying, at a nearby farm.

The scheduled surgery was elective, my staff usually cheerful and understanding. Because I had brought the ill foal into the world there was no question as to the decision. Surgery would be postponed until after I had reached my young patient and helped it in every way I could.

I drove to the farm in a matter of minutes and found the farm manager crouched over a still, dark form flattened in the straw. The tiny foal had the deflated appearance that is so characteristic of death, and the experienced manager repeated his impression that the foal was dying, even though he had seemed fine an hour earlier when brought in from pasture for the night.

I knelt beside the limp foal to examine him. His respirations were almost imperceptible. His nasal, ocular, and oral tissues had a discouraging bluish tint and the half-opened lids partially covered his dull eyes. He felt cold to the touch and did not respond in any way while I examined him, nor did he react to the activity in his stall.

Luckily I was able to recognize the symptoms I had often seen in foals before. How fortunate I felt with my prompt diagnosis of septicemia. As quickly as humanly possible I injected the specific intravenous broad-spectrum antibiotic and started restorative intravenous fluids.

The foal's condition was a completely familiar one and the history that was related to me while treatment was under way fitted the picture perfectly. As I watched the fluids run into the small body, I prayed that treatment had been started soon enough and that time had not run out for this young life.

With the passage of an hour his condition gradually improved. He became slightly aware of the movement and quiet conversation around him and began to move his legs. I had just finished running in the last vial of fluids and was watching the little foal when he raised his head and whinnied to his mother.

It was a miracle—the farm manager's face was almost split in two by his sudden happy grin. It was time for me to leave, for the foal needed a respite from treatment and time to rest. Assured that the foal's mother would be milked and a bottle offered to the still-reclining baby in an hour, I left the scene feeling a glow of hope and hurried back to the clinic and my surgical case.

Back at the hospital I found a somewhat impatient group waiting for me. Preparations for surgery had long since been completed and it was obvious that it would be late evening before they would be able to leave for their respective homes—even later before they would reach their destinations, for each one had a considerable distance to drive.

But when I told the story of the foal's precarious condition and his encouraging response to treatment everyone, as usual, became happily enthusiastic, volunteered to stay in the recovery stall with the postoperative surgical patient, and rushed me out so that I could return to the farm as soon as possible after we completed surgery.

A night-light had been placed near the small patient's stall door. As I followed the dim light, I saw a note on the door. I quickly read the note, looked into the stall with unbelieving eyes, then reread the scribbled words. Within thirty minutes of the time I had first left, the foal had struggled to his feet.

In spite of being weak and wobbly, he had managed several swallows of warm milk; his anxious mother had nuzzled him and guided him into position so that he could nurse. Then he collapsed and slept. Ten minutes later he awoke, *walked to his mother's side,* and nursed again.

The manager was ecstatic, as I was.

The foal was now alert, his respirations deep and regular, and his body temperature almost back to normal.

It took an intensive course of drugs administered over several weeks to be sure that he completely recovered. But he did.

This case represents more than just a fortunate series of events: the person in charge recognized the seriousness of the foal's rapidly deteriorating condition, and his urgent call made almost immediate treatment possible. No one will ever know just how narrow the margin of time and how great the danger of potential tissue changes were against which we were working. I know that I never want it to be any closer.

The drugs I used are expensive and relatively new, but without the research and development that made them available that foal would not have survived. Without the help of the good God, and the foal's innate ability to fight back, that colt would not be standing at stud today!

It would be considered foolhardy by any well-informed person to categorize foalhood diseases, entities, and abnormalities without considering the multiple interrelated influences of heredity, as well as the congenital, acquired, and even the ambiguous (yet ever-present) gray areas of influence.

Veterinary medical knowledge has shown us the unfathomable interplay of forces influencing not only embryonic, but prenatal, perinatal, and postnatal development. A definite clear-cut delineation of these multiple forces is virtually impossible.

In light of these facts and in an effort to clarify the complex collection of foalhood disorders, a simple chart follows that shows when we think such abnormalities develop. They fall into three categories—I, *Prenatal* (*in utero*); II, *Perinatal* (during birth); and III, *Neonatal* (immediately after birth) and *Postnatal* (early life).

Time designations are loosely specified as before and after birth. The precise periods are somewhat ambiguous and do seem to precipitate into a matter of opinion, so I have taken some license in this matter of categorization. Actually, these columns represent growing and changing manifestations for the foal within the mare, during delivery, and in the new external environment.

A complete physical examination of the foal should be conducted by a competent professional as soon after birth as possible.

Careful notation should be made of deviations or malformations of the head, mouth, jaw, eyes, and especially the legs and feet. Immediately check for completeness of all body apertures (oral, respiratory, ocular, auricular, and the navel area, plus the anus, sheath, penis, or vulva). It is vital that all orifices mentioned be present, obvious, and functional.

The foal should be examined for any indication of physical trauma sustained during delivery—facial or body bruises, fractured ribs, subluxation of limbs, capped elbows or hocks.

Injury can be sustained by the hocks and elbows during an unattended delivery. The floundering efforts of a newborn foal to achieve a standing position may result in internal capillary bleeding and edema (swelling) over these bony prominences. Bruised or capped elbows or hocks are startling to see but are rarely any cause for concern. Any abrasions of the areas can be treated with an application of topical ointment. The swelling soon subsides. (I have never seen a foal suffer any aftereffects in even the most severe of such cases.)

I PRENATAL
(*In utero*)

Constipation
  (Retained
  meconium)

Weak or crooked
  limbs

Contracted foal
  (Contracted digital
  flexor tendons)

Hernias
  (Scrotal)
  (Umbilical)

Locked stifles
  (Upward fixation
  of the patella)

Defective soft palate

Overshot and
  undershot jaw
  (Prognathism)

Jaundiced foals
  (Isohemolytic
  icterus)

Systemic infections
  (Septicemias)

Defective colon or
  rectum
  (*Atresia coli*)
  (*Atresia recti*)

Monster foals
  (Hydroencephalon)
  (Schistosomus
  reflexus)
  (Fetal anasarca)

Inflated guttural
  pouches
  (Tympany)

Heart defect
  (Interventricular
  septal defect)

Wobbles
  (Equine
  uncoordination or
  foal ataxia)

Cerebellar hypoplasia
  and degeneration
  (Arabian horses
  only)

Extra appendages
  (Polydactylism)

Retained testicles
  (Monorchidism)
  (Cryptorchidism)

Immuno-defense
  deficiencies
  (CID)
  (IgM)

Visual deficiencies
  (Ocular
  abnormalities)

II PERINATAL
(During birth)

Trauma to
  (Heart)
  (Lungs)
  (Ribs)
  (Limbs)

Body hernias

Ruptured bladder

Ruptured diaphragm

Obstetrical accidents

Contusions
  (Mouth)
  (Face)
  (Eyes)

Eye lesions
  (Corneal)

Inverted eyelids
  (Entropion)

Everted eyelids
  (Ectropion)

III *NEONATAL AND POSTNATAL*
(Immediately after birth and early life)

Absence of nursing reflex	Diarrhea Mechanical Infectious Rhinopneumonitis Influenza	Capped hocks and elbows
Simple constipation		Absence of urination
Urine leaking from navel (Pervious urachus)	Pneumonia Mechanical Infectious	Infectious arthritis
		Dummy or sleeper foal (Actinobacillosis)
Bacterial infections (Septicemia)	Naval infections and abscesses	
Viral infections (Viremias) Rhino influenza	Joint infections	Barker foal (Neurologic damage)
		Shaker foal
		Premature foal

Early recognition of trouble, followed by the earliest possible start of proper corrective measures, is the secret of a successful nursery. This procedure will increase the number of existing and healthy foals and considerably reduce the overall mortality rate.

The foalhood disorders listed in the chart are discussed below more or less in the order of their prevalence.

Simple constipation is a relatively common ailment and is due to the foal's retention of meconium. Most often it is indicated any time from the first half hour after birth until the foal reaches its third day.

The first symptoms of constipation are colicky signs of pain and discomfort—tail switching, straining, lying down, and rolling. This behavior in a foal is often caused by simple gastrointestinal pain created by a small, hard fecal mass in the rectum that cannot be passed easily. An ordinary soapy-water enema often solves the problem. Avoid commercial preparations. They create additional peristalsis, resulting in added discomfort in the newborn.

However, the same symptoms can indicate a more serious problem located higher in the gastrointestinal tract. The unmistakable (pathonomonic) sign of well-developed constipation is the unnatural position assumed by the foal. A stricken foal is found on its back in the straw with its head and neck extended in a straight line with the body so that the lower jaw is prominent and embraced by the front legs and feet. This position signals a serious condition and immediate treatment by a veterinarian.

Meconium is defined as the first intestinal discharge of the newborn. During the later period of gestation, some systems of the fetus are functioning independently. The waste fluids are accumulated, stored in, and expelled with the placental tissue at delivery. The semisolid waste materials that accumulate in the gastrointestinal tract await their arrival in the external world to receive the necessary stimulus to evacuate.

Retained meconium is almost self-explanatory. For some reason, frequently the meconium does not evacuate, as is required for a foal to remain healthy. Any protracted or stubborn case of constipation that develops within the first three days of life can almost always be attributed to meconium that has been retained.

Prompt treatment is essential. An enema should stimulate evacuation of the rectum, with consequent end of the discomfort in cases of mild constipation. However, if pain and all the symptoms persist, your foal requires a veterinarian's care.

Most successful treatments include sedation, oral laxative medication, intravenous fluids, and enemas administered with discretion.

There will be periodic signs of both distress and comfort. Around-the-clock surveillance, with treatment when indicated, is necessary for the foal's survival. At any time during the course of this disorder the veterinarian in charge my be placed in the position of recommending life-saving surgical intervention. Odds for the foal's survival are increased if a well-equipped surgical facility is within your reach.

It is astounding to see the size, length, and concrete consistency of some of the meconium masses successfully removed from foals. Many of the survivors develop into normal animals and never show a similar problem thereafter.

Colic in foals, as well as in adult horses, is defined as spasmodic pains in the abdomen. The term "colic" is overused and misunderstood, for it is only a symptom of many possible causes. The source of the pain can be located in the gastrointestinal tract, urogenital tract, liver, kidney, or any other area within the abdominal cavity.

Colic is not a disease entity: as a symptom it is a vitally important danger signal.

The cause of straining and the specific types of straining seen in foals are sometimes difficult to diagnose properly. Quite often straining from constipation can be confused with urinary discomfort, and this situation requires a veterinarian to determine the proper diagnosis.

Diarrhea is an abnormally frequent discharge of more-or-less fluid fecal matter from the bowel. Diarrhea can be caused by poor digestion, overindulgence, the quality and quantity of the mare's milk, ingesting water in place of milk, and feeding on manure (coprophagy).

Some conditions can be controlled with thoughtful stall management.

Diarrhea caused by infectious diseases falls into another category and definitely requires professional attention. Use of a rectal thermometer helps distinguish between mechanical and infectious causes.

The majority of infectious diseases (newborn septicemia) are associated with elevation of body temperature, although one very serious infection—Actinobacillosis—often carries a subnormal temperature initially. Together with other symptoms, the color, odor, and character of the feces will indicate the agent of cause to your veterinarian, its seriousness, and the appropriate treatment.

It is essential to remind yourself that *foals do not have a built-in margin of safety to count on*. They weaken quickly; dehydration with electrolytic imbalance can develop suddenly; and debilitation follows shortly.

One can expect foal diarrhea to develop simultaneously with the mare's heat period—commonly called "foal heat scours." The onset of scours can be expected any time from the sixth to the twelfth postpartum day of the mare, and should end about four days from its onset.

Weak foals routinely receive treatment to shorten this diarrhea and to reduce the degree of its stress.

Some strong, vigorous, overindulgent foals will be unduly affected; they too require aid. Irritation of intestinal mucosa in some of these foals can be the cause of protracted diarrhea (well beyond the mare's heat period) and will require professional attention.

The cause of foal heat scours has been highly controversial over the years. There are two schools of thought on the subject.

Some people think that hormonal activation and milk content are contributing factors to foal diarrhea.

Others believe in a theory which states that *E. coli* and other gram-negative bacteria found in the intestines are carried down to the udder and teats by fluids discharged from the anus and the vulva, especially during the heat cycle, and that the amount of these fluids will be markedly increased if the mare is covered by a stallion.

However, tests have shown that milk from a clean udder *does not result in diarrhea,* and when efforts are made to keep the udder clean during the occurrence of this period diarrhea is minimal.

If diarrhea from any cause is allowed to continue unchecked there exists the grave danger of a gram-negative intestinal bacterial invasion of the system, resulting in overwhelming septicemia (enterotoxemia).

We accept the onset of foal heat scours as a normal reaction and believe it should be treated as required; but *diarrhea in any foal at any time* should by looked upon with suspicion, quickly requiring professional assistance.

Septicemias are common in young foals and are the result of bacterial invasion of the circulatory system. Septicemias are systemic diseases caused by the presence of microorganisms, or their toxins, in the bloodstream; they can affect all parts of the body.

They may be acquired *in utero* and result in the abortion of a dead fetus. In spite of the infection, in some cases embryonic growth and fetal development continue in an infected uterus and placental membranes, and a sick foal is born. The fetal fluids and the placenta are stained or brownish in color from fetal diarrhea. But some of these foals are saved by prompt recognition and treatment of the acute form of infection.

A healthy foal can be born and then acquire a systemic infection in three known ways: microorganisms may enter through the open navel, be ingested, or be inhaled.

It is difficult to regulate completely what the foal ingests or inhales, but the navel is within the realm of control.

If the navel antiseptic is properly applied before exposure to contaminants occurs, this route can be at least partially closed. The accepted antiseptic contains a bacterial agent and its caustic properties stimulate tissue contraction, thus hastening closure of the umbilical tissues.

Some foals are completely cured of such an infection and never suffer any future consequences. Unfortunately, there are foals that survive the acute attack and appear symptomless, but still harbor a dormant residue of infection that reappears—cruelly—in a chronic form between eight to eighteen months. Gradual joint enlargements that are occasionally painful and stiff, grossly infected joints, and/or generalized arthritis are the conditions most commonly seen associated with the chronic form of the disease.

Systemic streptococcal infections in the newborn are not as common now as they were before the advent of antibiotics. Today, foals with streptococcal infections have a better chance for survival, as do foals with other formidable systemic infections. Appropriate and effective drugs are available and a better understanding of these overwhelming infections has improved survival statistics. Foal losses were enormous prior to the miracle drugs.

It is difficult to be specific as to how long a sick foal should be tube-fed, if needed, and treatment continued. Your veterinarian must weigh all decisions carefully and utilize laboratory tests to the fullest to supplement his own judgment.

As long as the foal's condition does not deteriorate, it is safe to say there *is* hope for survival and justification of continuation of the exhausting (and sometimes costly) treatment.

Foals suffering from *Streptococcus pyogenes* infections *in utero* are either aborted, delivered dead at term or, if alive, are very weak, dehydrated, and usually comatose. Such a condition represents an emergency—prompt and intensive treatment to replace lost fluids and electrolytes, and chemotherapy to combat the responsible microorganism, are imperative. The prognosis is poor for infected foals coming into the world from a diseased uterus and placental tissues, in spite of all treatment.

More typically, a foal appears normal at birth and then, within the first few days of its life, develops a fever, depression, and constipation or diarrhea. Hot, swollen, painful joints (called "joint ill") complete the picture of positive evidence of the dreaded Streptococcus pyogenes invasion. Joint swellings can be transitory and inconstant in location from day to day, but persistent. Cultures of the joint fluids will determine bacterial sensitivity and help in the selection of the effective drug for proper local treatment.

Blood studies are indispensable in evaluating septicemia and act as an indicator of the effectiveness of the drug being used. In addition, they help the veterinarian to assess the foal's defense-mechanism response and to determine the course and prognosis of the disease.

Navel infection is an additional (and consistent) finding associated with streptococcal infections. When the navel is involved, it is commonly called "navel ill." The navel stump is found to be hot and swollen, with evidence of intermittent discharges. Pain is shown by the foal's reluctance to move. This condition can be compounded by secondary invaders causing one or more abscesses to develop in and around the area of the navel.

The open navel cord represents the most direct route and greatest danger to the vulnerable abdominal cavity, especially the urogenital system. An infected navel should be treated locally, concurrent with the systemic treatment that should be under way for the streptococcus.

When the systemic infection becomes septicemic, following its entrance into the circulatory system, multiple secondary infection sites develop. These sites include pulmonary, liver, and kidney abscesses, and various types of pneumonia.

Pain, depression, and fever result in inability of the foal to stand and nurse. Such foals become progressively weaker and are commonly found prostrate in the straw.

If the foal survives the initial infection, *Streptococcus pyogenes* is notoriously obstinate in its resistance to treatment, and invariably a residue remains. The foal appears to have recovered because the infection remains quiescent until it becomes a young adult. Then, for no accountable reason, although it is predictable to veterinarians, an enlarged, hot, painful swelling appears in the hock, stifle, or knee. This presents a puzzle and a worry to the owner, who may have purchased a foal with no knowledge of its early medical history.

Such latent infection can be treated, but not very satisfactorily, and unless the situation is an exceptional one, it may result in irreversible chronic joint damage, called infectious arthritis.

More often than suspected, *Escherichia coli* is the active culprit in systemic infections. Usually found in combination with other infections, it appears to play a minor role until offered opportune conditions to make its presence known. Alone, *E. coli* does not possess invasive abilities; but the debilitating environment produced by other pathogens can induce it to leave the intestine (its normal habitat) and enter the bloodstream—producing a fatal septicemia.

The striking symptom of an *E. coli* infection is its effect upon equilibrium. Occasionally the foal's head and neck are slowly and steadily drawn to its side and sometimes it is unable to get up. Its legs move in a helpless, flailing, running motion. These neurologic symptoms lead veterinarians to conclude that the microorganism and its effects invade areas of the central nervous system.

Most of these cases respond well to treatment and recovery can be complete *if* the problem is recognized and treated before symptoms are too well advanced.

Actinobacillus equuli or *Shigella equuli* produce a deadly septicemia in foals that generates a syndrome variously referred to as "sleeper," "wanderer," or "dummy foals."

If the foal is infected *in utero*, it may be aborted or delivered dead. When these foals arrive in the world alive, they are very weak, semicomatose, and unable to stand. Regardless of all efforts to help, their survival is rare. If the foal is strong enough to stand, it may wander aimlessly around the perimeter of the stall. Habitually, it circles in one direction only, ceaselessly "nursing" on the boards of the stall, feed tub, or anything it can reach in its rounds *except its mother.* A trail of moist spots is often visible along the walls of the stall as evidence of the continuous, unreasoning sucking. When exhausted, such foals will stand as though in a stupor.

These foals, who will not nurse from their mothers, will take milk from a bottle, but they must be interrupted in their endless treadmill-like circling of the stall.

Subnormal temperature, severe dehydration, prominent bluish-white nictitating membrane (inner eyelid), and a yellowish, fetid, distressing diarrhea all help to confirm the diagnosis. In well-developed cases, upon entering the stall one can smell the diagnosis because of the particular fecal odor.

A few years ago 90 percent of these foals were lost. With increased knowledge and the advent of broad-spectrum drugs, combined with supportive therapy, the majority now survive with no apparent aftereffects.

The specific drug for "dummy foals" is truly a miracle drug, chloromycetin IV and chloramphentical capsules orally. Coupled with the necessary intensive regime of care, a foal often responds within a few hours. If the foal responds favorably, it will stop its aimless wandering and walk across the stall—perhaps for the first time! Its insistent need to stay near the wall gradually weakens. It approaches its mother as if it had been previously unaware of her existence. As progress continues, the foal touches and explores the mare with its outstretched nose. First attempts at nursing are usually misdirected and the foal may suck on the mare's front legs. Finally the foal seems to be able to locate the udder and actually nurses properly. The initial confusion and disorientation disappear.

Initial success is not a signal to discontinue treatment. Subsequent blood studies will guide the veterinarian and owner in determining the procedures necessary for complete recovery.

Corynebacterium equi or classified as *Rhodococcus equi* is another microorganism capable of causing fatal septicemia during intrauterine life or in young foals. However, this disease is most prevalent in foals that are three or four months old. This is not a neonatal problem.

This pathogen was not easily recognized for its capacity to produce severe disease in the young equine until recently. *C. equi* is most often associated with refractory foal pneumonia, yet has been isolated as coming from many other hosts—including humans. It is basically a soil inhabitant and once a farm is infected, the owner must face yearly outbreaks among the three- to four-month-old foals.

Its presence is insidious and its destructive effects can be misleading at times. Diagnosis of this disease has been somewhat elusive, hence difficult in the absence of a specific means of identification. The only helpful tool the practitioner had for years was astute observation, because serology studies and routine cultures are unrevealing.

There is no clear-cut symptom or precise combination of symptoms that permits a definitive diagnosis. Depression, coughing, elevated body temperature—with intermittent spiking fevers—and some degree of respiratory distress (panting respirations) are generally seen. It is sad, but interesting, to note that these foals continue to nurse and maintain exceptionally good body weight until just before death.

When the foal's defense mechanism can no longer contain the rapid multiplication and advance of the pathogenic microorganisms, in the absence of effective medication, an overwhelming suppurating infection is released throughout the entire body, causing death. The lungs, liver, kidneys, lymph glands, and intestines are literally covered with abscesses, and destructive tissue changes are present throughout the body.

Diagnosis today has been improved by a method of transtracheal culture. This transtracheal washing technique provides an accurate method of culturing and identifying the insidious microorganism. Other newer procedures have been very helpful as diagnostic aids in recognition and treatment of this frustrating foal disease.

In the affected foals, pulmonary pneumonia is the primary clinical manifestation. Sporadic in nature, this disease may affect only one or two foals in a large group. It is not highly contagious, but it is infectious, and thought to be transmitted by inhalation. These isolated cases are frequently lost because the course of the disease and its seriousness are neither reflected externally nor shown by the foal's physical condition.

I strongly recommend, in all cases of pulmonary pneumonia, a serum transfusion loaded with preformed antibodies administered concurrent with daily treatment of Ampicillin I.V. and capsules orally OR Neomycin, Erythromycin, and Rifampin. Do *not* hesitate to ask your veterinarian about these new effective treatments!

With early recognition and effective treatment, some foals survive. If the foal pulls through, the internal tissue changes seem to heal by themselves, for no functional or residual damage has been detectable in those cases I have followed.

Pseudomonas aeruginosa, Salmonella typhimurium, and *Salmonella abortus equi* are three offenders seen on occasion and known to be present in foal diseases. Their prevalence has been dramatically reduced during the last twenty years because of people dedicated to the care of their foals, and the enlightened though prudent use of vaccines and bacterins.

Hernias are defined as a protusion of an organ, or any tissue, through an abdominal opening. They occur either accidentally in nature or from an enlarged natural opening in the abdominal wall. The emerging organ or tissue is usually enveloped within the intact peritoneum and covered with the skin.

Foal hernias are not commonly found at birth, but become obvious within the first 24 to 48 hours of life. Umbilical and scrotal hernias are the two most common sites of herniation in the foal and are considered to be of hereditary or congenital origin.

A large percentage of these abdominal defects noticed shortly after birth will correct themselves by weaning time without any treatment.

Strangulation of hernias always poses a threat and can occur at any time without any advance warning signs. It is well to have your veterinarian assess the mass to determine the size, whether a loop of intestine is present or not, and the risk involved. Skillful palpation can distinguish a reducible from an irreducible hernia.

A *reducible hernia* is one that responds to manual reduction, though it still represents a potential hazard. An *irreducible hernia*, caused by either the development of adhesions or an entrapped loop of intestine, is one that requires emergency surgical intervention. Surgery is the only method of preventing the onset of peritonitis, which is always lethal.

An *umbilical hernia* is usually recognized as a small protruding sac hanging from the abdominal wall at the location of the navel. It is clearly visible.

A *scrotal hernia*, on the other hand, is well hidden high up between the hind legs, and is not discovered so easily. A number of these are present at birth. I have learned to sit quietly by and observe them as they efficiently correct themselves within a few days with no human interference. In my long years of practice with foals I have observed only two instances of scrotal hernia that required surgical correction.

Any hernialike protrusions of the abdomen, other than in the navel or scrotal areas, are usually of traumatic origin and should be looked at by your veterinarian.

Eye lesions from multiple causes frequently occur in little foals from irritated corneas. Hay, straw, and dust are the familiar offenders. The simple and frequent introduction of specifically prescribed ophthalmic ointments and drops usually is all that is necessary to correct the condition. Occasionally, corneal and conjunctival trauma develops during prolonged or difficult delivery. These conditions heal quickly following the use of ophthalmic medication to lubricate and soothe the globe of the eye.

Ocular lesions of congenital origin, including cataracts, are considered to be rare in the equine.

Entropion, the inversion of eyelids, is by far the most common eye lesion seen in the newborn foal. It most often involves the lower lid and is generally associated with premature, weak, and—especially—dehydrated foals. Entropion is characterized by a turning in or folding under of the eyelid, causing the eyelashes and outer hairy surface of the lid to come into intimate contact with the sensitive cornea, thus causing severe irritation. Discomfort, profuse tearing, frequent blinking, and photophobia draw attention to the condition.

Some cases can be relieved temporarily by careful manipulation. Lubricate the eyes and lids well with a bland ophthalmic ointment, then manually evert (turn out) the affected eyelid by gently rolling it outward using your thumb. Repeat this procedure as often as possible, preferably every hour around the clock. *Care should be taken to avoid further trauma.*

If permitted to go untreated for even a few hours, the corneal surface becomes dry and damaging secondary changes develop. A generalized bluish haze covers the cornea and minute local spots appear, indicating the result of continuous irritation and trauma. Keratitis, blepharospasm, or eventual blindness may follow.

If the degree of inversion is great, and manual efforts toward correction are fruitless after two or three days, surgical correction is indicated to restore the cornea to health. Correction involves a simple horizontal incision that reduces the excess of skin. A row of well-placed sutures achieves the desired correction by the tucklike surgical procedure.

Ectropion, or the eversion (turning out) of the eyelid, is very rare in foals. The only cases I have seen have been the direct result of trauma and were corrected quite easily by minor surgery.

Weak or crooked legs have always been of major concern to the brood mare owner. A normal foal arrives with a well-developed musculature and a God-given balance in the tone of the antagonistic flexor and extensor muscle groups. It is able to gain proper postural stance without undue effort and is the sought-after "straight-legged" foal.

Every year a certain percentage of foals is born with weak or crooked legs. Because they are not carbon copies of paintings or engravings of the ideal foal, their owners are unnecessarily yet naturally disappointed.

But many deviations from the norm correct themselves or are readily correctable with a little help, as long as the foal is able to get up and nurse. Even foals that require assistance, given time, do surprisingly well.

Foals with *weak pasterns* or, as we say, "down in the pasterns," represent the most common, yet least serious, in this category. Within a wide range of involvement, the extreme is the foal that actually walks with the back of its ankles on the ground. Do not despair: good nutrition and exercise have proved over the years to bring about miraculous improvement. Some of the most severely affected foals grow into useful adult horses that are able to compete effectively in performance events.

Weak pasterns are caused by a decrease in flexor muscle tone; stretched flexor tendons result in an overextended ankle that is allowed to drop back and down. But good nutrition and carefully regulated exercise permits the deficient muscle group to regain or establish its tone over a varying period of time. Foals with the slightest involvement correct themselves in a few days; those without severe deviations usually correct themselves within a few weeks.

Extreme cases, with the ankle dropped down so that it touches the ground, require protective padding and bandages to prevent the abrasions and soreness that may prevent a foal from engaging in much-needed exercise. Even these foals do remarkably well and within a few months achieve a stance approaching normal.

Note that I said protective padding, *not* supportive bandages. Any support given to flexor tendons adds to the weakness of those tendons. Do *not* apply any form of support.

Foals' limbs deviate in four distinct directions. Looking at the foal from the side, the deviations may be anterior (in a forward direction) or posterior (in a backward direction). Gazing at the foal from the front or rear, deviations occur medially (toward the midline or laterally (away from the midline). In cases of weak pasterns, the deviation of the ankle is in the posterior direction. Anterior-posterior deviations are essentially the result of an imbalance between the flexor and extensor muscles and tendons; medial-lateral deviations are primarily the result of skeletal deformities.

Foals with calf knees, or "back at the knees," are sometimes seen in conjunction with weak pasterns and sometimes as a separate entity. Posterior deviation of the knee is an indication of weakness of the flexor muscles and is often reflected in the anatomical structure of the knee joint. This condition, once present, will always represent a problem; very little definitive correction can be accomplished if radiographic studies show that the weight-bearing planes of the joint are genetically imperfect.

When foals have *sprung knees* or are "over at the knees," with an anterior deviation, it is an indication of an imbalance in tone of the flexors and extensors, with the flexors exerting the stronger pull. Unless the angulation is extreme, there is no cause for concern. Under the influences of normal nutrition and sufficient exercise, the deviation disappears by the time the foal is weaned.

Knees that deviate *laterally* (the reverse of knock knees) represent potential unsoundness. Unlike the other abnormalities discussed, this deviation is self-perpetuating. With normal exercise and work the condition usually worsens.

Knock-kneed foal or foals with knees turned toward each other face a much brighter future. When the deviation is slight, it is self-correcting; and in even moderately severe cases, self-correction is possible. Time is the essential factor, so "keep the faith!"

It is necessary to visualize the distribution of weight placed on the forelegs in order to understand why lateral and medial deviation respond in opposite ways.

Stand in front of the foal and imagine a plumb line dropped from the point of the shoulder to the ground. Ideally this line should bisect the forelimb into two equal parts, but unfortunately this is rarely seen.

Veterinary science theorizes that 90 percent of the weight and stress is placed to the inside of this perpendicular line, thus creating a laterally directed force onto the joint planes. Outward deviation would therefore have a tendency gradually to intensify the effect of these forces or, at best, to allow the leg to remain unchanged. On the other hand, a medial deviation seems to receive some benefit from exercise and growth.

Extreme cases of knock knees will not improve. I have seen foals so badly deformed that their knees were literally pressed against one another for support. The "growth line" or epiphysial line located at the distal end of the radius, or the top of the knee, is intimately involved with unequal weight bearing and areas subject to stress. An uneven epiphysial line develops, with medial spreading or separation and compression laterally.

A surgical procedure called "stapling" is effective in retarding this action. But surgical intervention is valid only if performed at an early stage to prevent the likelihood of still further damaging secondary changes developing in the ankle and foot.

An old rule of thumb usually proves to be quite accurate: experience has shown that *a medial deviation offers a good prognosis, whereas a lateral deviation carries with it only a guarded prognosis.*

If your foal *toes in* (pigeon-toed) or *toes out* (splay-footed), the ankle, pastern, and foot are directly involved.

A toed-out foot usually represents a reduced flexor tendon tone, allowing the ankle to deviate medially, which results in a lateral deflection of the pastern and foot. Quite often these foals have weak pasterns, for this position creates uneven stress on the joint surfaces and stretches the adjacent ligaments.

The altered gait causes interference, and trauma is then sustained in the form of bruising, for the opposite forefoot strikes against the medial aspect of the *opposite ankle* during movement.

If untreated, the possibility of future unsoundness is clearly evident. Good nutrition and regular exercise, combined with minimal but regular, conscientious foot care, are essential factors in order to retain control of or improvement of this condition.

For your convenience and to maintain the necessary regular care, obtain a blacksmith's rasp. Any owner can purchase one. Every week or ten days, two or three carefully guided strokes applied to the lateral side of the bottom of the foot—from the heel to the toe—will slightly lower the outside of the foal's tender foot. Then, if the rasp is guided around to the front of the foot to the center of the toe, one or two strokes will effectively remove the point that normally develops. This will square off the toe.

The foal will then be encouraged to "break over" at the foot's center, as is normal for the foot as it is brought forward. If unchecked and allowed to continue to break over on the inside of the toe, the foal's unnatural gait will place more and more damaging stress upon its soft, pliant bones and joints.

A toed-in position is much less frequently seen than the splay-footed position. In fact, a minor degree of toeing-in is considered to be an indication of strength, although severe toeing-in is comparable to severe toeing-out: both present weakening mechanical and conformational defects. Similar joint stresses are inflicted and the same threat of future unsoundness exists if either problem is allowed to continue unchecked. Although interference presents no problem, the resultant paddling gait is undesirable.

Here, too, the blacksmith's rasp is the best defense. With a toed-in deviation, the foal has a tendency to break over on the outside of the toe. The rasp should be used gently to remove the point of the toe, actually squaring the front. This time, the inner or medial side of the bottom of the foot should be lowered slightly; maintain the same balancing schedule as for splay-footed foals.

In spite of all your efforts, the degree of improvement achieved will depend upon the degree of initial involvement. But improvement *will* be seen.

Any conformational deformity of congenital origin carries with it the implication of consequences affecting the horse's future ability, but to what degree no one can predict with accuracy.

A few years ago a well-known race horse was successfully winning important races in spite of a deformed front leg. Such a deformity would be a legitimate excuse for any horse to fail in competition, but because of his heart, courage, the will to win—call it what you will—his performance was outstanding.

He is not unique. Many horses have this unusual drive and consequent ability. They are able to compensate for such handicaps.

Obviously, if you were considering the purchase of a foal, you would not want to acquire one with weak or crooked limbs; but if the foal God and your brood mare gave you is not perfect, it does not mean that its future necessarily is bleak. The genetic structure of any individual horse can supply that mysterious ability to achieve if his environment provides the opportunity for him to get on with his work.

Anterior-posterior deflections of the ankle produce a problem that is the reverse of that represented by deflection of the knee. Anterior deviations of the ankle are more serious for a new foal and carry with them a less favorable prognosis than do posterior deviations.

Casts and braces should *never* be applied to an ankle with a posterior deviation. Reduced tendon tone is the principal cause and immobilization only weakens the involved structures. The opposite side of the coin, *knuckling-over* or anterior deviations, often responds well to light braces or casts if applied *only during* the foal's first 24 to 48 hours. If knuckling-over persists beyond this brief period, surgical intervention may be needed to correct the uneven tendon pull that causes this abnormality.

A condition similar to knuckling-over occasionally is seen in the foal's foot. These foals travel on the toe and are unable to flatten the heel down to the ground. This toe-dancer posture also is caused by an even tendon pull.

When the tension on the tendon is somewhat less and permits the heel to touch the ground yet continue its pull, the position of the interior structures of the foot is altered and a *clubfoot* gradually yet relentlessly develops.

Both the toe-dancing attitude and the crippling and unsightly clubfoot are the result of undue pull from the deep digital flexor tendon. In my practice I have learned to recognize the varying degrees of foot involvement and I ponder over some fortunate, yet marginal, cases that have barely escaped the potentially crippling effects resulting from such problems.

Until recently, very little could be done for foals with such conditions, other than continuously rebalancing the feet. In spite of these efforts the basic structural problem remained. Braces and casts were of no value.

Now, miraculously, a new surgical technique has been developed. An inferior check ligament desmotomy corrects this crippling condition and totally restores the young animal to soundness, with no aftereffects or evidence of surgery.

Hind-leg deviations or abnormal angulations are a common finding in foals, and are especially common in large foals. Although they are seen more frequently, these less serious problems are associated with the hind legs rather than the forelegs. Perhaps the fact that less weight is carried by the hind legs is a factor. The position of the fetus in the uterus, the nutrition and exercise the mare receives during gestation, and, most important, the genetic makeup of the foal are the major causes believed to be responsible for crooked hind limbs.

Most common conditions found in the hind leg include *straight stifles, sickle and curbed hocks, bandylegs and cow hocks, weak or cocked ankles.*

Straight stifles represent a potential weakness leading to future unsoundness. *Everybody likes the appearance of a straight hind leg, but a straight hind leg must include a straight stifle.* Pony farms make a particular effort to breed for foals with straight hind legs. The desired angulation at the stifle necessary for soundness is lost or reduced in direct proportion to the straightness of the leg. With reduced angulation between the femur and the tibia, the patella is allowed extra movement and that causes pain and discomfort. Normal growth, condition, and exercise will sometimes bring about improvement; but quite often blistering, injections, or a simple surgical procedure called medial patellar desmotomy may be required for permanent improvement.

Sickle hocks and curbed hocks are usually very evident immediately after birth. When viewed from the side, the foal is much taller at the withers than at the croup, and it seems the hind end has a difficult time following the front end. From the stifle on down, the hind legs are curved under the foal and are shaped like the blade of a sickle—hence the name.

Almost invariably sickle hocks are accompanied by *curbs.* A curb is a protrusion of the plantar ligament at the back and bottom of the rounded hock.

"Rounded hock" is a "shotgun" lay term describing any combination of sickle hocks, curbs, or any and all weakened standing positions of the hind leg.

It is amazing to see how much improvement these foals show by the end of a few weeks, and an even greater surprise to see how much more improvement they show by the end of a few months. This is particularly gratifying, for there is no specific treatment to offer.

Even though these foals mature into serviceable adults, it does not take a particularly acute horseman to observe residual evidences of these early physical deviations.

Often when I see a big, good-looking colt come into the world my momentary enthusiasm wanes when the colt stands and his rounded hocks become suddenly, and depressingly, evident. This deviation predicts an almost-automatic exclusion from a future show career, even though it is not a serious deterrent so far as his performance goes. (I'm always pleasantly surprised when I see one of these large colts with "clean" legs and normal hocks.)

Other departures from normal in the hind leg are more easily seen from the rear of the foal, looking forward. This vantage point permits you to imagine a plumb line dropped to the ground from the whirl bone (tuber ischii) of each hind leg, effectively bisecting the leg and foot. A *bandy-legged or bow-legged* foal stands with the hind feet close together and with both hocks *outside* the plumb line. Time offers very slight improvement.

Occasionally a weak foal is seen with one bandy leg and the other leg following the contour of the curved leg in parallel fashion as if in imitation of the deformity. These foals have swaying hindquarters that seem to defy the forces of gravity, so they stand as though on the side of a hill.

In spite of the severity of this deviation, these foals straighten surprisingly well. Discouraged by the newborn's appearance, inexperienced owners have suggested euthanasia, but rapid improvement soon eradicates this idea.

Remember the old adage: as long as a foal is able to get up and down to nurse, exercise, and rest, the strides it can make in musculoskeletal improvement can be fantastic. Many newborn foals that appear to be cripples do grow into useful, happy adults.

Cow-hocked foals stand with the hind feet in a toed-out position, with the points of the hocks and the ankles falling to the inside of our imaginary plumb line. Even though there may be some improvement with exercise, growth, and good nutrition, this deviation will continue to plague the foal to some degree for the rest of his or her life.

It is a common problem for cow-hocked horses to brush or strike at the ankle with the opposite foot as that leg is advanced (interfering). Corrective trimming or shoeing will help to a slight degree, but such corrective efforts are of more help to the owner's peace of mind than to the horse. A square-toed shoe with an outside trailer is indicated.

Most limb deformities are of hereditary or congenital origin, and certain deviations are strikingly (seemingly unavoidably) present in some blood-lines, indicating dominant familial tendencies.

Some families carry specific talents, such as speed, jumping ability, or dispositional traits that may be hidden or unanticipated: these traits can be either reinforced or eliminated unknowingly in breeding programs. Crooked limbs or conformational defects are inescapably evident, but they may be avoided by careful study, combined with diligent research into the history of the produce of the dam and the get of the sire.

Locked stifles, or upward fixation of the patella, is a quite common con-genital condition. A straight hind leg predisposes to locking of the patella and its ligaments onto the femoral trochlea, causing backward extension of the hind limb.

Fixation of the rear leg in extension can be frightening to both the animal and the owner.

One or both patellas can be involved. Usually the animal will inadver-tently move and the patella will slip free, relieving the horse. If the locking is recurrent, local injections or surgery (a medial patellar desmotomy) can provide a permanant remedy before secondary changes develop.

In some cases, forcing the animal to back will quickly unlock the stifle. As a last resort, place one hand firmly on the stifle and push inward, while the other hand lifts the leg and pulls outward. This does require strength and ability on the part of the operator, so try to arrange to have a helper or two with you.

Trauma or physical injury to foals during birth occurs much more fre-quently than is reported. External injuries are visible and noticed quickly, but an obscure internal trauma may go unnoticed until its frightening results make the condition known.

Many injuries are sustained when mares foal unattended; but a pre-ponderance of injuries consists of bruises to the soft tissue that, although unsightly, heal quickly with little or no consequence.

Contusions of the gums, lips, tongue, and nose are those most fre-quently seen. After all, the foal does come into the world virtually leading with its nose!

The prominent structures around the eye, especially the supraorbital ridge, are also vulnerable. Occasional injury to the globe itself is not uncommon. Caution should be used when treating any area close to the eye, as well as the eye itself.

Medication applied to adjacent tissues has a tendency to run inadvertently into the sensitive tissues of the eye. Any irritation usually will cause rubbing or itching. Only prescribed ophthalmic ointments should be introduced into the eye or applied to the eyelids. It is important that adequate lubrication be provided for any condition in which heat and irritation are found, to protect the cornea from dehydration and consequent irreparable damage.

Usually the neck and shoulders escape bruising, but the thorax represents an area that can and does present a susceptible target for the compressive forces of delivery. Injuries range from minor bruising and bending to actual fractures of the flexible ribs.

With only the thin and fragile pleural membrane providing protection, any damage to the rib cage jeopardizes the safety of the underlying lung tissue—even the heart. Bruising and puncture wounds can be easily inflicted upon these structures.

Fractures of the ribs are sometimes difficult to diagnose. Grunting and groaning are characteristic symptoms of rib, heart, and pulmonary injury. *But if you even suspect the possibility of such trauma,* your veterinarian should be called. Reluctance to move, reduced excursion of the rib cage during respiration, and obvious soreness also are signals that should alert you.

A *ruptured diaphragm* occurs infrequently during parturition or from any physical compression that forces the viscera against the diaphragm. The diaphragm is a musculomembranous partition that separates the thoracic cavity from the abdominal cavity. In shape it resembles an open umbrella. Any defect in this powerful structure, ranging in size from a pinpoint opening to a major rent, disrupts the vital pulmonary pressures and creates discomfort.

A tear of this diaphragm can permit displacement of the viscera, or abdominal tissue, through the diaphragm into the thoracic cavity. The highly motile intestine is the most likely invader. Once this has occurred, the ruptured diaphragm has already progressed to become a *diaphragmatic hernia.*

Symptoms usually are depression, reluctance to move, reluctance to nurse, and mild colicky actions.

Diagnostic symptoms are shallow panting respirations, a slightly pendulous abdomen, and a tendency to use the abdominal muscles to aid in respiration. Most of these foals will insist upon remaining on their feet and will assume a "sawhorse" stance. Again, the diagnosis is elusive, but time is of the essence: immediate corrective surgery is the only alternative.

A *ruptured bladder* is not uncommon and is *very* serious if not diagnosed early. Compression of a partially filled bladder during delivery, or a sharp jerk on the intact umbilical cord because a startled mare jumps to her feet prematurely after delivery, have been reported as causes.

Such trauma results in a tear in the urinary bladder. If it is recognized early and proper surgical correction is instituted, chances for survival are greatly increased. The foal appears normal for the first 12 to 24 hours—which can be deceptive. Then it gradually becomes dull and progressively weaker. Occasional straining, in the absence of constipation, with distention of the abdomen, should alert the conscientious attendant.

If allowed to progress, breathing shortens, discomfort becomes evident, nasal and oral membranes become pale—then usually show a yellow tinge. Toxicity develops and the body temperature elevates because of the accumulation of urine floating freely in the abdominal cavity.

An obvious symptom of a ruptured bladder is the gradual enlargement of the abdomen so that it resembles a balloon full of water. In some cases, straining efforts might force some urine to escape and give the false impression that the foal is voiding. The small amounts of urine passed is the result of the build-up of internal pressure in the abdomen, not from the bladder.

Your veterinarian can aspirate a sample of the abdominal fluid for a positive diagnosis. Skilled surgery performed early results in a good survival rate. If untreated, uremic poisoning sets in—causing blindness, convulsions, and then death.

There are three possible causes for absence of urination in foals, other than rupture of the bladder. The first is *bruising of the urinary tract,* sustained during delivery, which can result in blockage. The amount of occlusion in this instance depends on the location of hematomas and the degree of tissue change. These factors also affect the eventual outcome.

The second cause is *dehydration,* usually associated with septicemias, resulting in diminution of the flow of urine. A total absence of urination does not necessarily result in septicemias, but volume is often decreased to a mere dribbling of urine. Reduced fluid intake, electrolytic imbalance, and faulty fluid exchange are all contributing factors limiting the volume and frequency of urination. In some septicemias, kidney tissue is damaged by the infection, either during the prenatal or the neonatal period, resulting in a discouraging prognosis.

The third cause is *congenital absence of urinary tract components,* which has not been reported in veterinary medical literature.

Absence of the nursing reflex immediately after birth is a serious warning and an indication of a very weak or very sick foal.

A strong foal is usually up and nursing within thirty minutes after birth and, even before it gains its feet, its curled pink tongue and lips search its surroundings for a source of nourishment.

If the newborn is unable to secure food independently, prompt assistance is needed. Without the ability to suck, it may be necessary for your veterinarian to obtain the mare's milk and "feed" the foal through a tube introduced directly into its stomach.

In the case of a weak foal, after one or two tube feedings the sucking reflex miraculously appears, and the foal then is usually able to stand and nurse by itself.

In an unattended delivery, a veterinary diagnosis is needed to distinguish between a foal that is simply weak from a difficult delivery or from delay in receiving nourishment, and a foal weakened by an intrauterine infection.

The weakened and very sick foal suffering from systemic infection or septicemia requires intensive drug therapy and intravenous fluids *in addition* to tube feeding. Tubing not only provides nourishment but also affords a means of administering essential oral medication. Unless a nursing reflex can be established, there is no hope for the foal's survival.

Several years ago I worked on a case that illustrated the tenacity some weak foals possess.

I answered a desperate call for help from an owner unknown to me: her newborn foal was dying. I had a difficult time locating the stable. Even from the outside, the small structure presented a dismal picture of neglect. Inside, with her owners standing by helplessly, I found a Standardbred mare who had foaled unattended in the worst possible surroundings. She was in a tiny, narrow stall in which it was impossible for her to turn around: it is questionable whether she was able to get up or down in the close confinement that was her home as well as her foaling stall. Very little bedding was provided routinely, let alone for the special occasion of the birth of her foal.

The pitiful creature lying beneath her was battered and bruised, and looked as though it had been beaten. Small and weak, the foal lifted its head and feebly moved its legs when I pulled it from between the mare's hind legs and placed it on some fresh, dry straw in the aisle—there was no room for me in the stall! The mare stretched her neck down over the makeshift gate of her stall and licked her new baby. She seemed relieved that he was in a safe, clean, dry bed.

While I began to run fluids into the tiny foal, the two owners, quick to follow any suggestion, found a heat lamp and rigged it up so that the gentle warmth covered the colt like a blanket. He fell into a light sleep.

We carefully cleansed the mare's udder and the owner milked a cupful of the precious colostrum for me. As I passed a small, soft polyethylene tube through the foal's nostril down into his stomach he made only the slightest protest. With a large plastic syringe I slowly fed 2 ounces of the colostrum through the tube. In a comfortable warm bed and with warm food in his stomach, the foal stretched out for the first relaxed sleep he had ever had.

The tube was left in place and secured with a couple of sutures, with the open end taped for safety's sake so that no air could enter and so that the owners could continue to feed the foal every hour. As I left, the owners were removing a partition to enlarge the mare's stall.

Later in the day I stopped by to see my young patient and found his vital signs had improved. After he had been treated again, we supported him on his weak and wobbly legs so he could walk a few steps. He promptly collapsed in a heap, slept for a few moments, then struggled to get up. With a little assistance he again got to his feet and managed to navigate a turn around his renovated stall. As yet he had showed no interest in or inclination to nurse. I left the owners with a firm caution to continue the hourly feedings throughout the night.

The next morning I received a call from the exhausted but elated pair. The feeding instructions had been followed during the night. In the early morning hours, while one owner was awkwardly trying to milk the mare to replenish the supply, the foal got to his feet, walked over to the mare, and nursed!

Although the intranasal tube did not seem to interfere, did I think it was needed any longer? I returned to the little barn and the foal checked out with flying colors. When the sutures and the tube were removed, he improved steadily. His progress and growth rate soon were normal.

A premature foal is delivered before it has received its protection, nourishment, and the time necessary for full development of those faculties required for survival in the external environment. Equine fetal growth is greatly intensified during the last two months of gestation and any reduction of this growth period lessens the chances for the foal's survival. The intrauterine time so necessary for the foal's vital systems to reach maturity and capacity to function is lost.

It is encouraging when I see a foal a few weeks premature that appears healthy and able to stand and nurse, but I invariably question the due date.

Premature foals usually require assistance to establish respiration, possess a subnormal body temperature, and show extreme muscular weakness. For any hope of survival, truly premature foals must be placed immediately in a warm environment, fed with a bottle if a sucking reflex is present, or with a stomach tube if it is not, and given total supportive treatment as needed.

The necessity for oxygen, humidity control, and environmental temperature can all be met ideally by the large animal incubator. These incubators are practically unheard of today, but I can foresee—in spite of the expense—that someday their use will become commonplace. At a lowered body temperature the premature foal's vital body functions are unable to operate efficiently and heat lost by radiation will result in death.

Foals four to five weeks early are usually dead upon delivery or, even under the finest care, live only a few hours.

If, however, your "preemie" arrives alive, do not panic. Keep the foal warm; even an electric blanket can be used. If you feel unable to adequately care for the foal at home, you have the option of sending it to a neonatal emergency care unit, commonly found at state universities. (Neonatal care units are *expensive*.)

While making arrangements to ship your foal to such a unit, perhaps your veterinarian will insert an IV catheter and tape it around your foal's neck. This provides for a slow drip of electrolytes during the trip, thus stabilizing the foal. Let me repeat: *Warmth is essential.*

Evaluation of such incidences should be considered during the long eleven-month gestation, allowing you to make intelligent decisions if the need arises.

Pervious or patent urachus or leaky navel is a relatively common condition in the newborn foal. The urachus is a small tubular structure contained within the umbilical cord that carries the fluid waste from the fetal bladder to the allantois or placenta during prenatal life.

After birth, when the umbilical cord ruptures, natural closure of the urachus should occur. When the urachus is closed effectively, urine is then permitted to pass from the bladder out through the urethra.

Failure of the urachus to close allows a continuous dribbling of urine from the area of the navel. Dribbling from that area develops into a flow of urine when the foal attempts to urinate. This condition is not difficult to recognize, for the urine can be seen escaping from the midline of the abdomen rather than through the normal opening.

In the case of a colt, it may have gone unnoticed for a few days because of proximity to the sheath, but in the case of a filly it is always a dramatic and shocking thing for the owner to observe.

As the result of leaking urine, a constantly wet, soiled, warm navel stump provides an ideal environment for pathogenic bacteria to grow and presents a continual threat of infection. Spontaneous correction is rare in untreated cases because the majority of these faulty closures require daily cauterization with silver nitrate or tincture of iodine. Medication should be discontinued only when the umbilical stump has shrunk in size, becomes dry, and shows no evidence of urine.

Never permit the urachus to be tied, for the urethra may not be patent (open). A leaky navel usually can be corrected within a few days, but it should be a warning sign. It is my opinion that a high percentage of pervious urachus cases are usually associated with various forms of intra-uterine origin. Treat it as a simple leaky navel, but *be alert* for hidden signs of systemic infection that may soon become evident and quickly overwhelming.

Jaw deformities. Parrot mouth and sow mouth are two jaw deformities seen in the young foal. Both are considered to be of hereditary or congenital origin and both constitute an unsoundness. To date no satisfactory treatment has been developed.

Parrot mouth, or brachygnathia, is a mandible or lower jaw that is shortened when compared with the upper jaw. This can be an unpleasant sight for the foal owner, who always anticipates perfection. It is controversial whether overgrowth of the upper jaw (the maxilla) or a defective lower jaw creates the parrot-mouth appearance.

Academically there remains a question as to where these defects lie. Similar to the classic question whether the glass is half empty or half full, here the question is which jaw is lengthened or shortened in relation to the other. In any event, the deformities discussed here are described as they appear clinically in the foal.

Sow mouth, or prognathia, is a jaw deformity opposite to that of parrot mouth. The maxilla, or upper jaw, appears to be shortened in this case. If you ever have occasion to look into the mouth of a pig, you will see how apt this description is. This defect is not as common as parrot mouth.

Improper opposition of the incisors results in abnormal wear and an uneven overgrowth of the tooth surfaces, involving not only the readily visible incisors but the large, numerous, and hard-working molars that are located well back in the mouth and out of sight. Any misalignment of the large dental arcades produces future uneven wear, with all its undesirable consequences.

However, it requires an extreme condition actually to interfere with the foal's ability to nurse and feed.

In the individual with an extreme deformity, grazing can become almost impossible because seizing of grass by the teeth is dramatically impaired.

These foals would not survive if left alone on the short grass of the range; but within a protected environment, with concentrates and lush pastures, they live to become useful animals. Frequent dental attention to remove the offending tooth edges that develop will always be needed to enable them to chew their feed properly.

Continuous eruption of the teeth throughout life is a phenomenon peculiar to the equine. All permanent teeth, with the exception of the canine and wolf teeth, are constantly pushed out from the root level by a continuous process of cancellous bone proliferation.

Essentially, the growth rate is controlled by the opposing teeth. Normal opposition is vital for even wear and to maintain a smooth dental arcade. In the absence of an opposing tooth, growth will progress uninhibited, causing discomfort, inefficiency in mastication, and may even progress to an unfortunate climax whereby the tooth locks into the opposite jaw.

Historically, dental care for horses has been substandard, in fact virtually neglected, not because of lack of concern but through lack of knowledge. Perhaps it is a case of "out of sight, out of mind." The horse's mouth is an area that the average person does not frequently—if ever—explore; and wisely so, for unskilled fingers can be lost.

Routine dental examination and care, performed by a trained person, should include the removal of caps and wolf teeth from young equines' mouths, and provide regular attention to "float" or remove the sharp edges of grinders or molars and any other rough, protruding tooth surfaces. This service is an essential one for the young adult as well as for the mature animal throughout its life. *Establish an annual dental checkup program for your horse, starting with its yearling year.* Four times a year dental attention is recommended for competitive or working horses.

A defective soft palate is of hereditary or congenital origin and is noticed at birth or shortly thereafter. The admixture of milk and nasal fluids oozing from the foal's nostrils, during and immediately after nursing, is pathonomonic (*the* diagnostic symptom).

The normal soft palate, if functioning properly, helps direct milk to the esophagus (the entrance to the stomach) and prevents it from entering the respiratory tract. In contrast, a defective palate is incomplete because it contains a rent or aperture in the palatal tissue. In some cases the palate is inadequate in length, creating functional inefficiency. A major portion of the nutritious milk misses the esophagus and is permitted to flow into the pharynx and out the nasal cavity.

Because of this loss of milk volume, these foals seem to be constantly nursing, choking, and gagging. Not only do they suffer a deficit in nutrition, but with such inefficient feeding they are busy nursing when they should be resting.

This condition, not to be confused with the usual, clearly visible cleft palate seen in human infants, is considered to be incurable in the foal and is the cause of poor nutrition, fatigue, unthriftiness, and grave weakness. Surgical correction, although quite successful in humans, has been attempted in foals with inconclusive results.

Defective colon or rectum—known, respectively, as *Atresia coli* and *Atresia recti*—are commonly classified as hereditary or congenital in origin and are relatively rare. The two conditions are similar.

In *Atresia coli* a developmental deformity occurs anatomically in a section of the small colon that ends abruptly in a blind pouch. The opposing section of the colon also ends in a blind pouch. In some cases several feet, or even sections, of the colon are missing.

In *Atresia recti* the rectum ends in an abrupt blind pouch, usually found relatively closer to the anus.

In both cases the foals appear normal at birth, only to develop symptoms of colic shortly after birth, especially after ingesting milk.

Any time I administer an enema that is nonproductive to a newborn foal I am apprehensive. Because of the substantial lack of tone in the rectum and colon, little if any liquid from the enema is returned; I then have to consider the grim diagnosis of *Atresia coli*.

In *Atresia recti*, the enema content may return lacking fecal material and coloration. Either of these findings should arouse suspicion and be a signal for the need for careful observation for any signs of discomfort.

These two conditions are untreatable, except for surgical intervention. The only hope of survival for such foals is early recognition and prompt surgery. Anastomosis or connection of the blind ends has proven successful if performed within hours of the moment of birth. Major abdominal surgery requires general anesthesia and a team of veterinary surgeons.

Monster foals. Compared to their bovine counterparts, monster foals are rare. Monster calves are not uncommon and seem to be accepted as a matter of anticipated percentages.

Equine fetal monsters are sometimes carried to term, but are usually aborted during the later months of gestation. Any arrest in the development of the embryo or the fetus results in intrauterine death, with subsequent abortion. The physical deformity, per se, does not necessarily terminate fetal life: it is the other conditions involved that prove to be collectively inadequate for maintenance of life.

If a deformed foal is extensively affected, that foal is considered to be a monster. A monster cannot function effectively in the extrauterine environment. So the degree of aberration determines whether the foal is considered to be deformed or a monster. The few times that I have delivered monster foals, they arrived in the world barely alive. As they were only "technically" alive, the decision to put them to sleep became somewhat easier.

I have seen some skull and spinal deformities so slight that a foal manages to live and grow, although most afflicted foals deserve the consideration of euthanasia.

There are three types of monstrosities found in foals that are usually born dead or die shortly after birth.

Hydrocephalic foals are characterized by an exceptionally enlarged cranium, a staggering unsteady gait, and other central nervous system symptoms. No treatment is known and euthanasia is indicated.

Schistosomis reflexus is a congenital absence of the ventral abdominal wall and skin covering, thus exposing the entire abdominal viscera. Even if carried to term, these foals are usually born dead.

Fetal anasarca or *hydrops amnion* is a condition of hereditary or congenital origin. An excessive amount of amniotic fluid is accumulated *in utero,* causing edema and ascites in the fetus and profound stretching of the mare's uterus.

Excessive stretching of the uterus often results in uterine inertia, regardless of whether the fetus is aborted or presented at term. A veterinarian is usually called to assist in the delivery and is rewarded by a bath of 20 to 30 gallons of amniotic fluid that gushes forth to soak clothing, hair, and shoes, as well as flooding the stall. This tepid, distasteful bath would be bearable if only the foal were not *always* dead!

These waterlogged foals have a bluish-gray tint and are slightly swollen in appearance. If a postmortem is performed, it usually will reveal one or many developmental defects.

Faulty placental circulation and a diseased uterus are acknowledged as the agents of cause; however, the fetus with a digestive tract that is faulty, being unable to swallow amniotic fluid, has been a constant finding by researchers. Did the diseased uterus, with its faulty circulation, cause the accumulation of fluids; or did the faulty foal, with its initial inability to swallow, cause the condition to develop?

Tympany of the guttural pouch is a condition of congenital or hereditary origin.

The guttural pouch is the saclike enlargement of the lower end of the

Eustachian tube, which is located relatively close to and opens into the pharynx.

Tympany in this special instance means "air-filled," and these foals are found with one or both guttural pouches distended with air. The distention is caused by a faulty flap of soft tissue that should be positioned over the pharyngeal opening of the Eustachian tube; this tissue sometimes acts only as a one-way valve. The flap traps the air entering the pouch and causes it to distend. Respiratory infection with a pharyngitis, strenuous coughing, or a foal's panicky screaming for its mother will cause air entrapment if such a predisposition exists.

In the few cases that I have observed, the foals were asymptomatic until circumstances developed that allowed air to enter the guttural pouch. The sudden onset of swelling in the parotid area—from the base of the ear to the angle of the jaw and under the mandible—closely resembles a case of strangles.

However, one's fears are allayed quickly when the swelling is touched. The underlying structures are soft, cool to the touch, and have the unmistakable feel of a partially inflated small balloon. The foals are not sick, have no elevation of body temperature, and do not show any signs of discomfort. Correction of this problem requires surgical resection of the offending flap.

Congenital heart defects are uncommon. About a dozen different conditions have been reported. Each requires careful professional examination in order to diagnose and predict an accurate prognosis.

Weakness, unthriftiness, and lack of tolerance of exercise—in combination—are a warning that a foal should receive an in-depth cardiovascular examination.

The heart condition found most frequently in young horses is known as *interventricular septal defect*. There is no known treatment or cure.

Cerebellar hypoplasia and degeneration has been thought to be of hereditary or congenital origin, but recent information suggests a possible viral cause. To date, this condition has been reported only in the Arabian breed of horses and, interesting to note, is more common in colts than in fillies. Arabian horse breeders are understandably concerned, and they are supporting and encouraging research in an effort to determine the cause of this disheartening entity.

Symptoms can appear at any time from birth to six months. Head and body tremors interfere progressively with the foal's ability to walk and, in the absence of any known treatment, they continue to degenerate.

Arrested pregnancy, about 35 days.

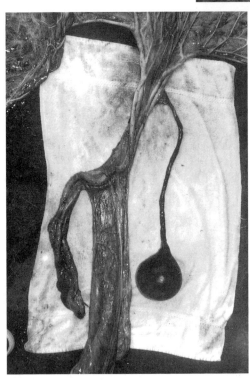

Amorphus globosus. Arrested pregnancy, 45 to 50 days. Mare produced one viable pregnancy.

Brownish color indicates septicemic foal. Also release of meconium during gestation—unnatural.

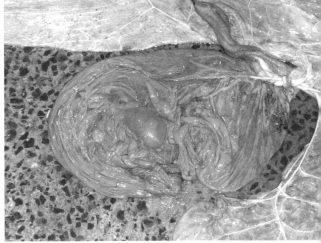

Diseased placenta: discolored, undersized, and torsion of some tissue, including the umbilical cord. This type of afterbirth membrane indicates the likelihood of a septicemic foal. This invaluable examination alerts the veterinarian to begin treatment early, or even before symptoms appear.

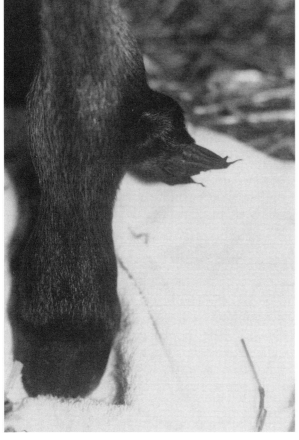

Polydactylism (extra appendage).
Evolutionary throwback to prehistoric three-toed eohippus.

Extra appendages or polydactylism is rarely seen in the equine. There has been one case reported in a Standardbred foal in Australia, one reported case in the United States affecting an Arabian foal, and just recently I had, as far as I know, the only Thoroughbred foal with a supernumerary digit.

In all three cases the extra appendage was attached to the forelimb and was successfully removed. The surgical correction had no adverse effect upon the foal's future soundness.

Retained testicles or cryptorchidism is failure of the testicles to descend at the proper time from the abdomen into the externally located scrotal sac, the normal position for optimal fertility.

When only one testicle descends, the condition is referred to as *monorchidism*. The retained testicle can vary in location from well within the abdomen to just inside the internal inguinal ring, or inside the inguinal canal proper and down as far as the external inguinal ring, yet still be considered retained.

This hereditary or congenital defect is not an uncommon finding and is frequently presented to veterinarians for their assessment.

I see many newborn colts arrive in the world with both testicles well descended into their scrotal sacs. Within a few days, the testes disappear back into the abdomen to grow and develop. Most colts' testicles have permanently descended by the time they are yearlings, but some animals are approaching their second year before both are permanently located in the scrotum.

In the case of an outstanding foal with show-ring potential or with a prospect of some day being stood at stud, good nutrition and plenty of exercise for the colt—and an abundance of patience on the part of the owner—are essential while waiting for the testicle or testicles to descend. Otherwise, prompt and complete castration is the most satisfactory solution.

As a rule, treatment has been unsuccessful. A heavily promoted hormone therapy has proved to be of little or no value. The use of a testicular prostheses, for cosmetic purposes, is unsportsmanlike, unethical, and detrimental to the betterment of the breed.

Any degree of retention results in partially arrested development of testicular tissue, with consequent reduction of fertility and hormonal imbalance. It is not unusual to see erratic behavior and undue aggressiveness—even to the point of viciousness—in cases of abdominal retention of the testicle.

Castration is necessary to transform these horses into safe, dependable, and useful animals, and to protect humans from unnecessary accidents. Safety is important for all concerned, but it is vital to prevent a stallion with a genital imperfection from breeding, thus perpetuating this defect.

In my practice I often see the end result of what I consider to be not only irresponsible but imprudent procedures in management of animals with genital-tract imperfections.

Many horses that appear to be geldings are referred to veterinarians because of their bizarre behavior. Upon examination, these "geldings" prove to possess a retained testicle that was ignored when a careless castration removed only the one obvious testicle. I have known a few unique cases of cryptorchidism of horses represented as geldings, but their unacceptable behavior quickly attracts attention and suspicion. The new owners are then faced with the expense of abdominal surgery or the nuisance of handling an unsatisfactory "gelding."

Jaundice or *Isohemolytic icterus,* also referred to as *Neonatal isoerythrolysis,* is a hemolytic anemia of newborn foals that develops as a result of the mare's production of antibodies which war against the red blood cells of her own fetus during pregnancy. The foal's blood type is actually incompatible with that of its dam, and the fetus can, in some instances, act as a foreign body within its own mother. A strange twist of nature's usual efficiency!

If the red blood cells of the embryo correspond with the blood type of the stallion rather than with that of the mare after conception, isoimmunization occurs in the mare while she is carrying a fetus with an incompatible blood type.

Because of the unique placentation of the mare, with its lack of antibody transfer, the effects (if any) observed during pregnancy are usually slight. Most of the mares are healthy and vigorous during gestation, disguising this hidden condition. In young mares who have never produced a jaundiced foal, this condition is especially insidious. Without a history to serve as an alert, the first jaundiced foal a mare produces is usually lost.

Contrary to what we know about the physiologic placental barrier, some mares do exhibit clinical signs of incompatibility during pregnancy; they then abort or deliver a dead or very weak foal.

I have known mares, particularly older mares with a history of sporadic isoimmunization, that are affected in varying degrees during gestation. They usually exhibit depression, progressive slowness of gait, a detectable yellowish tint in the mucous membranes, and inconsistent edematous areas over the entire body.

Considered collectively, these signs reflect the dynamic internal conflict taking place.

If your veterinarian is fortified with a history or a past performance sheet, there is no excuse to lose a foal because of lack of preparation.

When a foal arrives, having been spared the intrauterine effects of the disease, it appears normal and healthy *until it ingests the colostrum that contains the injurious antibodies* developed by the mare to react specifically with the foal's erythrocytes. Then the destruction begins. Her colostrum contains a six to eight times greater antibody level than the mare's circulating blood serum. It is indeed apparent that only a few swallows of this first milk can be lethal.

A few hours after the first meal the foal becomes depressed, weakens, and finally becomes prostrate. The mucous membranes of the mouth and eyes are pale at first, then they develop an icterus or yellow tinge within 24 hours. Most untreated foals die of acute anemia within 12 to 24 hours.

A foal's chances of survival are increased if an astute veterinarian can make an early diagnosis and take appropriate measures quickly.

The mare and foal should be kept together, but the foal should not be allowed to touch the mare's udder under any circumstances.

A partition of suitable height should be erected in the stall—allowing the mare to see, hear, and touch her foal, but preventing the foal from drinking the destructive milk.

As an alternative, a muzzle can be used on the foal, but I think the hazards of this method outweigh the advantages.

Constant supervision is required during this difficult period.

The mare should be milked every hour to remove the unwanted colostrum and to stimulate continued milk production. *This colostrum should be disposed of* and the foal bottle-fed every hour. Either a commercial preparation or, if available, a previously prepared frozen quantity of colostrum from other mares may be used. However, there is no way of ensuring that the frozen colostrum may not be antagonistic to the foal.

A mare may produce colostrum for as long as 72 hours, so the mare must be milked and the foal bottle-fed for as long as colostrum is produced. Before a foal is *ever* allowed to nurse, determination of the absence of the antibodies is vital.

A blood sample from the foal and a milk sample from the mare should be submitted to a laboratory for confirmation of compatibility. This test is the necessary assurance that the mare and the foal may be reunited as nature intended.

If your veterinarian suspects the existence of this problem during gestation, a blood sample should be obtained from the mare and the horse to which she was bred. Blood obtained during the later part of gestation allows the laboratory to determine the presence or absence of agglutination between the dam's blood serum and the sire's red blood cells. If the tests are positive, additional samples obtained much closer to parturition are essential so that your veterinarian will be provided with a life-saving time advantage.

When the foal arrives, blood counts, blood transfusions, and total supportive therapy will be in readiness and can, with modern medical knowledge, avert a disaster.

Since this disorder definitely carries the implications of loss of the foal, a quick, simple, on-the-spot test has been devised that can be made immediately.

Obtain one drop of blood as the umbilical cord ruptures and one drop of colostrum from the mare's udder. Mix these on a clean glass slide or surface.

After a moment or two, check for gross clumping of red blood cells, which is a positive finding; a pink solution is a negative finding.

I have watched foals that survive the initial insult—with the help of quick aid and definitive action—grow into perfectly normal adults.

Two very special individuals come to my mind:

A pregnant mare was shipped to one of my clients' breeding farms. Not only was the old matron extremely valuable in her own right, but also she was carrying a foal by Native Dancer. I was called as soon as the mare arrived and, I must confess, I was looking forward to the privilege of examining such a prestigious patient. I had never seen this mare before, but before my routine examination had progressed very far the pleasant anticipation I had felt turned into concern.

It was early fall and instead of the smooth and gleaming coat one would expect, the exquisitely bred Thoroughbred's coat was dull and stary. She seemed listless in her movements and her attitude was one of disinterest. Her oral, ocular, and nasal membranes were pale, with a slight yellowish tinge.

I drew blood from the mare, and a quick telephone call to Maryland brought a courteous reply from the farm and a swiftly drawn blood sample from Native Dancer. Both blood samples were rushed to a reliable laboratory. The results from the test were so overwhelming that the technician who gave her report over the telephone expressed concern at the amount of agglutination.

At this time the mare was in the eighth month of her pregnancy. From this moment on everything possible was done to help her maintain excellent nutritional status and to provide the exercise she needed. The same monthly tests were made until just before the mare was due. An unfortunate increase in her blood titer took place at this time.

Only now did we learn that the mare had mysteriously lost two of her foals very shortly after their births.

Because we were forewarned, the mare was never left alone for fear that she might deliver her foal unattended and the baby inadvertently reach the udder filled with poisoned milk.

As it turned out, the mare foaled with more help on hand than would ever be needed. When I responded to the excited call that she was foaling, the farm manager, three stablemen, and the apprehensive owner were all in attendance.

The foaling stall had been prepared well in advance, with slots installed on the walls to receive the precut boards to form a temporary partition. The boards were in readiness, neatly stacked outside the stall.

Shortly after I arrived, the mare got down and, like the old professional that she was, quickly and efficiently produced a near-perfect robust, bright chestnut colt. We allowed the mare to greet and check her handsome new son. Then the men began to put the barricade in place while I collected a drop of blood from the colt's ruptured umbilical cord and a drop of colostrum from the mare's teat.

The colt was placed close to the partition so that his mother could lick him and admire her latest effort while I carefully stirred the two insignificant drops that would give us such an important revelation.

Almost too soon the result of my crude test became startlingly clear. The two liquids separated into reddish semisolid forms to reconfirm what we had already known.

The big, strong, beautiful colt would have to be protected from the normally life-sustaining colostrum in his mother's udder that now contained antibodies that could destroy him.

By now the active colt had been rubbed dry and, even before I completed his routine neonatal care, he was up and insistently searching for food. A bottle was prepared for him, using a mare's milk substitute. It took very little encouragement for him to accept his first meal from this unnatural source. He was soon comfortably asleep in the straw, close to the partition and under his mother's watchful eye.

While he slept, I drew blood from a vein in his neck and collected a sample from the mare's udder to send to the laboratory. Repeated samples were taken every twelve hours and it was not until the middle of the fourth day that a negative report was given to us.

In the meantime the foal thrived on his bottles and the mare adjusted with calm acceptance to both the regular milking and the unusual housing arrangement. The foal even accepted his daily protective injections with little more than a curious interest.

When the good news was received from the laboratory that the mare's milk was no longer a threat to the foal, the stall partition was removed. After a brief exploration of the newly expanded boundaries of his world, the foal found his natural food supply and nursed as competently as though he had never eaten in any other manner. After switching her tail in annoyance a few times as the foal started to nurse, the patient mare shifted her quarters to make her udder more accessible to her fine young son.

This colt grew and continued to develop just as he had started—as an exceptional animal.

He raced successfully as a two-year-old and won many races during his third year. After receiving an injury early in his fourth year, he was retired and now stands at stud on a farm not far from the home of his illustrious father.

Wobbles or equine uncoordination is usually seen in young horses from 16 to 28 months of age. It may develop in foals and is then called *foal ataxia*. The onset either can be sudden or gradual, and is characterized by a wobbly and, in some cases, uncontrollable hind-leg gait. Varying degrees of uncoordination exist, but the most striking feature that is always noted is the complete absence of any sign of pain or discomfort. Once you have seen a classic case, it is not difficult to recognize the loose, free-swinging, swaying gait. Such horses appear to be relaxed, even uninhibited, and their actions can be compared with those of an inebriated human.

Early in the development of this condition, or in individuals involved to a lesser degree, identification is more difficult. However, foal ataxia is progressive and usually the symptoms become more obvious in a short period of time.

The hind legs are affected first. Various foreleg gait alterations are slower to appear, yet just as persistently progressive. A common observation is the foal's inability to control his hind legs during flight (movement), with resultant extraneous lateral motion. There is often telltale evidence of the uncontrolled feet to be found in uneven wear of the hoof walls—also a part of this dismal condition.

In early instances, if the foal is turned suddenly or abruptly, or backed, the symptoms will be exaggerated.

Colts are affected more often than fillies. Their awkward, loose, and pain-free movements are easily identified and then, sadly, diagnosed.

Various lesions, or tissue changes, are found in the cervical vertebrae and spinal cord. An especially common location is at the level of the third and fourth cervical vertebrae. Although there may be several causes, the location and clinical symptoms remain relatively constant.

Three overlapping, interrelated causative tissue and cellular changes can be seen at autopsy:

1. *Osteoarthritic changes in the bodies of cervical vertebrae* are found frequently. Such changes are caused by irritation or trauma to the vertebrae.

2. *Stenosis or narrowing of the bony cervical canal* causes undue pressure on the growing spinal cord, with resulting secondary degenerative changes. Bilateral, or symmetric, changes may indicate hereditary origin; this type of lesion has frequently been identified with classic clinical wobbler symptoms.

3. *Subluxation of faulty articular processes of the cervical vertebrae* is also thought to be of hereditary origin and to allow movement with resultant pressure and degeneration of the spinal cord.

4. A fourth, unrelated cause, although infrequently diagnosed, simulates the wobbler syndrome. Amazingly, an internal parasite—a cerebrospinal nematode—escapes its conventional tissue in the body and inadvertently burrows into the cerebrospinal tissue, causing an inflammatory reaction. A foreign-body reaction results, and degenerative changes follow.

I am convinced that parasites are the cause of wobbles more often than ever is recognized. Parasitic damage is so vast, appears in so many guises, and affects all classes of horses, so that it seems impossible to determine an accurate estimate of the losses suffered over any measurable period of time.

Although many causes for hind-leg ataxia have been proposed, popular theories include hereditary or congenital origin, and traumatic stress to the neck, especially in long-necked horses that are notoriously so predisposed. At present there is no known treatment.

When old horses suffer degrees of ataxia it is a different entity from that of the classic wobbler. Gait deviations with visible swaying are commonly observed. Some of these older horses continue to function in a limited way, while many others are no longer useful.

Degenerative changes develop in various sites of the spinal cord, but the most usual area to be affected is the lumbar section of the vertebral column. These chronic irreversible changes and their effects are reflected clinically.

This process differs from the ataxia seen in young horses because occasionally it seems to have been arrested—even to have become static at times.

Sometimes, when I am called to examine a new horse that is unfamiliar to me, and while I listen to the heart and lungs, I seem to sense an ever-so-slight swaying body movement. This movement, in combination with the seemingly ceaseless replacement of all four feet, is a condition that should never be overlooked.

When these horses are asked to move out for a soundness check, invariably the horse exhibits some degree of ataxia. Unfortunately, this constitutes an unsoundness.

I have learned to expect and have witnessed an increase in the incidence of wobblers in specific equine families, as one would anticipate in any disease for which hereditary influences are suspected as a factor.

A contracted foal is generalized terminology that embraces a conglomeration of diverse kinds of contractions involving different locations in the foal's body. The term is inaccurately used to cover such a large variety of conditions that it is, at best, confusing and misleading.

In a truly contracted foal, the contorted members are *ankylosed* or rigidly and permanently fixed into position. These irreversible changes have developed during intrauterine life. In describing these foals, the terms "contracted" and "ankylosed" are used interchangeably. Most often the thoracic spine is scoliosed, being twisted and locked into position, with accompanying distortion of the cervical spine and cranium.

These contracted or ankylosed foals-to-be are frequently found in aborted fetuses; those carried to term are always associated with difficult deliveries (*dystocia*). Because of the fixed flexion of the forelimbs, the overall diameter of the shoulders and thorax is greatly increased; for purely mechanical reasons, passage of the foal through the pelvic canal cannot be accomplished.

Such impossible deliveries require a *fetotomy, embryotomy,* or a *caesarean* to remove the unyielding mass in order to save the mare. The frustrating fact about these contracted foals is the veterinarian's inability to reposition the rigid fetus, making normal manipulation impossible, plus the fact that the forelegs cannot be straightened for delivery. These two facts alone call for reevaluation of the situation, for foals that are severely contracted *in utero* cannot be delivered through the normal birth canal.

This situation constitutes a *dystocia*, a difficult birth, which is always a red alert: total attention, energy, and knowledge are now required instantly to relieve the mare quickly and considerately and to deliver the foal by performing a fetotomy or caesarean section. See chapter on dystocias.

A fetotomy performed with expertise is acceptable, but a caesarean is much to be preferred if a suitable equine surgery is available. This surgical procedure offers the most humane and advanced method to provide for the well-being of the mare and her reproductive future.

Seventy-five percent of the dystocias encountered in my practice have been caused by contracted foals. If the fetus is less than term, hence undersized, it provides a definite advantage for both the mare and the veterinarian.

When these rigid, abnormally twisted, and dead foals are finally in the world, other areas of body and extremity contractions will be visible. Varying degrees of thoracic vertebral deformities, asymmetric cranial distortions, and torticollis (wry or contorted neck) are also found.

If these foals are delivered alive, they are unable to stand to nurse and consequently attempt to walk on their malformed knees. It is a tragic sight to see these otherwise apparently normal foals scrambling around on their knees searching for food—demonstrating a grim determination to survive. Unfortunately, they invariably possess additional hidden spinal lesions and are therefore hopeless cripples. For humane reasons euthanasia is indicated.

But this same entity may also remain as an insidious, hidden time bomb, not revealing its crippling effects until a certain predictable timetable is fulfilled.

Two separate, distinct manifestations occur.

The first is seen at birth, or within the first few months of life. During this early postnatal period, one or both forefeet gradually assume a club-foot appearance.

Classified as a *coronopedal* contraction (club foot), this deformity is caused by the relentless pull of the deep digital flexor tendon attached to the bottom of the *os pedis* or coffin bone. Tension from the associated muscle group creates a backward pull on the tip of the *os pedis,* making the foal travel on its toe, with the heel elevated.

The resulting break or subluxation in the longitudinal skeletal axis produces dorsal pressure on the coronary band, causing sufficient discomfort to create lameness.

In addition, the tip of the coffin bone is forced into a position that requires it to support the entire weight of the forelimb—similar to a human walking on very high heels or the tip of the toes.

With this painful, stilted gait and continuous internal pressure, the naturally tough and durable hoof tissue soon thins and gives way at the toe. A separation (or opening) develops, carrying with it the threat of infection and osteomyelitis.

A recently developed surgical procedure to relieve the excessive pull of the deep digital flexor tendon has produced gratifying results. Called inferior check ligament desmotomy, this procedure provides dramatic relief of the signs of coronopedal flexure deformity in the young horse. The long-term results are exciting.

A second manifestation—a flexure deformity of the metacarpophalangeal joint called *nutritional contraction*—is not usually seen until the foal reaches twelve to eighteen months. It is depressing to see a fine young yearling, ready to be broken, gradually develop knuckling-over of the ankles and knees that appears to be self-perpetuating. As a rule both forelegs are involved.

As the contraction progresses, the animal has difficulty supporting its weight in a standing position and its reluctance to move is only too evident. These yearlings show a desire to get down and rest; then it becomes difficult for them to regain their feet. Tremors, with instability, are frequently seen in their deformed and weakened limbs.

The unbalanced pull of the superficial digital flexor tendon causes the ankle to flex and, at the same time, straightens the pastern. Concurrent flexion of the knees is thought to be a reciprocal or compensatory action. Neuromuscular involvement is thought to originate in the thoracic spine and to be of hereditary or congenital origin.

Many researchers believe a muscular imbalance is caused by unequal growth and development between the skeletal and muscular systems. Bone growth outstrips tendon growth.

An increasing incidence of contraction has been found where excessive protein is fed to encourage rapid growth and development—perhaps for sales or show possibilities. Coupled with an hereditary predisposition, nutrition versus growth rate is gaining in acceptance among veterinarians as a contributing factor in contraction problems. Hence the name "nutritional contraction" as it differs from foal (one limb) contraction.

Often when I am first called to see an affected yearling, the owner is concerned because of what appears to be a weakness of the hindquarters. Because of the difficulty these yearlings experience in getting up, once the forefeet are extended, they are hesitant to continue to rise; they may remain in a sitting-dog position before finally rising to their feet. This gives the erroneous impression that the hind legs are involved. Stall rest combined with a near starvation diet has produced favorable clinical signs of remission. Pain and tendon contraction subsided within mere days. Many fine large colts have been saved simply by the reduction of dietary protein.

In the attempt to grow a super colt, horsemen literally fed them to death.

I have never seen a contracted foal or yearling in a poor man's barn!

A surgical procedure, similar to the coronopedal surgery, is available; it is producing good results. Superior check ligament desmotomy has produced immediate and sustained relief.

Rhinopneumonitis. Another serious disease to be reckoned with is the two-pronged rhinopneumonitis virus. This sneaky, destructive virus causes upper respiratory problems in the young horse but death to the not-so-lucky unborn foal.

While the degree of upper respiratory infections varies greatly in the young horse, the rhinopneumonitis virus has an affinity for the allantois chorion of placental tissue, attacking the exact spot where attachment to the maternal uterine lining occurs. Spontaneous abortion is the outcome. This insidious virus becomes more invasive and hazardous as the placenta increases in size and growth.

A commercial injectable vaccine is available, with injections beginning in the fifth month to be followed through on the seventh and ninth month of gestation. This schedule seems to confer a fair and safe immunity to the brood mare. Currently the vaccine of choice is Pneumobort K (Fort Dodge Laboratories).

As for the young foal, his series of vaccinations begins at fourteen to sixteen weeks of age. It is wise to note that a good schedule of vaccinations for young and old is the key to good health.

Streptococcus Equi. Young horses have no defense against bacterial invasion, especially the streptococcal diseases. Almost every young foal suffers through a period of fever, muco-purulent nasal discharge, and swollen glands which results in the production of its own antibodies.

Streptococcus equi is the causative agent of "strangles" and can make a foal very uncomfortable because of sore and swollen glands around the head, eyes, and jaw. This disease is highly contagious and will spread rapidly through a barn, affecting even older horses if they have reduced immunity.

Strep-equi bacterin (Fort Dodge Laboratories) is not a new product, but it is a very useful one when an outbreak threatens. It is irritating to muscle tissue and sometimes results in a sore injection site because its compatibility with certain individual horses is unpredictable. However, with prudent use and careful dosage, this bacterin can be safe and effective and has a valid place in the protection program for your foal.

Equine influenza is another relatively common viral respiratory disease that affects horses in all age groups and plagues humans as well. As presently interpreted, this viral disease is caused by either of two subtypes of *Myxovirus influenza*: M. influenza A-equi I type virus and M. influenza A-equi II type, each being clinically similar but antigenically different.

Highly contagious in nature, this respiratory viral disease is normally seen as epizootic. The sick animals exhibit depression, a dry hacking cough, elevated body temperatures, and a characteristic clear, watery nasal discharge. The nasal mucosa is inflamed and appears scarlet. By lifting the nasal flap, the moist flaming mucosa is uncovered and proves to be a reliable finding. Sore throats are commonplace. These horses continue to eat hay as usual, but there is a marked reduction in their grain consumption and in the volume of water they drink.

With frequent and uncontrollable coughing episodes, this airborne virus spreads rapidly and is capable of invading an entire barn (even assaulting an entire farm) within hours.

Equating the M. influenza A-equi I type virus with the human cold, almost all equine residents become ill; yet no losses or deaths are recorded as attributable to this agent.

The unwanted intrusion of complicating secondary bacterial invaders, however, can occur with any malady where an exceptionally weak, undernourished, or parasite-ridden horse may succumb to the additional insult to its overall defense mechanism.

In treated cases, the virus of A-equi I type usually limits its effects to the upper respiratory tract.

It is a different story with A-equi II type virus, which seems to demonstrate a distinct affinity for lung tissue. Bronchitis and pneumonia occur, accompanied by high fevers. Fortunately the prevalence of the II type virus in the United States is less frequent.

A safe and effective bivalent influenza vaccine is available today which, if correctly used, produces a strong first-line antibody defense in young horses. In foals, this vaccine is most beneficial if administered at about four months, then repeated one month later to establish adequate immunity. Monthly boosters are recommended through the first year.

Equine influenza is erroneously used as a catchall term for other viral diseases. Rhinopneumonitis, just discussed, and Equine Viral Arteritis, which principally affects adult horses and can cause abortion in mares, are now acknowledged to be separate diseases caused by different viruses.

Foal pneumonia, as discussed earlier, can be caused by an array of bacterial or viral infections or combinations of the two.

Mechanical foal pneumonia originates from many causes. It can follow the aspiration of any foreign substance. Aspiration of fetal fluids during a difficult or prolonged delivery, accidental aspiration of milk by a weak foal, or the aspiration of oral medications administered by inexperienced handlers are obvious causes.

Any thoracic trauma sustained during, or immediately after, foaling can also contribute to pulmonary congestion.

Symptoms of pneumonia are the same and remain constant, regardless of the etiologic agent. Common signs are depression, respiratory distress or limited rib cage movement, fever, and disinterest in nursing.

Rapid action in obtaining veterinary help can be decisive here.

When your foal has an infected joint regardless of cause, the joint manifests specific red alert symptoms, i.e., enlargement or swelling of the joint capsule accompanied by heat and acute pain. An elevated fever with overt lameness are constant findings along with reluctance to bear weight on the affected limb. Please recognize this as a serious condition and act accordingly.

Summon your veterinarian at once on an emergency basis! First observed is a swollen joint with reduced range of motion. Untreated, this infection can cause crippling and even require euthanasia for humane reasons. Foals that survive the acute state undoubtedly suffer with a chronically enlarged joint that compromises its future.

Infectious arthritis can be seen primarily in older foals or young adults as a sequel to or a residue of a previous navel infection, usually streptococcal in origin. Veterinarians must make a differential diagnosis. A microorganism known as *Escherichia coli* is commonly isolated as the destructive agent in these infected joints. *E. coli* is a normal inhabitant in all gastrointestinal tracts and is harmless and in fact quite helpful in its role in the intestinal contents. Fecal material is literally loaded with *E. coli*. When this bacteria enters any place other than the intestine and fecal material, it is transformed into a deadly pathogen or disease producer. When it gains entrance into a wound or especially a joint space, no matter what its course, an intense, destructive infection ensues.

A strict aseptic approach to treatment by a professional is vital to the outcome and should be handled by an equine veterinarian.

After consulting with the owner, a decision must be made to either institute immediate "on the spot" treatment or to rush the young patient off to the nearest modern equine hospital where intensive care "around the clock" can be administered. Unfortunately, availability of a facility and cost factors must be addressed.

Suggested treatment:

1. Draw blood and submit to laboratory for a complete blood count.

2. Begin a body temperature chart.

3. Administer IM and IV antibiotic of choice (Amikacin, Gentamicin). Do not wait for laboratory results.

4. Aspirate some synovial joint fluid and submit to laboratory. A mild sedative given to the patient can be helpful to both patient and attending personnel.

5. Joint lavage (flushing) with copious amounts of Ringer's Solution will remove infected synovial fluid and cleanse the inner joint. Ideally this should be followed by an intra-articular injection of the antibiotic of choice.

When the laboratory results are back, the practitioner can evaluate and be guided by this information. Based on laboratory findings, a treatment program can be organized or reorganized with a prognosis forthcoming. Most infected joints are categorized as guarded to poor for future soundness.

Suggested manner of preparation to invade any joint space:

The area on the joint skin surface to be entered must be scrupulously cleansed and prepared in an aseptic manner, abiding by all precautions to avoid introducing new contamination and thus complicating an already serious condition. This is the only place where time is well spent! To assure asepsis, clip the hair, shave the skin, and scrub with antiseptics and presurgical preparations (Betadine, Xenodine, Novalsan). Your veterinarian will most likely apply alcohol and tamed iodine via sterile 4″ x 4″ sterile gauze sponges, immediately prior to the introduction of a sterile needle for aspiration and introduction treatments. This is the accepted front-line treatment.

6. Routine radiographs of the infected area can aid in the assessment of articular cartilage damage.

7. In addition, I prefer, in times of stress, to administer a serum transfusion loaded with preformed antibodies to support and perhaps stimulate the foal's questionable immune system. This is a reliable and safe procedure and, although time-consuming, it does produce results.

8. Hyaluronic acid is a normal component of joint fluid and its contents are low in infected joints. It is known for its ability to protect articular cartilage and synovial membranes. Lately, the practice of including a small dose (25–50 mg) of hyaluronic acid has gained popularity among veterinarians. Although there are many commercially available HA products, the ones containing the highest osmotic pressure seem to produce the desired effects and provide longer duration. Of course, it is also more costly!

9. In my opinion, the only treatment is prevention.

Osteochondritis Descecans. Another joint condition rapidly gaining in incidence is osteochondritis descecans, or OCD, which is thought to be an inherited condition. It can easily be confused with an infection. The primary symptoms of OCD are enlarged swollen joints containing principally synovial fluid. It is easy to differentiate this from a septic joint simply by palpation—it is always cool to the touch and lameness is inconsistent in the early stages. OCD attacks the articular cartilage inside of the joint and erodes the tissue in ulcerlike lesions literally extending down to the bone surface. At this period in time it naturally causes lameness. It is commonly found in large well-bred fast-growing colts and the high incidence found in certain bloodlines cannot be ignored as coincidental. Certain stallions are known by the high numbers of affected get. Treatment is discouraging yet the local use of hyaluronic acid injections into the affected joint on a regular schedule, coupled with oral powdered perna shells and weekly injections of specific polysulfated glycosaminoglycan (PSGAG) has shown some promise in these usually large and handsome colts. Invasive experimental surgery has to date produced better results than conservative treatment. The disease process however seems to continue showing resistance to most of our efforts. Sad to say, our better families of runners carry the highest incidence of the elusive OCD.

OCD is another crippling entity of principally young horses.

Esophageal, gastric, and duodenal ulcers. Although ulcers of the gastrointestinal tract have been common in other species, including the human, not until approximately ten years ago did the question of their presence in the equine become controversial. With nothing but clinical symptoms on which to base a diagnosis, ulcers continued to elude the veterinarians, until increasing numbers began to be recognized in the postmortem room.

The veterinary profession became alert and began to recognize classic clinical signs of suspected ulceration of the digestive tract. "Shotgun" therapy ensued consisting of copious amounts of antacids on a daily basis. This trial and error treatment brought encouraging responses and relief from abdominal pain and distress. Ulcers have been known to be painful and very destructive if untreated.

We now know the telltale symptoms of gastrointestinal ulcers in the foal or even an older horse: depression, even withdrawal from people and other horses; abdominal pain or cramping often called "colic"; excessive salivation; and relentless teeth grinding. These individuals are usually underweight and have an unthrifty appearance. Whether observed in a weak foal or even in an older, poorly conditioned horse, the common denominator has been *stress* from either disease or environmental conditions.

GI pain is translated by horse people as "colic." Consequently, the individuals receive treatment for colicky symptoms. When the veterinarian passes the nasogastric tube, a diagnostic reflux of hot acidic fluid usually occurs as the tube enters the foal's stomach. With the release of stomach fluids and gases, signs of relief are usually evident. (Remember, the equine is incapable of eructation.) Most doctors will then include a therapeutic dose of antacid through the tube along with routine treatment for abdominal discomfort.

With the advent of the fiber-optic gastroscope, mucosal erosion and varying degrees of ulceration can now be visualized, assessed, and treated accordingly.

The fiber-optic gastroscope has been a wonderful step forward, allowing a definitive diagnosis affording early treatment, and thus improving the chances of successful treatment. Accuracy of prognosis also increases. So-called stress ulcers in foals are similar to the peptic ulcer so commonly experienced by humans.

A blood test is another diagnostic aid. A recent study showed that foals with ulcers consistently had a higher content of pepsinogen in the serum than those without.

Another diagnostic procedure includes the use of barium in the upper gastrointestinal tract. Although this has been quite successful in humans and other species, to date no literature on the equine has been forthcoming.

Ruptured stomachs and perforated intestinal walls are not uncommon as a cause of death.

When ulceration is even suspected, begin treating with copious amounts of antacids—stat. Tagamet (cimetidine), at a dose of 600 mg four times daily is recommended. Also indicated are other antacids such as milk of magnesia, Maalox, and the newer and more expensive Carafate, (recommended dosage, two 1-gm boluses, three times daily).

Short course therapy is never successful! Continue daily liberal doses of antacids for perhaps six to eight weeks and insist upon serene and quiet handling and surroundings. Some foals have responded to this regimen so it is surely worth the effort.

Barker foal is a highly descriptive lay term for neonatal foals that suffer convulsive seizures and literally bark like a dog. The syndrome is observed in some foals not yet dry, while other foals—after a few hours of life—may suddenly convulse and bark ceaselessly until exhausted. Convulsions consist of involuntary head jerking, with spasms of the limbs and body.

These sounds are such a departure from what is expected from the foal that the eerie primitive cry emitted by a small wet body convulsing in the straw once heard is never forgotten!

If a barker foal can survive repeated convulsions, be tube-fed, kept slightly sedated, and given intensive antibiotic and supportive therapy, incredibly some afflicted foals reportedly survive.

In my practice I have not been fortunate enough to see this. Literature states that it requires four to five days for symptoms to slowly subside, a weak sucking reflex to appear gradually, and for the foal's other faculties to return gradually.

The true cause of this entity is not known. Human intervention was first thought to be a factor because the incidence of barker foals is slightly increased in attended deliveries. Now a popular theory is that deprivation of oxygen to the brain is the cause of convulsions and seizures.

In nature there are three events during delivery that can cause oxygen deficiency. Any prolonged or delayed delivery almost assures the possibility of oxygen reduction. The early separation of the placenta from the uterine wall—*placenta previa* or *abruptia placenta*—creates a premature shutdown of the foal's life-support system.

Finally, the rupture of the umbilical cord before the foal receives its essential 500 to 700cc or pint of placental blood can cause a dramatic drop in blood pressure, reduce aeration of lung tissue, and result in diminished available oxygen in the blood.

Early, untimely umbilical rupture can occur by the action of a high-strung matron suddenly rising just as the neonate lands in the straw. I have seen mares who apparently cannot wait to greet their foals jump to their feet, spin, and rush back to nuzzle and inspect them.

Another cause of ill-timed umbilical-cord rupture is the ignorant, outrageous act of a well-meaning attendant who is overly conscientious and feels undue concern in his job. In an unnecessary attempt to protect the foal and show it to the mare, the foal is snatched from the recumbent mare and briskly dragged around to her head. This abruptly breaks the navel cord, allows the escape of the precious placental blood, and may produce a devastating drop in the foal's blood pressure.

Shaker foal is a term for a highly fatal, neuromuscular disease found in young suckling foals approximately three to eight weeks old.

The cause is unknown and the incidence is on the increase. Although the big-business Thoroughbred breeding farms in Kentucky have experienced isolated cases for years, the incidence of shaker foals in Thoroughbreds seems to be on the increase both geographically and by number.

Diagnosis is determined by the physical evidence of the foal's inability to rise, along with profound muscle weakness and flaccidity. With assistance the foal can gain its feet and, perhaps, nurse, yet generalized muscular trembling makes it difficult to stand so the foal drops back into the straw.

Intense muscular trembling progresses to well-developed shaking, which then prevents the foal from standing, or even rising. Complete prostration soon ensues, and death occurs, treated or untreated, in approximately three days.

Recent information has related the deadly *Clostridium botulinum* microorganism to the mysterious shaker syndrome. (*C. botulinum* is the cause of a fatal disease, called botulism, in adult horses and humans.) A new vaccine has recently been developed for use in the brood mare.

Aminoglycosides, tetracyclines, and procaine penicillin are contraindicated and *should not be used*. Potassium penicillin, oxygen support, and a serum transfusion are our front line until further and more effective treatment is forthcoming.

Immuno-defense deficiencies, in the form of CID (combined immuno deficiency) and IgM (immuno-globulin deficiency), are two newly identified conditions found in foals.

CID is a recently recognized fatal, hereditary disease of young foals that results in a combination of immuno-globulin deficiencies. The symptoms are weakness, pneumonia of viral origin, and other various secondary infections.

Lymphopenia, the profound reduction of circulating white blood cells—specifically, lymphocytes—is a most remarkable diagnostic symptom. Lymphocytes play a major role in the formation of antibodies and immune responses of the body.

Microscopic tissue changes are found in the thymus, spleen, and lymph nodes, and are characteristic of this perplexing disorder. At present the only diagnosed cases that have been laboratory-confirmed have been found in Arabian foals.

Research is sorely needed in this field.

IgM deficiency is also a fatal and relatively new finding. Thought to be of hereditary or congenital origin, it is found in young foals whose lives are unpredictably shortened. IgM is only one immuno globulin identified amongst other globulins and lymphocytes. Its deficiency is of major importance as it relates to CID and an effective immuno-protective mechanism. A deficiency such as this is known to be associated with respiratory and pulmonary infections, and with Klebsiella, the dreaded bacterial microorganism capable of causing a deadly septicemia.

If I suspect a substandard neonatal foal, I do not wait for symptoms to convince me. I quickly run a routine blood count to see if the white cells are increased in number, indicating a bacterial infection. If the white cell count is depressed, that indicates either viral or immune deficiency. If body temperature is one degree higher or lower than the 101.0° F, I begin antibiotic therapy concurrent with 1 pint of hyperimmuned serum intravenously—slowly. This greatly increases the foal's chances for survival, regardless of the cause.

When I first entered practice I saw foals lost because of improper diagnosis, yet-undiscovered medication, and inadequate surgical techniques. Such strides have been made during the past two decades that our foal loss has been drastically reduced. Progress will continue, I am certain.

10

A Closer Look at the Mare

The process of evolution has not been kind to the mare. When compared to other breeds of livestock, mares are endowed by nature with a reproductive system that is more complex and less dependable than in any other known species. This is clearly demonstrated by her anatomically primitive uterus, her unstable antiquated type of placentation, a fragile cervical closure, a tendency to hormonal imbalance, and the long period from fertilization to implantation of the vesicle embryo.

The courageous horse breeder should be aware of and learn to recognize several well-documented problems that are inherent in today's brood mare.

Nidation, or the implantation of the vesicle embryo, occurs only after the embryo floats free in the uterus for an unusually long period of time.

The embryo remains unattached for a minimum of 110 days after conception. This protracted and hazardous period is unique in the equine. Early embryonic loss is high during the first three months of gestation, for during this period the mare's inefficient placenta grows and gradually attaches itself to the maternal endometrium or the inner uterine lining.

Nutrition and waste products are then more easily coped with and uterine stability becomes more reliable (and proficient) as each day of gestation passes.

Early in my practice I strove to detect pregnancies as early as possible and was exuberant when I finally learned, after many years and thousands of examinations, to determine pregnancies at 18 days.

Now I look on this ability with mixed emotions. Because of the typical mare's high rate of embryonic death, with subsequent abortion, and her unstable reproductive system, this information is only informative rather than confirmatory. In other words, this is a very valuable tool that permits one to determine what the mare is doing, but *not* the final word that the mare is safely in foal.

When early detection of pregnancies first became possible, because of the average mare's instability, some brood mare owners were highly skeptical. One of the typical nonbelievers was a very critical and not overly intelligent owner of a mare I had examined and found to be in foal at 18 days. On the fortieth postcover day the irate owner called to say that the mare was exhibiting strong indications of being in season. He was absolutely positive that the early pregnancy examination was just so much hocus-pocus and that the mare had not conceived.

I answered the call and during a careful examination of the mare discovered a tiny embryo on the floor of the vagina. The timing must have been perfect, for in all my years of practice this was the only time I had retrieved such an early abortion. In a matter of minutes the soft, watery vesicle would have been lost in the stall bedding or in the pasture.

It was certainly fortunate to have evidence in hand to convince *this* owner that his mare had indeed been in foal.

A year or so later I had another unusual experience and, interestingly enough, it involved the same owner. It was November, and he had just brought a filly home from the track that he wanted to retire to his brood mare band.

Even though she had showed no promise as a race horse, he valued her bloodlines and was anxious to determine her gynecologic soundness in anticipation of the approaching breeding season.

When I arrived at the farm to examine the filly, the stableman led out an attractive, slim, fit young Thoroughbred. She had run her last race just three days earlier and still looked a little drawn. She had run a poor race; in fact, she finished well back, showing even less willingness than in her previous attempts.

I started a routine examination and was startled when I put my hand on the head of a well-developed foal! When I told the owner that his race filly was pregnant he was as shocked as I had been, and stated in no uncertain terms that it was absolutely impossible for the young mare to be in foal.

Looking at her sleek sides, with no abdominal enlargement, it *was* difficult to believe that she was carrying a foal. Driving out the lane, I smiled as I remembered the earlier episode involving that owner.

Several hours later the office telephone rang; then the story came out. In the middle of the summer the filly had been sent to a farm for three weeks to be allowed to relax and "freshen" in hopes of improving her racing performance. That farm did have a stallion and nature had prevailed.

To repeat: evolution has not been kind to the mare. This is clearly evidenced by her poorly positioned, suspended uterus. The large, sagging uterine body, with two long projecting cornua (horns), assumes a "Y" shape that permits little, if any, normal physiological drainage. With each ensuing pregnancy efficiency is further reduced and can limit the number of lifetime pregnancies. With no provision for natural drainage in the poorly placed uterus, exudates develop and pool, circulation stagnates, and infection is invited.

Uterine ligaments attached to each of the long horns are responsible for the suspension of the uterus in the abdominal cavity. The normal position of the uterus in the average maiden mare is well suspended above the pelvic rim, permitting effective drainage and circulation that results in a condition of excellent health.

The normal uterus is a hollow muscular organ, weighing approximately eight to ten pounds when empty or nongravid. It is situated partly in the pelvic cavity and partly in the abdominal cavity. It is attached and suspended from the lateral walls of the abdominal cavity by broad ligaments, which then attach to the borders of the cornua.

The average mare's uterus can hold approximately one liter of fluid in the involuted stage.

Its location is altered by successive pregnancies to a lower, less efficient position in the abdomen. The tone or vigor of the suspensory apparatus decreases progressively with each new pregnancy, allowing the horns to sag. They, in turn, exert a pull on the uterine body, distorting its position and disturbing its circulation. Uterine tone is decreased—especially after parturition and during involution.

So the large, antiquated, and poorly positioned uterus suffers with each pregnancy; each gestation takes its toll by compounding the extent of sagging until the uterine body is eventually found below the pelvic rim, resting on the abdominal floor.

The cervical canal is the entrance to the uterus. The cervix is the structure that, under hormonal control, opens as if it were a door to permit semen to enter during the estrous period and then closes again under hormonal influence.

The state of the cervix accurately reflects the stage of hormonal activity, opening and closing appropriately.

When pregnancy occurs, the cervical closure becomes as effective as its capabilities permit. Somewhat fragile at best, the closure is consistent with other areas of reproduction in the mare—a condition that is unstable and inconsistent.

Cervical closure is responsible for maintenance of pregnancy. Any patency (openness) in the cervical canal immediately signals either barrenness or an impending abortion.

For a pregnancy to progress normally, a constant and absolute cervical seal is imperative. Any deviation in the closure pattern is *always* an ominous sign and should be interpreted as such.

Unfortunately, the mare was not blessed with as efficient a cervical closure as that seen in all other domestic animals. Cervical location and color can vary somewhat during pregnancy and warrant no concern, *but the closure must be unvarying.* Most disturbing is the fact that the cervix can be rather freely dilated manually at any stage in the mare's cycle—even during pregnancy. This fact may account for many abortions occurring during the early stage of pregnancy.

Adequate exercise is the only method known to promote drainage and aid involution in the postpartum mare. Combine good husbandry with conscientious veterinary assistance and then—perhaps—your mare's productivity can be prolonged.

The placenta of the mare is categorized as a *diffuse deciduate* type of placentation. Placentas are classified into types mainly by their method of attachment to the maternal endometrium, or inner lining of the uterus.

The method of attachment, whether secure or insecure, has the awesome function of maintaining embryonic life. The slightest change or aberration can easily cause detachment, resulting in embryonic death and subsequent abortion.

"Diffuse deciduate" is defined as the falling off or peeling away of a membrane. This describes well the mare's placenta, because the entire outer surface of the placenta is weakly but intimately attached to the uterus during pregnancy by millions of microscopic villi that project into the inner lining of the uterus.

This feeble attachment represents the main nutritional supply and sustenance for the embryo, and will separate or peel away at the slightest provocation.

Cervical closure is affected by humoral (blood) factors and hormonal control, with only a mucus plug or seal to retain the precious cargo for eleven long months. It is a sad fact that the bovine's cervical closure is at the pinnacle of efficiency and the mare's closure the exact opposite.

At this point it seems appropriate to touch on the highly misunderstood endocrine system, better known as the hormonal system. This complex —a powerful, effective interplay of hormonal secretions accurately dispersed into the body from the ductless glands—totally controls all phases and actions, both stimulating and inhibiting, of the reproductive tract.

Endocrine glands, usually small in size, are located at various positions in the body, and their chain-reaction function is to secrete yet another hormone. Balance is maintained and regulated by the stimulation or inhibition of one hormone upon another.

It is quite clear that a very fine balance must exist in order to maintain systemic stability. A complex system of checks and balances imposed upon each hormone, and its opposing hormone, efficiently maintains harmony in the multifaceted production. Any slight imbalance obviously can result in failure for a link in the reproductive chain of events, reflected by clinical manifestations that vary from a very slight symptom to a profound cyclic change. Cessation or elongation of normal cycles, or strange and unusual behavior, are obvious indications of endocrine upset.

The synchronized production of secretions governs a wide range of critical functions in the body: regulation of the estrous cycle or heat; responsibility for production of the follicle in the ovary (with the egg or ovum inside the follicle), with subsequent ovulation or egg release; promotion of egg fertilization; preparation of the uterus for pregnancy; and production of the corpus luteum to replace the ruptured follicles' crater in order to maintain pregnancy during early gestation.

The corpus luteum is a firm yellow body that remains in the ovary and produces progesterone (the main known hormone involved in maintenance of pregnancy).

The hormones also initiate parturition, prepare the mammary gland for lactation, and aid in involution of the uterus after delivery. Altogether it is a massive assignment for this group of small glands!

Evidently this profound hormonal system has an overwhelmingly authoritative control of the functions of the entire reproductive tract. Every small "cog" in the endocrine machine, unless in perfect order, can create havoc and result in varying degrees of subfertility, infertility, or sterility.

The mare is notorious for possessing a known imbalance in her hormonal makeup. This imbalance, which shows itself relatively often, lies in the innate inequity that exists between the follicle-stimulating facet and the luteal phase of the reproductive process.

There exists a highly developed ability to produce gonadotropic hormones that stimulate follicles, ova or eggs, and estrogen production. The actions of estrogens are responsible for manifestations of heat or receptivity in all mammalians.

Conversely, the weak luteal phase produces progesterone, which is directly involved in the maintenance of pregnancy and the security of the embryo—the least desirable place for any weakness to exist.

The functioning luteal phase aids ovulation, and establishes and maintains the corpus luteum in the ovary. There is an interplay of conflicting forces between the estrogens and progesterone function, but (with efficient function) complementary action can eventually be achieved that should result in a successful pregnancy.

A large number of mares today suffer from a poor luteal phase. These affected individuals have been recognized in the past only by a history of early abortion, in the absence of other causes. Instead of relying upon an educated guess, today we have laboratory tests available to assess the hormonal quantity in the mare's blood; these tests are of some value (and comfort) by helping us avoid the frustrations endured previously. The chance to recognize a deficient mare in time to avoid a costly loss more than justifies the use of such tests.

Moreover, upon recognition of such deficiencies, prudent use of the previously discussed drug progesterone can help preserve the pregnancy.

Contrary to early opinion, the administering of progesterone has no known adverse effect upon the fetus. It does not appear to interfere with initiation of parturition, nor does it affect the postpartum mare or delay subsequent conception.

This conclusion is based on years of observation, though we do not yet have scientific data. When the two main hormonal factions are not synchronized, it then becomes evident that the forces to maintain pregnancy in the mare are not so efficient and, therefore, not equal to the dynamics of developing the pregnancy.

Faulty or insufficient luteal hormone levels can also be responsible for failure of the establishment of a corpus luteum in the ovary; this results in low progesterone production and, of course, inability to maintain pregnancy. At a later date in gestation, the growing placenta ultimately assumes the role of producing vital progesterone.

Currently, a mare with a known weak luteal phase or lowered progesterone levels can be prudently checked for pregnancy via a portable ultrasound machine on the twelfth postcover day. This method provides positive proof of pregnancy by producing a photo of the embryo *in utero* and perhaps more importantly allows the initiation of repository progesterone injections beginning the same day. Many pregnancies have been saved by this early treatment!

Experts recommend 3cc (150 mg) of repository progesterone administered deeply IM into the gluteal muscles (rump) every other day throughout her gestation.

Cleanse the area well and be sure to alternate injection sites and sides in her huge gluteal muscles.

If all appears well, cease injections a few weeks before her scheduled parturition or due dates.

In the absence of conception, progesterone stabilizes the cycle and prepares for another estrous. *Deficient progesterone can result in early undetected abortion.* As a rule, the minute embryo and its vesicle, consisting mainly of fluid, passes out of the unstable cervix unobtrusively.

The pregnant mare experiences several hormonal crises during her first 100 days of gestation. The first such crisis occurs around the eighteenth postcover day, when the stability of the luteal phase is first challenged by the follicle-stimulating hormones. This is the time when the corpus luteum in empty or barren mares should give way to estrogen influences, followed by development of a subsequent heat period. The second challenge to luteal efficiency occurs during the twenty-eighth to the thirty-third postcover day, when a flight of small follicles can be found, but are held at bay by a competent corpus luteum. This flight of follicles can actually cause a pregnant mare to exhibit light signs of estrous, which usually disturbs the mare owner much more than it does the mare.

There *is* an occasional mare whose estrogen level is sufficient to cause receptivity. Such an unusual mare—who will receive the stallion at this time—is in jeopardy and likely to suffer a subsequent abortion.

The next danger periods exist, with varying hormonal levels, around 45 days, again around 62 days, and then continuing until nidation takes place at about the 110th day. Each of these critical dates represents fluctuations in the normal hormonal balance. The dates coincide loosely with estral cycles which appear to be, during pregnancy, suppressed by luteal forces.

The number of mares "showing in" during the twenty-eighth to the thirty-third day seems to outnumber those of other unstable periods. Certain pregnant individuals will experience light estrogen influences during these periods. By all means, call your veterinarian and have your mare's status checked. It is the wise stud manager who checks his mares and knowingly keeps his foals instead of unknowingly aborting his mares.

Three generations—a granddam, her daughter, and her granddaughter—of an equine family observed over a period of twenty years have caused their owners and caretakers great consternation by exhibiting regular cycles throughout their *entire* gestations.

It is a shock, even to trained people, to see a near-term mare, huge and pendulous, reacting as strongly as a cycling, barren mare during the height of the breeding season.

But don't jump to erroneous conclusions. When you see what you consider to be abnormal behavior in your mare, previously diagnosed as pregnant, call your veterinarian and determine the animal's status before rushing her back to the stallion.

An unnatural breeding season is imposed upon the equine industry by the arbitrary birthday of January 1 for all Thoroughbreds—as required by The Jockey Club—that appears to be the final insult to the breeding business by creating unnatural problems.

Breeders, in their efforts to obtain foals delivered as close to the mandated birthday as possible, are tempted to try any method to breed their mares early—contrary to the brood mare's innate physiologic makeup. *This is absolutely opposed to Nature's cycle.*

Although a small number of mares do conceive, there are not enough to justify the continuance of this date with all its inherent problems.

The professional breeder is faced by conflicting factors: a rigid registry date, the known gestation period, and the natural breeding season of the equine. Considering the size and power of today's industry, it seems these unreasonable breeding requirements could be amended by industry legislation.

According to The Jockey Club, breeders cannot "cover" a mare prior to February 10 without the risk of a foal's arrival in December, and the unfortunate possibility of owning a tiny 75-pound *yearling* just a few days old! The Jockey Club continues to show its power by standing firm on its rigid birthdate rule, which is in direct conflict with the normal breeding pattern of the mare. Could this be just a matter of convenience for office recordkeeping?

The Standardbred registry is taking a fresh look at its inflexible birthdate rule by considering giving greater latitude in dates permitted for the breeding season. Foals that arrive by November 1 of one year are not considered yearlings until January of their second calendar year. Allowing foals to be dropped over an additional 60-day period and still considering them equal in age provides some advantage over the former system.

Yet, while this effort is laudable, it seems to represent a backward move into an even earlier breeding season.

The ideal birthdate for *any horse of any breed or registry,* considering the length of equine gestation and climatic conditions conducive to reproduction, should be February 1. One month, or thirty days, may not seem to be that critical at first thought; however, the obvious advantages clearly demonstrate the importance of that extra month.

Greater numbers of mares are cycling more consistently and with increased efficiency by the beginning of March, with its increased number of daylight hours, more sun, and warmer temperatures—and some green grass is visible. Foals would still arrive during the cold, short days of February, but the period until spring's pleasant weather would be shortened.

The breeding season would benefit greatly if The Jockey Club and farm and stallion owners would cooperate with the natural requirements of the animal world. It could be so simple: by moving the fixed birthdate one month forward, we would move that much closer to the physiologic breeding season, instead of backing away from nature's dates.

Consider the problems caused by breeding in the dead of winter, in snow and ice, with not a blade of grass or a robin to be seen. Most mares—appropriately—are in their most inactive breeding condition—a deep anestrous. Low vitamin A levels and short daylight hours with little sunlight all contribute to the bleak breeding record for the month of February.

The stallion seems to be the only truly adaptable, flexible, and well-adjusted part of the situation. He appears unaffected by the adversities borne by the mares and their foals.

Recent studies have revealed, however, that the stallion also reflects the seasonal changes. Being of the male species though, he refuses to outwardly succumb to the inward truths!

Biological study reveals that the modern mare is an excellent example of transition from a polyestrous animal to a monestrous animal. (A polyestrous animal is one that experiences two or more reproductive cycles each year; the monestrous animal cycles but once a year.)

Mares vary greatly in their breeding habits, but there are certain brood mares that will cycle effectively year round, while others insist upon a specific season of the year. External behavior, induced by teasing (or reacting to the presence of any horse), can be quite misleading.

Cycles may occur regularly with or without follicle formation, with or without ovulation, and with or without external manifestation of the heat.

An examination to determine the mare's breeding condition is obviously required in order to increase breeding efficiency when a large horse population must be cared for.

Mares are less consistent early in the year than they are as the season progresses; but do remember: the only consistent thing about a brood mare is her inconsistency! Usually her estrous periods will be long and inefficient early in the year, but shorten progressively, becoming more intense and more effective as summer approaches.

It is not unusual to see mares in season for a period of from one week to one month early in the year. Finally they may go out of season without even developing a productive follicle. The normal estrous period extends from six to eight days early in the year and will decrease to a surprisingly short period of three days by midsummer.

In order to have a fertile cycle, the mare must first develop a capable follicle formed by the ovary, followed by ovulation to release the ovum so that fertilization can take place. (Late-occurring ovulation in a longer-than-average estrous period is characteristic of the equine.)

Ovulation usually occurs late in the estrous period and, if all is well, results in termination of receptivity. The sudden switch from a mare's receptive attitude to teasing to her hostility or outright rejection, after a well-timed cover, is looked upon by experienced owners and breeders as a happy sign.

Over the years I have watched maiden and barren mares sent to the farm very early in the year in hopes of an early foal, only to have to wait weeks or even months for the mares' natural response. Without the use of artificial methods, which are of questionable value, the average mare will not cycle productively until midterm of the Thoroughbred-regulated breeding season, or until the days lengthen, depending upon your geographic location.

Today, we have an injectable drug called Prostiglandin. It has the capability of shortening the mare's cycle provided she is cycling. This drug has little value if a mare is in deep anestrous.

If you have a noncycling mare and the season is moving along with no hope of a cover in sight, discuss with your veterinarian the use of combined amounts of estrogen and progesterone. Programs astutely followed can bring about the desired results and soon your mare is on her way to the breeding shed.

This same method is commonly used to synchronize donor and recipient mares in embryo transfer programs.

The incidence of ovulation within an estrous period usually increases in frequency as the length of daylight increases. More nonovulatory cycles are detected by veterinarians in the early months of the season. It has been reported that conception rate per cover, per month, increases progressively with each month of the season and peaks during May and June.

Mares whose owners do not concern themselves with the problems (mostly economic) resulting from early foals are at a definite advantage. By the time their mares reach the breeding shed, fertility and breeding efficiency are at a peak because the mares are functioning naturally. It is sadly amusing to see the amazingly high produce record amongst the amateur pleasure-horse breeders, compared to the professionals who must struggle to overcome their self-inflicted handicaps.

The breeding farm comes alive about February 15 and systematically begins to cover mares. A preponderance of mares, however, are still in deep anestrous or at the lowest level of fertility at this time, as noted. This rigid, medically unsound, initiation of the breeding season makes it appear an uphill struggle. Admittedly, a small, select group of exceptional mares exists, which does cycle actively and produce valid follicles: they do conceive early. But, without these few exceptions, this would be a very discouraging time for professionals.

By approximately the middle of March, fertile cycles begin to appear with some frequency in the other mares. As daylight hours increase, so does hormonal activity in the average mare, although the degree of effectiveness varies with the individual. Certain mares seem to "settle" first each year in a regular pattern, unless some external development alters their schedules. (These easy-to-settle mares usually belong to highly fertile families.)

Interestingly, it is well documented that the length of daylight hours has a direct effect upon the pituitary gland by means of the retinal vessels of the eye. (Retinal vessels, located deep in the eye, relay the effects of daylight to the pituitary gland.) The pituitary gland responds to this stimulus and in turn activates other endocrine glands that are directly involved in the reproductive process. The activated endocrine glands cause the mare to experience cyclic activity, and follicle development ensues.

Research has shown clearly that neither intensity of light nor degree of temperature, nor any other stimulus *other than the number of daylight hours of exposure on the eyes' retinal vessels* has any appreciable effect on cyclic activity.

The winter solstice begins on December 22, the day with the shortest number of daylight hours in the year. This is the time of year, owing to the annual revolution of the earth, when the sun is at its greatest distance from the equator. Sixty-five to 75 percent of our mares are in deep anestrous at this time and the number increases to about 85 percent by mid-January. February will see some of these mares begin to develop *some* cyclic activity. The remaining small percentage represents the extraordinary minority that occasionally remains in a light anestrous or that may even cycle.

As we know, May and June, the months with the greatest number of daylight hours, are the months of highest fertility.

Can one ignore such a coincidence?

By way of contrast to the fixed beginning date of the Thoroughbred season, the other end of the season is quite flexible. Here the limiting factor is governed by the wishes and goals of the individual breeder. The undesirability of having a late foal, with its disadvantages in size and strength, has its effect upon the closing date of the breeding season. However, as we have observed, the pleasure-horse breeder is relatively unconcerned with early dates and therefore avoids the pressures on the commercial breeder.

One must remember, however, that the late foal, throughout its first three years of life, constantly encounters an obvious inequality. But the chronological "lag," so conspicuous at an early age, seems to even out during the third year of its life.

11

Fertility and Preparation for the Next Foal

Returning the mare to a stallion involves many considerations. If you are delighted by the new foal your mare presented to you and wish to repeat this breeding combination, many factors should still be weighed.

Foal Heat Checkup

Supposing your mare enjoyed a normal, uncomplicated delivery with no postpartum consequences and your foal is in excellent health, you are at least halfway toward making a decision.

It is imperative that the mare passes the critical (and revealing) foal heat examination and qualifies to be bred back. Then by all means pick up the telephone and confirm your breeding arrangements. If the mare's genital health is questionable or if she experienced any undue trauma during parturition that requires rest for her reproductive system, your veterinarian will issue a certificate to the stallion owner that will effectively cancel your stallion contract obligations.

You must be ready to face the care of the mare during her eleven months of gestation again, together with the expense of transporting her to and from the breeding farm with your precious foal at the mare's side—incidently exposing the baby to the possibility of physical injury or infection, or both. Too, there are the expenses incurred by your mare and foal while at the farm; and if she conceives, there will be the inevitable stud fee.

Assuming that your mare's only useful role is that of brood mare and she is *not* bred back for any reason, you will face an unproductive year and the ever-present expenses, although they will be somewhat reduced. Nothing is more costly than a barren brood mare.

Many findings are important in determining when to breed your mare, but most important is the decision when *not* to breed.

It is my personal opinion that one indiscriminate, poorly timed cover can jeopardize the mare's entire reproductive future.

Postparturient mares are especially sensitive and susceptible to irritation and infection within the 30-day period following delivery. Because of one unreasoning act, an impatient stallion owner or an insistent, overanxious mare owner may be willing to trade away the mare's future fertility by a greedy gamble for the poor risk of an early foal.

Ignoring the economics involved, if I could do one thing for the brood mare that would enable her to produce more foals and enjoy a longer reproductive life, it would be to *eradicate forever from the minds of all breeders any possibility of a foal heat cover.*

Statistics dictate that the disadvantages far outweigh the advantages. Physiologically, the foal heat serves as a continuation of the cleansing and repair of the mare's reproductive system. It is a rare mare, especially of the Thoroughbred breed, that recovers sufficiently from parturition in time to justify a cover within nine or ten days after delivery. It is this unusual mare that encourages owners to engage in the unsound practice of foal heat covers.

Following eleven months of gestation—regardless of your veterinarian's medical evaluation—common sense alone would seem to dictate the need for additional time for the mare's reproductive system to heal and prepare for her next pregnancy. Exploitation of "quality" mares, disguised as efficient use of breeding stock, in order to produce early foals is unforgivable.

Records show that the majority of mares that are covered during their foal heat do not conceive and require additional servicing by the stallion to eventually "settle." Often extensive and unavoidable treatment is needed to restore the well-being of the mare's uterus, cervix, and vagina if she has been abused by an injurious cover.

Thus, time is lost rather than saved during the relatively short breeding season. I'm happy to say that lesson is usually learned by those thoughtless people who are responsible—as shown in their red faces and feeble excuses; but unfortunately the damage does exist and will take its toll on future fertility.

Often the quality mares are the ones that suffer such maltreatment, for their owners seem to be the greediest and most indifferent to their mares. Small owners and those who lavish attention upon their pleasure mares seem to be able to overlook the pressure of the economics of breeding with its often disastrous consequences.

Perhaps this is inevitable. Quality mares *are* costly, but one can hope that someday there will be an end to this heartless practice by absentee or unfeeling owners who use flesh-and-blood mares as if they were pieces of machinery. Far better to listen to the advice of your veterinarian and reward your mare for the gifts she has already given you.

Statistically, foal heat conceptions average about 40 percent and sustain a much higher rate of abortion than do conceptions following covers during subsequent heat cycles. The later cover allows the mare additional time to regenerate and establish her genital health—namely, the second heat, which is seen most often from the twenty-eighth to the thirty-first postpartum day.

I can't resist saying again that if commercial breeders and owners of many animals were not placed in the position of competing for the artificially imposed date of the first birthday, such violations of good medical practice would be reduced substantially. If that arbitrary January 1 deadline were only moved toward spring, more consideration would be given to practices leading to increased fertility, and many invisible benefits would be enjoyed by the mare and the owner or custodian.

The circumstances of the delivery and the details of the postpartum period, combined with the individual mare's ability to recover and regenerate, will affect the practicality and scheduling of breeding dates for your mare. This precise information should be compiled by your veterinarian and then discussed with you, as owner, or the farm manager.

Ideally, on the seventh or eighth postpartum day—and I beg you, not before—your veterinarian will examine your mare with a speculum to determine the condition of her reproductive tract, and (with the use of a sleeve) perform a careful but thorough pelvic examination in order to palpate and evaluate the condition of the uterus and the ovaries.

The examination should include external determination of damage in the form of bruising, hematomas, or lacerations to the vulvar lips and the adjacent perineal tissues. Lacerations or tears in this area are found most often in maiden mares because of their failure to achieve sufficient relaxation—a deficiency that is rarely a problem for the experienced *multipara* mare.

It is absolutely essential to defer the necessary suturing of vulvar lacerations until all swelling and edema subsides; otherwise the tissue will not maintain the sutures and may tear again, so that the repair will have to be repeated at the appropriate time.

With the aid of a mare speculum, deeper tissues can be seen and appraised. The vaginal vault should be checked for the presence of bruises, hematomas, and abrasions. The condition of the mare's delicate cervix, essential for maintaining pregnancy, should be painstakingly scrutinized for any indication of minute hemorrhage, for the slightest inflammatory changes, or other indication of any infection—whether chronic or low-grade.

Only an experienced eye can assess accurately the mare's condition and degree of regeneration, and so determine whether or not it would be an optimum fertility period, hence proper to cover her at such a time.

Even if the speculum findings are favorable, their importance does not outweigh the significance of the pelvic examination. Either one of these examinations alone is not sufficient to evaluate the mare's condition properly. Interpretation of both examinations in combination is essential. A cervical culture is seldom required at the foal heat examination unless gross evidence or the history of the delivery dictates this need to your veterinarian.

The pelvic examination is essential to determine the degree of uterine involution. If the uterus is not totally involuted, it can be an indication that proper drainage and cleansing are incomplete, that regeneration is still taking place, or that a residual or low-grade infection exists.

If the mare *is* covered in the presence of any contraindications discovered by the detailed gynecologic examination, prepare yourself; this is an open invitation for damaging tissue changes to occur. The physical damage and the consequences of a poorly timed cover can trigger an explosive intrauterine infection.

During the pelvic examination the two ovaries are inspected to determine the presence of the follicle that contains the potential to produce and release a viable ovum.

In order to avoid a nonproductive cover, it is essential that the mare be presented to the stallion *only at the time she is able to conceive.*

A cover at any other time is a mere exercise in futility. The mare is unnecessarily exposed to possibilities of injury and/or infection, the stallion is placed in possible danger from an unreceptive mare as well as being subjected to needless stress, and the time spent by farm personnel is costly and completely wasted.

An overt teasing response by the mare may be misleading and perplexing. As we have seen, the fact that a mare does or does not act "in season" can be inconclusive. Teasing-response patterns often bear no relationship whatever to the actual physiological or hormonal state of the mare's reproductive system. It is not unusual for a mare to accept willingly the presence and overtures of a teaser horse at any time during her estral cycle.

Conversely, a mare may be at the height of her estrus and reject violently any approach by the stallion.

Only the mare's unique unpredictability is predictably consistent.

The combination needed to succeed in any breeding venture with horses is knowledge based upon experience, complemented by competent veterinary assistance.

A stallion's annual fertility percentage often reflects the competency of the stallion manager and the veterinarian, rather than the actual potency of the horse or fertility of his mares. The teaser horse, with an experienced, sharp-eyed stud groom at hand, is an integral part of all successful breeding programs. The information gathered every morning by the stud groom describing each mare is indispensable when interwoven with the gynecologic findings of the veterinarian.

But, in spite of all of these skills, occasionally there is the unusual mare who will continue to confound and elude us all.

The mare with a suckling foal at foot is recognized as a distinct challenge to the stud owner. The built-in hormonal variations and their influences are completely different in the lactating mare, compared with the barren or maiden mare.

Hormonally, the foal heat—if it occurs as early as the sixth postpartum day or as late as the twelfth postpartum day—imposes a strong estrogenic effect upon the average matron. High estrogen levels perhaps are nature's way of facilitating the generalized cleansing process of the reproductive tract, which is necessary after eleven long months of pregnancy. However, increased estrogen blood levels also cause a more intense sexual drive that can adversely affect the preservation of genital health if the mare is not observed carefully.

The mare's maternal instinct to remain with and protect her foal is pitted against her overwhelming hormonal drive to mate. This may account for the intense degree of receptivity exhibited by the mare during foal heat, as opposed to subsequent heats, with or without a viable follicle in the ovary, with or without involution of the uterus, and with or without infection or in the presence of a completely healthy hygienic reproductive tract. All the favorable ingredients are necessary for a pregnancy to result, but, most important of all, they must be present for the pregnancy to survive.

I am convinced that innumerable conceptions that are impossible to calculate occur during cycles accompanied by imprudent covers. The tiny, undiagnosed pregnancy is terminated by an undetected abortion. When the mare returns to her normal estral period, it is incorrectly interpreted as a lack of fertility.

Ovaries may form follicles and release them into the upper reproductive tract ready for fertilization. It is here that conception takes place, in this well-protected and relatively distant location.

But when the fertilized ovum descends into the less secluded uterine horn, it is positioned in a more vulnerable spot. The uterus must be involuted, free of infection, and prepared physiologically by the action of hormones to receive, protect, and nourish the fragile beginnings of new life.

If the uterine environment is not precise in its preparedness for the new pregnancy, the mare's delicate cervix will not close and the minute fertilized ovum will be washed out of the mare's tract because these two separated areas in the same reproductive tract are not in harmony. (It is as though a beautifully prepared loaf of bread were placed in a faulty oven to bake.)

At the foal heat checkup take advantage of your veterinarian's visit to arrange for your mare to be placed in as near perfect gynecologic condition as possible. Minor lacerations, not corrected previously, can be repaired at this time. Low-grade infections should be evaluated, cultured, and, if necessary, treated. In my opinion the most valuable service that can be rendered to your mare at this time is a perineal suture to prevent intake of air loaded with contaminants into the vagina, and to avoid the ever-present danger of impurities from fecal material.

Perineal suturing affords an effective protective closure of the upper edges of the vulvar lips. This is a very simple and inexpensive surgical procedure. Caslick's operation, as it is called, is without question the most rewarding action one can take to protect, preserve, and maintain fertility in mares.

The mare's anatomical makeup creates a predisposition to the entrance of air, with all its impurities, and allows fecal material to drain down over the vulva and accumulate between the vulvar lips. Many factors can add to the inefficiency of the vulvar closure: repeated pregnancies, reduced tissue tone, poor nutrition, and individual anatomical structure. Any or all of these may compound the problem.

Inspired contaminated air can create irritation to the mucosa, then inflammation and, finally, infection. Any provocation can cause vaginitis, cervicitis, and eventually lead to infection in the uterus. Low-grade inflammatory changes will affect adversely the efficiency of the cervical closure—hence presenting a direct threat to pregnancy.

Infertility begins when outer air enters, stretches, and actually balloons the reproductive tract. There is no hope for a successful pregnancy unless this condition is corrected. I have frequently seen uterine irritations and early infections in postpartum mares respond favorably to perineal closure with no need at all for drug therapy.

Let us assume that good judgment prevailed and the mare was not covered during her foal heat. Adequate daily exercise and proper nutrition are all the concerned owner can contribute while waiting for the mare to reach the optimum time and condition to be bred.

If you plan to breed the mare back, it is important that she be in professional hands and at the stud farm *no later than the eighteenth postpartum day*.

It is impossible to predict exactly when the mare—back to her old game of inconsistency—will experience a fertile cycle. Subject to a bombardment of hormonal imbalances, astute observation and critically timed gynecologic examinations are needed to cope with the not-uncommon variations in the reproductive cycles of the mare with a foal at foot.

The second heat period ranges from the twenty-seventh to the thirty-second postpartum day. This is considered by many to be the most favorable time to breed the mare back. By now most mares will have recovered from parturition. This 30-day cycle, as it is referred to, is considered most reliable and dependable for fertility.

When all is normal the average lactating mare will begin to come into her second estral cycle around the twenty-seventh postpartum day and will develop a viable follicle by the twenty-eighth or twenty-ninth day. She should accept the stallion and—if conditions are ideal—ovulate by the thirtieth or thirty-first day, then promptly go out of season. *Everyone* is delighted when the matron is able to follow this schedule and perform as expected.

I would like to stress again the behavior pattern of a mare with a foal at foot. Most mares tease intensely at their foal heat, but the maternal instinct is very strong and dominates any overt expression of being in season as the majority of mares during subsequent estral cycles. Preferring to play the protective maternal role, the "in-season" mare may even exhibit hostility toward the teaser in the presence of her foal.

But once in the breeding shed, away from the baby, she unaccountably becomes receptive. Such a mare is called a "silent" or "spec" mare; she requires careful surveillance and regular examinations to disclose just where she is in the pattern of her cycle.

A surprising phenomenon is occasionally seen about the eighteenth to the twenty-first postpartum day in some rare mares. They inexplicably come into a full, well-developed fertile cycle, with a respectable follicle capable of ovulation and conception.

This split cycle is not seen often enough for wide recognition or acceptance. And a mare that goes through this unorthodox cycle undetected can create havoc. Imagine the silent mare that has had a split cycle—either before being shipped to the stud farm or has been unobserved while at the farm. The usual 30-day heat will not appear on schedule and the next heat period will be expected around the fortieth to the forty-fifth postpartum day. Although the mare may continue to cycle in a regular rhythmic way, her expected calendar dates are thrown off, and in inexperienced hands she could conceivably be missed for the entire breeding season.

It is helpful if a bright, intuitive stud groom is aware of the possibility of a split-cycle season in silent mares.

An indirect alert to the possibility of a silent heat is the development of foal scours that coincide with the appropriate calendar dates. If the foal is found to be otherwise healthy, this clue should lead one to shift attention to the mare. Foal scours have led to the discovery of many silent mares.

It is obvious, too, that well-kept teasing records combined with judiciously scheduled veterinary examinations will increase the number of silent mares that are presented to the stallion at the correct time.

All too often at the second heat period I see intrauterine infections, slow-healing traumatic lesions, and mere delayed involution—all of which cause postponement when scheduling the mare's presentation to the stallion. Poor involution usually occurs in the older *multipara* mare, who needs the consideration of time and a little therapy to recover from her recent foaling.

The most frustrating medical entity facing me at the 30-day heat is the mare with small inactive ovaries and a tightly closed cervix. She may be lactating profusely and have a large, well-developed youngster at her side, yet she displays a persistently cold and often hostile teasing pattern.

A very different problem from the mare with a split cycle, this mare reflects a hormonal imbalance. Reduced estrogen blood levels are principally responsible for her behavior.

Hormonal assays prove that the hormone from the pituitary responsible for lactation is hyperactive and inhibits the follicle-stimulating hormone. Treatment, including hormonal injections, is futile as long as the foal is kept with the mare and continues to nurse.

Experience has strongly suggested that early weaning results in a spontaneous follicular response in the mare. Once it is established by a veterinarian that the lactating mare is out of hormonal harmony, one satisfactory recourse is to wean the foal promptly. Shortly after the foal is weaned and the mare's udder ceases full milk production in the absence of stimulation, she will resume fertile rhythmic cycles. So do not hesitate to act if it is important to you as the owner to have your mare pregnant again, but only with a strong healthy foal.

Here is an opportunity to wean and provide optimum nutrition for the foal while permitting your mare to regain her hormonal balance and conceive before the breeding season comes to a close.

As a child I often heard about "every-other-year" mares. I never received a satisfactory explanation as to exactly what that term meant until I was personally involved in an intense brood mare practice with daily observation (around the clock) of their many idiosyncrasies.

Time and education have shown me the importance of a hormonally well-balanced mare. Because of the mare's delicate makeup it requires little to upset her cycle or ability to regain her normal cycle, especially with foal at foot. Obviously this can cause havoc in the breeding shed and in many instances if the problem is not recognized and properly addressed, you find yourself in the dilemma of the "every-other-year" mare.

Through experience, I was well aware that all efforts, and most often-used hormonal drugs, proved ineffective—horse people were forced into early weaning, a practice learned by trial and error. The decision to wean early, even with high-tech milk substitutes and nutritional feed, still remains highly controversial among horse people.

An alternative treatment became available to veterinary medicine a few years ago. The drug Prostiglandin precluded the need to prematurely wean when facing this situation. Prostiglandin, an injectionable drug, reportedly could produce a viable follicle within five days postinjection!

The breeding industry heralded it as a wonder drug and openly accepted it, but with every positive there seems to be a negative. Although the mare's ovaries responded to Prostiglandin, the matron reacted with a frightening side effect to this strong drug.

Predictably within twenty minutes postinjection, the mare stood motionless with a lack of expression and total unawareness of her surroundings, even as to the welfare and location of her foal. Sweat streamed from the bottom of her abdomen and no matter what her registered color was, at this moment, she assumed a black color, actually a black cold sweat. Although no overt or clinical signs of pain seemed evident, this overall unnatural picture was most upsetting to the suckling, the owner and all caring personnel.

Thankfully, most reactions were short-lived, and within approximately thirty minutes the brood mare's coat and total reaction returned to a more natural texture, substance, and stature.

Today's Prostiglandins have been better researched and more highly refined. They are virtually free of side effects and are better understood as possessing a much broader spectrum of medical use. This drug should be administered only under the direction of a licensed veterinarian.

Let us not overlook the other side of the coin. No mare should ever be permitted to enter the breeding shed without a clean bill of gynecological health and, most emphatically, a certification of breeding readiness. No matter how badly you want another foal or how tantalizingly attractive the terms of a stallion contract may seem, *do not* gamble away your mare's complete future fertility. Abide by the rules!

One year's rest, if deemed necessary by your veterinarian, may be a bitter disappointment, but it could be repaid many times over by additional future pregnancies that might be impossible otherwise. This could be a great advantage calendar-wise, especially in the case of a late foaling mare.

Let us assume that your mare was successfully covered in the presence of a fertile follicle, ovulated on schedule, then subsequently rejected the teaser or stallion. A large step has been taken in the right direction. Yet even with all these favorable indications, it is much too soon to jump to the conclusion that conception has occurred. Dangerous periods of instability will exist at intervals throughout her early pregnancy.

The first precarious period appears about the twelfth postcover day, together with the possibility of a split cycle being demonstrated by the mare's coming back into season. To repeat part of my earlier description of this risky period during early pregnancy (or supposed pregnancy), if the mare does come back in season at this time it means that one of two unfortunate conditions exists: either the mare's hormonal balance is upset, or a quiescent deep-seated uterine infection was stirred up by the cover and is just now showing itself. *Both conditions require treatment and solution of the problem before the mare can be returned to the stallion.*

At approximately the eighteenth postcover day, even in the presence of a conceptus, the pregnancy is challenged by the formation of estrogen-containing follicles in the ovaries. Even if pregnancy is stable, the mare may react with an "estrogen flash" and briefly act in season.

The majority of mares will reject the stallion during the estrogen flash, but the occasional mare that is receptive will undoubtedly abort if covered. These mares require a gynecologic examination by a veterinarian in order to determine whether they are indeed pregnant and their actions are due to the presence of a small amount of estrogen, or whether they are behaving in this strange way because they are barren and are actually experiencing a return to an estral period. Today's ultrasound machines can confirm pregnancy or barrenness on the twelfth postcover day.

If the mare does not tease or remains cold and nonreceptive until the twenty-first day, a manual or ultrasound pregnancy examination should be performed to determine her status. *An examination scheduled precisely on the twenty-first postcover day can be conclusive.*

If the mare is found to be in foal, the pregnancy is more stable and more sure of diagnosis than at any earlier date. When the veterinarian finds the mare's cervix tightly sealed and the mucosa of the reproductive tract responding appropriately, it is certain that a pregnancy exists.

Competent veterinarians on breeding farms are able to palpate the tiny embryo in the uterus even at this early stage of development. Such service by the veterinarian is invaluable and should be employed in order to eliminate the possibility of a false pregnancy (*pseudocyesis*) and confirm the supposed true pregnancy. The use of ultrasound images can rule out pseudocyesis.

The percentage of false pregnancies in mares is high enough so that a determining examination is essential. A mare can "believe" she is in foal for months before her hormonal system reacts to the biological ruse and returns her to her proper rhythmic cycling.

An undetected false pregnancy can last from forty-five to seventy-five days unless unveiled by a veterinarian. Usually the condition is self-resolving within these time limits. It is both sad and unfortunate if a mare is thought to be in foal near the end of the breeding season and the hoped-for pregnancy is discovered to be a "pseudo."

Although many 21-day pregnancies do not survive and the loss is undetected before the usually conclusive forty-fifth-day examination, disclosure of whether or not the mare is truly in foal justifies the time and effort spent in the earlier examination. The validity of the 21-day examination has been questioned in the past, but the information provided is of such value in determining the condition of the individual mare that more and more breeding farms are utilizing this practice to serve as a guideline and to increase their efficiency.

Between the twenty-eighth and the thirty-third postcover days it is not unusual to see a pregnant mare exhibit signs of estrus. Even though breeding farm personnel expect to see this behavior in an occasional mare, the potential threat never fails to be alarming. This is the normal time in the pregnant mare's cycle for the flight of estrogen-producing follicles in the ovaries to show their influence, as mentioned earlier. If the mare has been examined and declared safely in foal on her twenty-first day, try to ignore her. These actions will subside quietly.

By the time a mare's pregnancy has survived for forty-five days, most of the major anticipated threats to embryonic life have been overcome by her healthy reproductive system. This is not to say that one can guarantee the foal being carried to term; but positive findings from the forty-fifth-day pregnancy examination are reassuring. Breeding farms are reluctant to allow a visiting mare to leave the farm before this arbitrary date. Once this hurdle is cleared and the period of greatest instability safely behind, most farm managers will release mares to their owners.

Your Pregnant Mare

It is an exciting day when the manager calls to tell you that your mare has been examined in foal on her forty-fifth day and that you may take her home.

By all means call well in advance to make transport arrangements so that you can discuss with the farm manager any medication prescribed or information provided by the veterinarian that you should be aware of. Here is your opportunity to review any recommendations for suggested medication, and to question the need for additional perineal sutures, as well as learning the details of any problems that were encountered and that might require follow-up attention.

Ask about any special requirements your mare might have during gestation to help maintain her pregnancy. Now is the time to absorb as much information as you can. It may be your mare has no problems and needs no special attention; even so, there are a few reminders that the farm manager should pass on to you.

Apparently the awareness that hormonally unstable mares are quite common has grown. Today, the farm veterinarian quite frequently recommends injections of repository progesterone—the hormone responsible for maintenance of pregnancy throughout gestation. Your mare may require this help to keep her foal.

The drug Repository Progesterone is injected deeply (1½-inch needle) into the rump muscles (gluteal muscles) at the prescribed dosage of 3cc every other day, beginning with the twelfth-day ultrasound diagnosis. This regime has reportedly helped mares retain their pregnancies. *Caution*: Inject Repository Progesterone only in the mare's rump muscles, alternating sites and sides regularly as it has serious irritating reactions in almost all striated muscles.

Cease the injections one month prior to due date.

If your mare has been sutured, you should be reminded of this. She will need to be opened about ten days before her due date.

The stud fee will be payable in the fall, in lieu of a veterinary certificate of barrenness. Remember, it is wise to have your pregnant mare reexamined just before the stud fee is due and before you send your check to the stallion owner.

A further word about suturing might be helpful here.

Most postpartum mares that require perineal repair and the routine partial closure are customarily sutured closing the upper vulvar edges, whereas mares that have already been bred and are pronounced in foal are sutured lower on the lips of the vulva. Unless a postparturient mare has a special problem that requires more complete closure, this routine, protective, but partial suturing is done to conserve fertility in the mare, to protect her from *invasion by contaminants. It will not interfere with a stallion's cover.* An adequate but not excessive space is provided for coitus, and immediately after pregnancy is determined, the vulvar lips are skillfully opposed by your veterinarian down to the level desired to maintain that pregnancy to term.

Worming

The proper and safe time to worm your mare is around the seventy-fifth postcover day. Remember that the embryo floats freely in the uterus until implantation (nidation) occurs at about the 110th day. Equine embryos are notorious for their instability until implantation takes place.

Worming your mare is extremely important—not only for her sake, but also for her early new pregnancy and for the valuable suckling at her side. In essence, you are protecting three prized lives from the everlasting plague of endoparasitism and its ravages.

If the mare has enjoyed the advantages of a good parasite-control program, she undoubtedly can afford the time to deliver her foal, be bred back, and wait to be wormed until her seventy-fifth day after conception.

At this time it is advisable to submit a fecal sample to your veterinarian or laboratory for identification of the species of enemy parasites. An analysis and count of their respective numbers is invaluable for the decision as to what anthelmintic or combination of drugs to use and what route of introduction into her system is preferred. These decisions should be left to your veterinarian.

Exposure to parasite eggs is tremendously varied. With monthly fecal inspections, protection for your mare does not have to be reduced to a guessing game. She can be protected from internal parasites through her entire gestation period, and while her suckling foal is by her side.

Do not worm her more often than every two months, if specifically indicated, and do not continue the worming past the ninth month of gestation.

One exception to this rule exists: because there is no laboratory test for determining the presence of bots, your mare should receive a single, annual, specifically formulated tubing medication for eradication of bot larvae from the stomach lining.

Traditionally, this worming is timed to take place shortly after the first few killing frosts, thereby making certain that all of the bot flies are dead, for they are the predatory egg layers and the only source of this infestation.

It is futile to have your horse tubed for bots and still allow the all-too-visible brownish-yellow eggs to remain attached to the horse's hairs. With a straight razor shave off the eggs, which are usually attached to the inside of the forelegs, to the long hairs around the muzzle, and on any other location at which they can be seen. *Unless the eggs are removed, the horse will promptly be reinfested.*

It is incumbent upon every owner to worm whenever bot fly eggs are seen on your animal's hair in late summer and through the fall.

Remember that the pathonomonic sign of a well-established bot infestation is very clear. After swallowing a minute amount of grain, your mare suddenly ceases eating and drops down in the stall in evident pain. Most affected animals will not remain down for long; as their discomfort seemingly disappears, they are soon back up at the feed tub to finish their meal unperturbed.

Some studies have revealed that the pressure of bots is not so harmful to digestion as is its degree of tissue damage to the stomach walls—eventually revealed by future gastric changes.

Unwormed adult horses eventually will discharge some of the bot larvae in their manure with the arrival of February or March. When larvae are so numerous that the gross physical sight of them is evident, one can only speculate in horror about the irreparable damage that is taking place in the animal's gastrointestinal tract.

If a pregnant mare misses her regular wormings during gestation, her physical demeanor will reflect the neglect. I have found it smart to pass a tube and worm her around the eighth or ninth day postpartum, with no ill effect upon her newborn. You are now assured that your mare is in good shape and ready for her next breeding commitment.

Vaccinations

Your adult mare has been exposed during her lifetime to almost every virus and disease-producing microorganism that exists. She possesses a respectable number of protective antibodies, so—excluding out-and-out exposure to a virulent infection or an epidemic—her vaccination requirements are few.

With the exception of EEV and VEE vaccination during the insect season and the rhinopneumonitis vaccination, a simple tetanus booster in the fall, coupled with an influenza booster as added protection for the cold months ahead are all the mature brood mare needs. See list page 10 for Potomac fever, botulism, rabies, and strangles.

Rhinopneumonitis (see page 190) is caused by a virus that attacks the upper respiratory tract of both young and adult horses, but—most important to be aware of—causes devastating abortion in pregnant mares. The young ones usually recover from the viremia with no serious after-effects, but in the pregnant mare it is a different story. Separate pregnant mares from other horses, especially young horses.

If pregnant mares are exposed to rhinopneumonitis any time from the seventh or eighth month of gestation through to term, they can abort shortly after exposure or maintain their pregnancy for an undetermined period of time only to abort at a later date or deliver a weak or dead foal.

Mares suffer an undetectable, asymptomatic infection and usually abort with no warning. There is no muscle relaxation or mammary build-up, as seen in a mare preparing for a normal delivery. The significant sign is when the placenta is found to be delivered intact with the dead or very weak foal inside the sac. This can occur as late as the tenth or eleventh month of gestation.

The rhinopneumonitis virus exhibits a profound affinity for embryonic and placental tissue. The viral infection causes a generalized viremia in the embryo or fetus because it characteristically attacks the placental uterine attachment, causing a decrease in the supply of oxygen and nourishment to the fetus. The fetus dies, which ultimately results in detachment of the life-providing placenta from the uterine lining and abortion ensues.

The mare, unless other unrelated foaling problems are superimposed upon this situation, generally cleans uneventfully, seems quite well, involutes on time, cultures clean, and when bred back conceives with comparative ease. Authorities explain that she is safe for one year by means of the natural immunity she has acquired through this unhappy experience.

It is unlikely that one lone mare would be attacked by this deadly virus, for it does not behave in this manner. As a rule, when the virulent virus appears, its pattern is to involve the complete barn, farm, or band of brood mares.

Brood mares are consistently symptom-free, so one can only *suspect* the exposure after knowing of the history of an outbreak. The probability of the virus being spread from farm to farm by horses or on the feet, hands, and clothing of personnel, or even feed trucks, is a frightening fact.

Twenty years ago, before the advent of a specific vaccine capable of conferring immunity, spontaneous abortion "storms" occurred in areas of horse concentration. If the disease struck, it was not uncommon for *all* the mares in one location to abort within twenty-four hours. What a shocking experience!

Accurate diagnosis can be determined by the history, the physical appearance of the mare, the fashion of delivery, the gross appearance of the placenta and of the dead fetus or very weak foal. A detailed postmortem of the fetus can be carried out to confirm the diagnosis.

Even a remote chance of exposure—conceivably by an infected new young horse arriving on the premises or a seemingly innocent but undiagnosed abortion—is an ominous hint that the very worst may develop. Suspicion of exposure to a group of pregnant mares creates a cruel anxiety, for at this moment there is absolutely nothing that can be done except to wait it out and pray.

To combat this deplorable disease vaccinate all pregnant mares at their *fifth, seventh* and *ninth* month during gestation, using Fort Dodge Lab– Pneumobort-K injectable vaccine.

The Maiden Mares

A maiden mare is usually, but not necessarily, a young mare that has never produced a foal. She may have experienced one or more covers without a resulting conception. If a veterinary examination discloses an intact hymen, the mare is a "true maiden." An unruptured hymen is an indication that she has never been covered and has not suffered the subsequent exposure to various traumas, contaminations, or infections that are found in barren mares and mares with a foal at foot. If nature has been kind, and her reproductive system is normal, the maiden mare will conceive readily.

In my early years I recall hearing that a maiden mare was always considered a challenge to the breeder and was, consequently, viewed with a wary eye. My experience has shown that this opinion of the maiden could not be further from the truth.

A young mare who has never been covered obviously has never been exposed to all the undesirable circumstances that adversely affect fertility. She has not experienced the problems created by a cover, conception, and birth. Eventually, she may be subjected to genital-tract damage, genital infections from infected stallions, production of a diseased foal, or the entrance of pathogens as a result of the poor hygienic practices of breeding shed personnel—as well as a host of other human errors.

To me, a maiden mare is clean, untouched, and full of potential, with the organs and tissues of her reproductive tract undepreciated by misuse. I feel an obligation to shield and sustain her innate fertility and to foster her future reproductive years.

It is my opinion that 85 percent of infertility or barrenness is the fault of human error, mismanagement, and abusive practices. The remaining 15 percent is undoubtedly the operation of nature's law of attrition.

How shameful it is to lose any individual's productivity because of man's thoughtless intervention.

There are essentially three groups of maidens.

The first group is composed of mares of varying ages that are physically unfit and are not under any stress, either physically or psychologically. This group could include lightly used pleasure horses or ponies, hunters, show horses, or horses from any walk of life. Unraced, even unbroken, fillies may be sidelined for one reason or another and are then assigned to the brood mare ranks. Because of the lack of strenuous demands upon them, and their consequent complacency, this group can be expected to enjoy a higher fertility rate. If the animals in this category have been inactive long enough to become sufficiently relaxed, demanding, and slightly spoiled, they are already well on the way toward acquiring the personality of brood mares.

The second group is usually young and honed to fitness for the racetrack, the show ring, or the hunting field. A physically and mentally "tight" young mare represents a poor breeding risk unless allowed ample time and the environment in which to let down to avoid both physical and mental problems. After analyzing breeding farm records, this fact has become quite conspicuous. Many tense young maidens are frequently "missed" unless they are allowed time to relax, to become acquainted with the leisurely life of the farm, and to run free in pasture with other mares. This period of physiologic adjustment improves the maiden's compatibility with her new way of life, as well as her overall fertility.

The third group is essentially the same filly or mare just described, but she has now found herself cut off from her young athletic career because of some sad or desperate circumstance. A dreaded accident is the most common cause, but any change that abruptly uproots her may displace her into the brood mare group.

Quite by accident these tragedies often strike during mid- or late breeding season—leaving her no time for relaxation and adjustment. (Sometimes there is not time to lose the sweat and sand from her coat or even evidence of the saddle mark!) There is only time to strike off her racing plates or competition shoes, then hurry her to the breeding shed.

No opportunity is permitted for the necessary physiologic changes and the interrelated corrections in her mental attitude—absolute prerequisites for the mare's acceptance of her new role.

I do not mean to imply that success is never achieved, but circumstances such as these are certainly not conducive to pregnancy. As Shakespeare put it, "Too swift arrives as tardy as too slow."

A maiden can, if normal, begin to cycle, form a respectable follicle, accept the stallion, ovulate, and promptly go out of season. This is real cause for celebration, for to well-informed people it is considered a most favorable sequence of events and should lead to conception.

Contrary to popular opinion, it *is* advantageous for you and your mare to have your maiden examined by a qualified veterinarian. She could possess hidden anomalous conditions that, if not discovered, could effectively interfere with or actually prevent conception. Some of these concealed conditions can be extremely harmful if the mare is covered before they are corrected. Five such conditions are described below:

Incomplete reproductive tract

On gynecologic examination it is not unusual to find a mare with an incomplete reproductive system. In some instances nature has failed to supply all of the components needed for reproduction to take place.

Man also contributes to the problem by having an *ovariectomy* performed on a race filly or show mare to escape the inconvenience of inconsistent performances. In either sad case an internal examination is a matter of necessity to reveal deficiencies caused by nature or meddling humans before costly arrangements are made to send a hopeless sterile mare to a stallion.

Infantile genital tract

An infantile genital tract is found in some older mares, but is most often present in fillies younger than three years. It is characterized by a constantly open cervix (indicating inability to close), a small uterus, and undersized, inactive ovaries—all exemplifying immaturity.

There is no known therapy for a mare with an underdeveloped reproductive tract and organs. Time is the only recourse. However, it is advisable to check these mares monthly for any detectable change during the breeding season. In certain cases it is wise to wait until the next year for the prospect of reproductive maturity.

Imperforate hymen

The hymen is the thin membrane just inside the vestibule that covers the external opening of the vagina. It is the duty of a conscientious stud groom to see that the maiden mare is "respectfully opened" prior to cover.

A number of mares' hymens are ruptured by the stallion at the time of service with no noticeable interruption. Some mares are endowed with a tough, almost impenetrable hymen that absolutely requires human assistance to open manually, and with consideration. A veterinarian should painlessly remove the membrane and, in so doing, avoid any fragmentation or the presence of any remaining sections.

Unless this simple procedure is performed correctly, the filly or mare can become justifiably frightened and resentful. In the future she may be very difficult in the breeding shed.

There is always the possibility of trauma, inflammation, and resulting infection.

"Stallion frustration" induced by an imperforate hymen can result in a poor or inadequate cover.

Vaginal septum

The vaginal septum is a strong membranous partition, usually vertical, that divides the vagina into two equal compartments. Occasionally this aberration is found in maiden mares and is of congenital origin. Septums found in the vagina are considered rare, but are discovered often enough to warrant discussion here.

Mares can conceive and carry a foal with this partition intact, but it does present a formidable problem at the time of delivery. It is advisable to have your veterinarian surgically remove the awkwardly positioned membrane well in advance of sending your mare to the stallion. And sufficient time should be allowed for proper healing to take place.

Remember that if this partition is torn during service, it conceivably can injure the stallion, affect the quality of the cover, and cause injury to the mare, resulting in inflammation and the possibility of infection.

Anestrus

Maiden mares are notorious for their anestrus, which may appear in either of two forms.

A true anestrus occurs when a mare is in the inactive phase of her reproductive cycle, demonstrating luteal influences with low circulating estrogenic hormonal blood levels. Outwardly she is cold when teased and exhibits no indication of being in season—an accurate reflection of the condition of her endocrine system.

Such inexperienced mares often require medical aid either to enhance or activate their endocrine systems in order to increase the chances decisively for conception. Only an inexperienced person will wait for a mare, especially a maiden mare, to come into season naturally. Time during the breeding season is too precious.

Quite often, the pendulum swings the other way and maiden mares will react to *any* teaser or *any* member of the horse family—appearing to be in season, though this can be false. Such semblance of receptivity, or false response to the teaser, can be misleading to the novice horse breeder. These disturbed and hormonally unbalanced mares will accept the stallion even though a veterinary examination reveals an out-of-season mare.

On large breeding farms, such mares can cause a calamity if allowed to continue their games, exasperating and confusing the personnel with their antics. Fortunately today, with our modern veterinary techniques, these wayward ladies can be outsmarted.

A large proportion of maiden mares, particularly early in the season, will not tease or show symptoms of heat to the teaser horse or to a gentle stallion.

Some mares, although in season and cycling silently, are frightened by the stallion and refuse to show the slightest indication of receptivity. *This is a false anestrus.*

False anestrus is only too common and sometimes even the most experienced breeders are deceived.

All these peculiar mares require that two special stratagems be employed to expose the true state of affairs. First, these special individuals should be carefully watched and methodically teased by a gentle horse that is accompanied by a sharp, intelligent handler who keeps written records. Second, a well-timed gynecologic examination is essential to determine the stage of the cycle and condition of the mare.

Only in combination can these two procedures uncover and effectively disclose the silent, indifferent, cool mare. Once the veterinary examination determines that the mare is physically, physiologically, and hormonally prepared to be covered, her attitude and behavior—amazingly—will fall in line when she is confronted by the stallion in the breeding shed. Wary and unbelieving horsemen's fears vanish when they see the metamorphosis of a skittish, sometimes hostile maiden into a quiet, normally receptive mare.

As a famous song put it: With all your faults, I love you still.

With all of the maiden mare's elusive conduct to contend with, she is a much better risk still and has a better opportunity to settle in foal than does the barren mare with her many unknown problems, or the foaling mare with her built-in, yet-undiagnosed problems that an incomplete history may conceal.

I must admit that maiden mares have been responsible for some peculiar incidents during my practice. The barren mare and the mare with foal at foot provide endless gynecologic problems, but little novelty in the situations they may present to those of us responsible for their well-being. After all, they have produced foals.

The unexamined maiden is a complete unknown, and at times unexpected findings within this group of mares can be disquieting.

As a young veterinarian, recently graduated, I had a consuming interest in brood mares and a driving desire to become an accurate and skillful equine gynecologist. It wasn't long before an opportunity came along to test my competence.

A nearby neighbor, a grand old gentleman, called to ask me to look at his mare. The homebred had failed to conceive after many attempts at impregnation by his fine old stallion.

Here was a chance to test my ability and a challenge to my stock of knowledge. When I arrived at the barn, I was impatient for the mare to be placed in the stock so I could examine her. I was fairly confident that I could discover her fertility problem and was hopeful that it would be one that could be solved.

Well into the gynecologic examination, embarrassment overcame me. For the first time since I had been examining mares, I was unable to locate *either* ovary! After several moments I forced myself to stop, review, and reconsider my findings—or, more appropriately, lack of findings.

At last I was compelled to conclude that the mare was a victim of congenital absence of both ovaries.

This young mare had been foaled at the farm and had never been in any other hands than those of her present owners. This precluded the possibility that an ovariectomy could have been performed.

It was a momentous occasion for any veterinarian to be able to make this uncommon diagnosis. Young as I was, I could not contain my momentary excitement at having discovered the mare's condition.

Suddenly I realized what my diagnosis meant to the owner and mare. I was saddened by the thought. The mare was, of course, hopelessly sterile, so her future capabilities were very limited. To the owner the disclosure meant that the years spent in vain efforts were lost, and that he would have to purchase another mare in order to have a foal by the stallion he prized so highly.

I couldn't help but feel sorry for the mare and for the dismayed owner; but at the same time I did experience a feeling of gratitude for the thrill of uncovering a rare congenital gynecologic finding.

Among my many experiences with maidens, there is one other mare that I will never forget.

Since I was not the farm veterinarian for the small, private breeding establishment, the fertility problem that had provoked the call to me was certain to prove complicated, at the very least.

The foreman greeted me as I drove up to an attractive and well-kept barren mare barn. While a groom was placing the mare in a stock, the concerned foreman told me about the mare and how she had puzzled him.

After winning sixteen races, the mare's earnings had placed her in the ranks of a potential producer with considerable monetary value. The owner had brought her home from the track so that she could have a foal that might inherit her racing ability, together with the bonus of her excellent bloodlines.

The foreman explained that on the farm they had been unable to settle the mare the previous season. Now, near the end of another breeding season, he wanted to ascertain the mare's status. She had been last covered twenty days earlier and, because she had not come back in season, I am sure he believed the mare was pregnant.

A classic Thoroughbred was in the stock, her tail bandaged and a groom at her head. I scrubbed with the hot water that had been provided and began the examination.

After twenty years of practice in equine reproduction I do not shock easily, but I was stunned by the bizarre condition the mare presented.

Instead of a vaginal vault, the mare had only a blind pouch. There was no cervix or opening of any sort into the uterus. There was only a cul-de-sac. The irritated mucosa that lined the pouch was still inflamed from the recent covers. Further examination revealed the complete absence of uterus or ovaries.

This astonishing condition is a rare congenital anomaly of hereditary origin.

This beautiful mare, who had proven ability and highly desirable blood-lines, was absolutely unable to perpetuate her outstanding qualities.

Although the mare was still young, the temperament that had helped her win races enabled her to run her best in spite of leg problems. Now that temperament, once an asset, and her unsoundness would deny her the chance of any other useful role.

I have since heard that her legs had been "patched up" and that she had been returned to racing. She was the sort that would give her all, as long as she was able. I still wonder about her fate today.

The Barren Mare

The term "barren mare" is used for any mare who has at some time or other produced a foal and either has not been bred back or has been unproductively covered by a stallion. She is always considered to represent some degree of risk by stallion owners because of her barrenness.

The empty mare is comparable to a new car. One anticipates unknown weaknesses or difficulties that may crop up unexpectedly at the least opportune moment, but a barren mare (like a used car) represents a group with multiple (and diverse) reasons for their problems. Collectively these mares possess one very evident finding—their inescapable and incriminating barrenness.

A brood mare has but one use or purpose in life, so it can be said with accuracy that the barren mare symbolizes a very costly animal in terms of return for money invested.

A mare can be barren from many causes, but the most ordinary is a genital-tract infection, which may have many origins. A difficult delivery produces mechanical and physical reproductive unsoundness, and if uncorrected predisposes the mare to infection.

Foaling accidents and their unfortunate aftereffects can result in genital-tract infection. Environmental influences or abuses inflicted by unknowing or uncaring human beings can also contribute to the destructive evolvement of infertile or barren mares. And there is the not uncommon instance of diminished stallion fertility. Stallion owners are reluctant to acknowledge or even discuss this possibility—therefore, a mare may receive the blame for something for which she could not possibly be responsible.

There is a reason for every barren mare's infertility. Although barrenness can be perplexing and quite discouraging to everyone involved, it does not have to be an insoluble mystery.

Equine fertility studies have advanced in recent years to a point at which a satisfactory solution may be found in 95 percent of all cases. The concerned owner or breeder is obligated to search for the reason for any mare to have missed a year, unless it was a deliberate choice. For her needlessly to miss two or more years of her relatively short producing life is truly shameful.

If one elects to give a mare a year's rest because it is required by some individual peculiarity, that is one thing. But when a good producing mare, capable of making her unique contribution, is sidelined because of carelessness, inefficiency, or neglect, it is unforgivable.

In evaluating a barren mare, look closely at her produce record and present every bit of available information to your veterinarian to aid in an accurate assessment. With luck and good planning, a rapid and definitive diagnosis, coupled with specific treatment, will bring your empty mare back to optimum breeding health.

In my opinion the major cause of infertility in barren mares is the grave mismanagement of postpartum care—and, especially, the lack of good judgment as to when a mare is ready to be returned to the stallion.

Experience has taught us that patient observation, without haste, will allow the wise owner to decide upon that optimum time for the next cover. The mare then will be permitted to maintain her fertility comfortably and successfully. A direct and *certain* road toward sterility is unquestionably achieved by blindly subjecting any mare to repeated covers without full knowledge of the condition of her genital health and without accurate determination of where she stands in her reproductive cycle.

It is far, far better to do nothing than to take irreparably destructive breeding steps.

Breeding shed practices also are a major factor influencing fertility. If a mare is properly prepared for a cover, thoroughly scrubbed, with her tail covered by a sterile bandage before she is presented to a perfectly cleaned stallion, you are well started.

The floor and atmosphere of the breeding shed should be clean and dust-free. The stud groom should be immaculate in his person and his practices. Ample light, preferably sunlight, uncluttered open space, and adequate ventilation round out my suggested list of requirements.

In natural surroundings, in a grass-covered field under the beneficial sun, the unconfined animal was constantly on the move and was never subjected to unsanitary conditions. The artificial situations imposed upon today's horses intensify the presence and prevalence of pathogens. Every effort must be made by all of us to compensate for this risk.

A treatise could be written on breeding shed hygiene and the many, many failures to maintain the cleanliness required to support the efficiency of stallions that have a court (or contract with perhaps fifty mares).

Rigid rules of hygiene must be followed daily to stay one step ahead of the ever-present, unaccountable pathogenic bacteria, which will exert their full destructive forces upon the breeding proficiency of both the stallion and the mare.

The mare that suffers early loss of fertility is invariably the better-quality mare. There seems to be a tragic parallel between the quality of the mare and the loss of her fertility.

This must be more than mere coincidence. So often it is the mare with the most precious gifts to offer her breed—priceless bloodlines, conformation, intelligence, and ability—who is selfishly exploited and prematurely reduced to the ranks of barren mares. Greed, anxiety, and financial exploitation must not be allowed to control those most important decisions that affect the brood mare's future.

This book has been dedicated to the growth of increased respect on the part of all of us who people the horse's world for the mare, the foal, and the stallion.

I have tried to guide and encourage horse owners in the achievement of their goals, while at the same time I hope it will help those serious members of the breeding industry to enjoy the rewards of conservation of equine fertility and the precious genetic capacity for reproduction by the most attractive and valuable members of our equine world . . . which is a blessing to us all.

12

In Conclusion

Nothing beats experience as a teacher. Even with the benefit of medical and obstetrical training, there are unexpected twists and endless variations to the unpredictable brood mare's approach to parturition.

I can assure you that after two decades of practice I am always prepared to be unprepared to encounter a unique experience presented by circumstances, the mare owner, or, as is usually the case, the mare herself. These experiences are often startling, sometimes amusing, and—I'm sad to say—frequently tragic; but together they combine to demonstrate the brood mare's unique ability to confound or disconcert those who associate with her.

Perhaps the most common occurrence is that of the brood mare who unintentionally foals alone. The experienced mare owner and the rank beginner alike are unwitting victims of the mare that manages to accomplish this deception. It is a marvelous surprise to walk into a barn and discover a live, healthy newborn foal nursing vigorously or sleeping contentedly at its proud mother's feet. Fortunately, this scene more often than not greets the person who had inaccurately read the signs of approaching parturition and, after a routine late-evening checkup, assumed it was safe to leave the expectant mare for just one more night.

One of the farms I attend has a completely conscientious staff and a very workable system for keeping a close check on their mares during the foaling season. The mares are carefully examined each afternoon when they are brought in from pasture and positioned in various stalls near or far from the foaling attendant's observation room. Their positions are arranged to match with their scheduled due date, thus their (seeming) closeness to foaling.

At the night check the mares are again closely scrutinized, and if any changes have taken place, an additional attendant is assigned to spend the night observing the mare. If no mare appears to be on the brink of delivery, members of the farm team are allowed the luxury of an uninterrupted night's sleep in their own beds.

There was a desperately sick foal at this farm occupying a stall at the far end of the aisle that contained the foaling stall. I had returned very late at night to continue essential treatment and to administer additional intravenous fluids.

I was alone in the huge barn, working by flashlight so as not to disturb the entire barn full of heavily pregnant mares. I had finished treating the foal and was carrying my equipment back to the veterinarian truck when something about the attitude of the mare in the foaling stall attracted my attention. I went to the pump house, washed my hands quickly, scrubbed my boots, then returned to the stall to find the mare down and well along in labor.

In short order she delivered a strong, active filly. I treated the foal's navel, dried her well, and was pleased to see the mare back on her feet in a few minutes. I automatically tied a knot in the hanging placenta to keep it safely elevated above the mare's hocks. The filly found the dam's udder, which I had carefully cleansed, and she nursed successfully, so I wearily climbed into my truck just as dawn was breaking. The men would be appearing at any moment for their early morning chores and I hoped to get a few hours of rest before my scheduled return to re-treat the sick foal.

On the way home it occurred to me that the mare that had just foaled was one of the farm's most valued matrons and I was grateful to have been on hand, even though the old lady had obviously needed no help.

Next morning, when I drove up to the foaling barn, the owner, the manager, and several of the farm hands were lined up in a row with sheepish smiles on their faces. I was completely unaware of the reason for this unusual reception. It wasn't until they spoke that I understood.

"Do *we* have a clever mare," the owner said. "She not only foaled by herself, but she treated her foal's navel and tied a knot in her own placenta!"

Only then did I realize that I had neglected to leave a note for them. The fact that these professionals were caught in the embarrassing, but not unique, position of having had a prized mare foal almost alone accounted for their chagrin.

It would be difficult to recall the number of times (in my practice alone, and in all the different barns with which I am familiar) when owners have entered their barns in the morning to be met by a newborn foal wandering up and down the aisle.

Unattended mares frequently get down to foal in a position that allows the force of the delivery to spring even a sturdy, well-secured stall door —which may propel the foal right out of the stall!

Unless the delay before the foal receives nourishment is overly lengthy, or unless it becomes chilled, little damage is sustained, amazingly enough. Capped hocks and elbows may result from trauma to the foal as it struggles to stand without benefit of the protective padding of the stall's straw bedding, but this is rarely serious.

The mare may become overanxious at this strange separation from her new baby, and the owner may be annoyed by his poor powers of observation; but *this* is one foaling misadventure that almost always ends happily.

Sometimes even the best-laid plans misfire because of a mare's unpredictability. There is a scene still vivid to me that I will never forget though it took place many years ago.

A charming young couple had bred their only mare and were grateful and excited when it became obvious that she was pregnant. They were painfully aware of their lack of experience and called my office seeking help and advice to prepare them for the mare's approaching due date.

They were new clients and I had never visited their barn. The directions were clear and precise, and I found the recently purchased small, well-kept farm with little trouble.

When I entered the roomy old stone bank barn, their loving touch was very apparent. Though the interior was in poor repair, the barn was immaculate and the odors of fresh clean straw and sweet hay filled the air.

Their mare, about a month from term, looked to be in fine condition. She was glowing with good health and contentment, as many pregnant mares do.

After I had finished my examination, the young couple drowned me in a sea of questions. They wanted to be sure that *everything* was right for the mare. We discussed many aspects of the mare's care, and they were pleased to learn that the prenatal routine they had been following was near perfection.

A proper foaling stall was the only missing ingredient needed to complete their preparations. The stall the mare occupied was enclosed by widely spaced boards and an elevated half-door. Its location, chosen for their convenience, was next to the big sliding door, permitting drafts of cold winter air to enter. The stall at the back of the barn was even larger and in a more protected area. When I suggested that it could be made into an ideal foaling stall, the young couple enthusiastically accepted the suggestion. After a detailed description of a properly pre-pared delivery stall, I left, promising to be on call when the mare foaled. As I walked through the big door, I could see the young man busily taking measurements in order to purchase the lumber to build a safe, secure stall.

I received a worried call from the apprehensive owners about a week later. The mare was restless, getting up and down, and had not finished her morning ration.

It took less than an hour to reach the neat little farm. But by the time I arrived the mare was more comfortable and beginning to relax. A small pocket of gas in her intestines, rather than early parturition, was respon-sible for her distress.

I treated the mare and quelled the fears of the young man. Then he showed me the stall he had been constructing. It was nearly completed and as perfect as he could make it. Strong, thick, smooth planks formed the solid walls. He had rounded and reinforced the stall corners by cutting the ends of short lengths of lumber at an angle and securing them, across the corners, to the walls on each side. All that remained to be done was to hang the sturdy stall door and paint. He planned to schedule his annual vacation in order to finish the last touches and then be with the mare when she foaled.

Only a few days had passed when tragedy struck. On a Friday my office relayed a message that reached me between early morning calls. All the office had been able to learn from the shocked and sadly disappointed couple was that their mare had foaled and that they had just found the foal dead.

That message turned me around in my tracks. I drove as rapidly as was safe on the twisting, narrow back-country roads. My heart went out to the two young people who had made such a tremendous effort to have things in perfect order for their mare. It seemed that fate had been unkind; but just how unkind I would not know until I reached the farm.

I walked into the little barn to find the couple holding hands discon-solately as they stood side by side looking helplessly at the lifeless foal. When I spoke to them they looked at me with still-unbelieving expres-sions.

They had come to the barn earlier than usual and found all of their hopes unexpectedly destroyed.

The mare had been checked carefully at midnight, more out of curiosity than real concern. She had given absolutely no indication of shaping up to foal and the visit to the barn had been more to admire the completed foaling stall, with its fresh paint still not dry. They inspected her stall to be sure the mare had plenty of water and enough fresh hay to last her through the night. Now, the morning after, they just could not comprehend that the mare had foaled and they had not been there to help.

The dead foal was literally entwined in the weak, widely spaced boards of the old stall. Obviously the mare had foaled from a position against the boards, and the explosive force of the delivery had sprung the boards apart just long enough for the foal's small body to pass halfway through before snapping back to close in a death trap.

The dam, a maiden, had been a "sneaky" mare. Still showing no external signs of parturition at midnight, she had rapidly made all the necessary changes by about 5:00 A.M. and then foaled.

She had not been due for another eight days.

The young man sadly explained his plans to start his vacation the next day, move the mare to her newly prepared stall, and begin sitting up nights with her in expectation of the coming birth.

I looked again at the dead foal, now freed from the boards and lying at our feet. As I lifted my head, the gleaming, white, perfect foaling stall came into view down the aisle. The foal at our feet was a tragic sight but the empty foaling stall was, somehow, the real tragedy.

Brood mare practice is both fatiguing and rewarding. Its unexpected variations are endless and fascinating. Mares that I know well and have cared for over the years or mares newly acquired by regular clients that I attend for the eleven months of their pregnancy can present ever-new challenges in spite of my feeling of familiarity with them.

The casual client who owns a pregnant or foaling mare and who calls only when worried or in dire need is cause for consternation on the part of any veterinarian. Under these circumstances the medical history of the mare in question is either incorrect or sketchy, and the veterinarian must rely on on-the-spot clinical findings to resolve any problem.

This was the case with a mare I had been called to see. The mare in question was only a few days past her due date and her behavior had not been unusual, so I was not overly concerned as I drove to this farm. When I arrived, the owner was waiting anxiously and led me to the mare's stall.

An impressive chestnut matron, the mare stood well over 17 hands. She had unusual breadth across the chest, which I usually associate with Native Dancer get, and large powerful quarters. She was quietly and comfortably eating her hay, oblivious of the colostrum that was streaming from her udder down over her hind legs. I suggested that the escaping colostrum should be collected and refrigerated. She was the type of mare that could carry a foal almost undetected, yet her abdomen was the largest I had ever seen! No obvious problem could be found. I tried to be reassuring, and after a talk with the owner and foreman in charge I agreed to be available for a hurry-up call whenever the mare foaled.

Five days elapsed and I was called again to see the mare. The general picture was much the same except that her huge abdomen was even larger. I was concerned about her size, the increasing length of her gestation, and the continued loss of the invaluable colostrum.

There was much discussion between the owner and the foreman about the mare's cover dates. The two men were unable to come to any agreement and there remained a two-week discrepancy between their opinions as to the mare's due date. The mare was either *just* due to foal or was ten days to two weeks overdue.

There were many questions in my mind about the big matron. Her general health remained excellent, although her heavy, pendulous abdomen caused her some discomfort. The questionable due-date complication also entered the picture. Could some hormonal imbalance or a nonfunctioning uterus be causing the delay? Was the mare carrying a diseased foal? Could her foal be *extremely* large or, perhaps, some gruesome monstrosity? Could her uterus have ruptured? Last, but not least, was the shocking thought of the possibility of a twin pregnancy.

Nothing could be done at this late date except to prepare mentally and physically for the eventualities that might occur. My veterinary truck was always kept completely equipped for me, but I went over it carefully to be sure that everything was in order.

All medicines and drugs were in good supply. The oxygen tank and resuscitator were in their usual places. All other equipment and instruments that would be needed in case of a dystocia requiring an emergency fetotomy or caesarean were packed carefully and conveniently positioned, and bore recent autoclave dates. I was as prepared as I could be.

Days went by. The big chestnut mare's owner called regularly but could report only that there was essentially no change. Finally, the mare was thirty days overdue by any calculation. The watchman and foreman were close to exhaustion and the owner was so worried that he was almost incoherent on the telephone. This mare had succeeded in unhinging all the people involved with her and her belated foaling. I was not much help, for I could offer no reassuring explanation.

One early evening, 38 days after I had first seen the enormous mare, I received the long-anticipated call. The panicky owner, not knowing what to expect, reported that the mare was down and foaling. "Please, for God's sake, come quickly!" he asked desperately.

At the precise moment that the message came to me over the car radio I was farther away than usual from the farm. Apprehension and concern combined forced me to drive faster than was prudent. At times I felt I should push the accelerator pedal through the floor of the car to gain more speed. Familiar curves were manipulated, but not very well. The well-known traffic light at the crossroad ahead seemed more than usually slow in changing. I rounded the approaching curve just in time to see it turn red.

All my life I have respected law and order, and have never taken any joy in even the most minor infraction. I was aware that my patient was in an explosively dangerous position and seconds were precious. This first time I felt justified as I looked for traffic in both directions, then gunned across the intersection against the red light.

At last my car screeched to a sliding stop at the barn door. Unbelievably, the foreman and watchman were outside the barn, puffing on cigarettes and obviously shaking with fear. The barn was pitch black, with all doors and windows closed. The frightened men seemed to be hiding from whatever was taking place in my patient's stall.

As I jumped from the car, the foreman quickly explained in a quavering voice that he had decided to leave the mare alone so he would not disturb her. I threw on the stall lights from the switch outside the stall door and flew in to the foaling mare. A large bluish-black sac was just behind the recumbent matron. I remember tearing at the sac with my hands and feeling the foal move inside. Seconds counted: opening the sac in time could mean life or death for the foal.

After a futile try, I reached in my pocket for scissors and made a hole in the tough, durable membrane. Thank heaven, the large black colt that flopped out of the sac was alive!

The foreman and watchman, braver now, had found the courage to come into the stall. Following instructions, they were briskly rubbing the big colt dry. I stood up and looked at the mother.

There was something unusual about the tired mare lying there before me. Her attitude was, somehow, different from other mares I had attended, yet it was undefinable. Call it intuition or medical knowledge, or maybe a combination of both, but I felt that the mare should be examined in spite of all the rules to the contrary. The need for an examination justified exposing her to all the hazards it could inflict.

I asked for a pail of hot antiseptic solution and a tail bandage. Quickly they appeared in the stall: the two men had recovered their mental equilibrium to some extent. I prepared the mare carefully, scrubbed myself meticulously. While she was still down in the straw, with a man at her head, I examined her to try to detect her problem.

My hand first touched, then felt, and—astonishingly—confirmed the presence of two little hind feet. They were high in the left horn of the mare's uterus and upside down. Long as my arms are, I could barely reach the small ankles. The alarming possibility of a dead foal was almost too much to bear, and the thought of any delay for lack of assistance— while the two frightened men had stood *outside* the mare's stall—had strengthened my determination. The small body had to be repositioned before it could be delivered.

It seemed that every move was a nightmare of slow motion, but with the two hind legs crossed, the foal was finally rotated into a position proper for a breach delivery. Each step had to be precise, yet it was important that the second foal be brought into the world before the available oxygen was depleted.

At last a tiny chestnut filly lay beside me. She was alive! Muffled exclamations of disbelief could be heard from the growing gallery of spectators as they stared at the almost perfect miniature foal.

The foreman came to assist with drying the newest arrival. She needed additional medical attention beyond the requirements of a normal foal, but it soon became evident that her strength, stamina, and will to live were out of proportion to her size.

The mare finished her well-earned rest and got to her feet. She nickered softly to the big black colt already standing and dropped her head to investigate the squirming chestnut bundle at her feet. After a moment her large soft tongue began to put the finishing touches on the rubdown the filly had been given. The mare accepted the unique presence of her twins much more quickly than did her audience.

It wasn't long before the black colt found his mother's udder and started to nurse. His twin sister, only minutes younger and much smaller, was still going through the trial-and-error period in her attempts to stand. The amazing brood mare alternately encouraged the tiny filly with a soft whinny, then turned her head to lovingly inspect the colt who was busy enjoying his first meal.

Here identical (split-egg) twins, healthy and normal until about 7½ months.

Identical female twins. Both survived.

Finally the filly mastered the herculean task of arranging for all four of her feet to be firmly planted at the same time. Soon she was hungrily searching for food. She worked herself to the proper location, but found a dilemma: her lifted head—with her neck fully extended—was two feet below the enticing, milk-filled teats above. The 17-hand mare's undersized filly was unable to reach the mare's udder and nurse!

At least the foreman came through with flying colors: clean nursing bottles were produced and filled with the proper amount of vital first milk. The sharp little filly was shortly swallowing the irreplaceable nutrients and antibodies from the mare's mammary gland by way of the bottle.

Perhaps those seconds saved by running the red light had made the difference. But, by whatever miracle, both of the twins were fine.

Plans were made to feed both foals by bottle for the first few days to ensure that the filly received her share of colostrum. The colt was allowed a certain amount of time at the udder, then fed a commercial milk substitute. The mare's milk was collected, stored in sterilized bottles, then refrigerated to be used as an alternate with the prepared formula for the filly.

The demanding hourly feeding schedule was followed absolutely until a larger volume of milk could be tolerated by the foals and the feeding schedules were stretched out. Both foals thrived. It was a marvelously curious sight to see the huge mare with the big colt and the dainty little filly romping at her side.

At twelve weeks the large, well-developed colt was easily and successfully weaned. The filly, now able to nurse exclusively from her mother, was allowed to stay with the mare for another two months.

It is unusual when a Thoroughbred mare delivers live twins because the uterus and placenta normally cannot support a twin pregnancy. Usually one fetus dies from lack of nutrition and the stronger twin is indirectly killed by the death of the other. Then abortion occurs.

The twins were an event. They were the only surviving pair born in the area in thirty years, so the trio attracted a great deal of attention and admiration. I need hardly to add that it is even more of an event when each twin is able to mature and fulfill its role in life.

The mare's owner kept the colt and I was able to follow his career to the race track and the winner's circle. I was his doctor throughout his life.

The little upside-down filly was sold. She grew into a 15.2-hand child's hunter. The last I heard of her she was still winning her share of ribbons in local shows.

What follows is not precisely a foaling experience, but because it so clearly illustrates a little-known fact it is pertinent, and I do want to include it with my other tales about the mystery and fascination of the birth process.

It was early morning. I had just finished treating a very sick horse and was on the road with a long list of visits to be made. Sometimes it seems that the most unusual calls in a veterinarian's practice always take place either very early in the morning or very late at night. Because of the predawn hour I turned the volume dial of the car's radio-telephone to "high."

It has been my custom to start each day at the most distant farm and, barring an emergency, work my way homeward. This minimizes the chore of driving at the close of a long day.

The crackle of the radio-telephone was no surprise. And the voice reporting was faint because of the many miles that separated the car's unit from the home-base station; but the message was clear. A client of many years' standing had a cow that was calving, in trouble, and he wanted me to come.

A cow calving—I could hardly believe what I heard. Equine medicine and bovine practice are as different as night and day. Equipment, drugs, and techniques vary drastically. This man didn't need a horse doctor, he needed a cow doctor. I asked my office to call back and suggest that he reach one.

The man apparently had little knowledge of cows himself. He raised and trained Quarter Horses and had purchased several steers to use in their training program.

One of the "steers"—or supposedly gelded bulls—was responsible for his present quandary. His venture with horses had been successful, but obviously he had gone far afield with his purchase of the steers. He had either been too disinterested to inspect his purchases or had been hood-winked by some canny dealer.

Hours went by and, even though I had made a number of my scheduled calls, I was still far from home and the steer owner's farm. A serious conversation with a new client was interrupted by a second call from the office. This call was to let me know that there was not a cow doctor who would come to the now thoroughly worried owner's aid. What should he do? I looked at the lengthy list of patients yet unvisited and conjured up a mental picture of the miles of twisting, rutted, country roads to travel. It seemed reasonable that a local veterinarian specializing in cows should be located and at the patient's side before I could get to the scene. I had my office tell the man to keep trying to reach someone else.

The day wound on and the sky was filled with stars by the time I was back in the vicinity of home. I called in to see whether there were any imperative messages that would turn me around at the last moment and further delay a hot bath and a hot meal. I was aghast to hear that the cow still had not calved and no help had been secured for her. The owner had given up after many futile tries to reach someone—anyone—and was still begging me to come to the farm.

I looked at the clock on the dashboard. It was 8:30 P.M. and the cow had been in labor for over twelve hours. It seemed very unlikely that her calf could have survived, but I was sure that she would need help. The few miles to the farm were traveled as quickly as possible.

The black-and-white cow was down when I arrived and one small cloven hoof was presented. When I grasped the foot, it was icy cold. Heaven only knew how long it had been exposed unprotected to the chill air. I was positive the calf was dead.

My examination revealed that one foreleg was flexed and folded back under the calf's body. It was a simple matter to reposition the leg. Once I thought I felt some movement, but the lack of muscle tone in the legs that I was manipulating seemed to belie that possibility.

Once the calf was in the proper position, it was delivered with ease. The coal-black bundle lay in a limp heap. Its eyes were shut. There was no question that it seemed lifeless. But as I bent to examine the tiny animal, the rib cage moved and the calf took a few ragged breaths. The blunt, blocky head lifted, shook from side to side, and then the eyes opened. The durable calf was alive! It was soon standing spraddle-legged at its mother's udder, nursing.

The tough, efficient placenta of the cow, with its "button" attachments to the lining of the uterus, had sustained the calf through that long period of time while the cow remained in labor. What a contrast to the equine!

The mare's placenta, with its fragile attachment by means of hundreds of villi, would never be able to support any equine baby through such an ordeal. If a mare were in labor for more than one hour, she, her foal, and the veterinarian would be in near-disastrous trouble.

All species are different. Any experience with the birth process in any other animal, including the human, is virtually useless when applied to a brood mare. For all her size, the mare's reproductive system is more fragile and less durable than that of any other mammal of which I know.

Cows and women are tough. Mares are delicate. Such a statement does not always endear me to my female clients, but nothing can alter the truth of the facts.

No one, especially a veterinarian, should ever forget to *expect the un-*

expected with the unpredictable brood mare. Even after all the years I have been in practice, when I feel a little confident about having been exposed to the innumerable behavioral twists that a foaling mare can contrive to confound humans, some new and unexpected experience crops up.

The exposure I enjoyed while growing up on my family's farm served as a very limited introduction to the world of the brood mare. The few mares we owned usually foaled uneventfully and the rare misadventures, with one or two exceptions, were resolved by intuitive responses, a little knowledge, and help from Mother Nature.

I became involved with breeding farms and brood mares very early in my practice. Even though I have always been vitally concerned with equine medicine and surgery, the bulk of my time during the breeding and foaling season has been taken up by those blessed brood mares.

As my practice grew, it was not unusual for several hundred mares to be placed under my care and supervision during the brief and hectic segment of time represented by the annual breeding cycle.

There is some mystical force always present in a foaling stall that involves the very soul of everyone present. Perhaps the end of the long wait and sharing in the wonder of the appearance of a new life are part of the feeling. The satisfaction felt by all with the presence of a live foal—especially after a difficult delivery—is magically transferred from the mare to the humans in attendance. Somehow all feel a sense of pride and accomplishment.

Even the inevitable tragedies, which represent both personal and financial losses, unite the human and animal participants with an inexplicable bond.

Any person who has ever taken part, even as a spectator, in the awesome experience of attending a foaling mare and has shared in the deep pleasure of watching an innocent, precocious live foal stand and nurse shortly after it comes into the world, will understand the title of this book.

The uninitiated will understand it instantly after they have lived through this beautiful experience themselves.

Glossary

aberration   deviation from the normal or typical.

abort   expulsion of an embryo or fetus before it is capable of maintaining extrauterine life.

abruptia placenta   *see* placenta previa.

actinobacillus equuli (shigella equirulis, shigella equuli)   a gram-negative microorganism causing infectious disease in newborn foals (known as "dummy," "sleeper," and "wanderer"), primarily noted for its generalized systemic disease in the neonate.

A-equi I, A-equi II   abbreviations of two strains of the influenza virus causing "flu" in the horse.

agglutination   to cause red blood cells or microorganisms to clump together. (Also called clumping.)

alfalfa   legume hay.

allantois chorion   a membranous sac of the placenta that is most intimately attached to the maternal uterine lining.

amniotic fluids   the fluids in which the embryo is bathed and ingests during gestation.

amniotic sac   the sac that encloses and is most intimate with the foal; the first membrane visible during birth; the inner of two sacs.

anaerobic   growing only in the absence of free oxygen.

anaphylactic reaction   an unusual or exaggerated reaction (hypersensitivity) to a foreign substance; may be induced by a small sensitizing injection of that substance; or a severe reaction to a substance inhaled or ingested.

anastomosis   a surgical or pathological connection of a passage between any two normally distinct spaces or organs in order to form a continuous channel.

anesthesiologist   a specialist in the administration of anesthetics in order to induce the desired level of insensibility.

ankylosed   abnormal immobility, stiffening, or fixation of a joint.

anomaly   marked deviation from the normal condition.

anthelmintic   a vermifuge or agent that is destructive to and causes expulsion of intestinal worms. Worm medicine.

antibody   a disease-fighting serum globulin substance produced by the body in response to an antigenic or foreign stimulus.

antigen   a substance or complex usually in protein form that stimulates the body's immune system to react to it by producing an immune response.

appetence   natural and recurring desire for food; appetite.

apposition   when the opposing surfaces of upper and lower teeth meet in proper position to inhibit improper overgrowth and permit proper mastication.

arteritis   inflammation of an artery.

articular   of or pertaining to joints.

ascarids   intestinal parasites responsible for a variety of symptoms and diseases. (*See also* nematode.)

ascites   abnormal accumulation of serous fluid in the abdominal cavity.

aspiration   the act of breathing or drawing in; also, removal of extraneous fluids or gases from a cavity.

asymptomatic   symptomless.

ataxia   locomotor imbalance; failure of muscular coordination.

atonicity   insufficient muscle tone.

autoclave   to sterilize by means of steam under pressure.

bactericidal   that which destroys bacteria.

bacterin   a vaccine prepared from dead bacteria.

bag   the mare's udder.

bandy legs   bowed or bent in an outward curve; bow-legged.

barren   a mare that has produced at least one foal, but is presently not pregnant.

biceps femoris   biceps muscle of the thigh or powerful, double-branched muscle on the back of the leg. Its general action is to extend and/or elevate the limb.

bilateral or symmetric   having two symmetrical sides.

bivalent, trivalent   medication capable of immunizing a horse against two or three known variations of neurotropic viruses that attack the nervous system.

blepharospasm   uncontrollable winking caused by involuntary contraction of the eyelid muscle, producing more or less complete closure of the eyelids.

blister   to apply a counter irritant (internally or externally) to increase circulation; thought to tighten, toughen, and strengthen tissue in the area so treated.

bloodworms or strongyles   *See* nematode.

botulism   poisoning caused by a toxin from the bacillus clostridium botulinum that affects the nervous system.

brachygnathia (parrot mouth) shortened lower jaw in relation to the upper jaw.

break out a sudden sweat.

break over flexion of the ankle preparatory to the leg being lifted from the ground.

breech presentation presentation of the buttocks of the fetus during labor; posterior portion of the foal's body with the hind legs appearing first.

caesarean section a surgical procedure in which an incision is made through the abdominal wall into the upper segment of the uterus in order to extract a fetus.

cardiovascular pertaining to the heart and blood vessels.

cartilaginous pertaining to cartilage.

Caslick's operation suturing together the upper edges of the vulvar lips.

castration removal of the testicles, thereby neutering or gelding a male horse.

caudal coccygeal pertaining to the tail and the region of the coccyx.

cerebellum the posterior brain mass; that part of the brain mass concerned with coordination of movement.

cerebrospinal pertaining to the brain and spinal cord.

cerebrum the front and largest portion of the brain, consisting of two hemispheres.

chemotherapy treatment of disease with chemicals and drugs.

cholinesterase an enzyme directly involved with nervous impulses.

chromosomes intracellular rod-shaped bodies that carry genes or hereditary factors within the nucleus of a cell at the time of cell division.

cilia hairlike tissue projections inside the oviduct leading from the ovary to the horn of the uterus.

"clean" legs normal, undamaged legs.

clover hay legume hay.

clumping *See* agglutination.

cocked ankles a broad nonspecific term that describes an anterior subluxation or any degree of anterior (forward) deviation from the normal articular surfaces of the ankle joint (from variable causes).

Coggins test a blood test to determine changes in blood caused by exposure to the equine infectious anemia virus (swamp fever); a negative Coggins test is required by more and more states before a horse may be shipped across state lines or from farm to farm.

colostrum a thin, milky fluid secreted by the mammary gland a few days before parturition; a mare's first milk, essential to the foal's health because it transmits vital passive antibodies, although for a limited period of time (48–72 hours).

concentrate   grain.

conceptus   the early product of conception from the time of fertilization of the ovum.

conformation   the anatomical structure and external appearance of a horse.

congenital   existing at birth, but not hereditary.

contagious   transmission or spread of disease by direct or indirect contact.

contracted foal   generalized description of many kinds of contractions.

contusion   to bruise without breaking the skin.

coprophagy   the act of eating manure (considered a vice).

cornea   a transparent membrane forming the outer coating of the front of the eyeball and containing the aqueous humor or fluid in which the iris is bathed.

cornua   the two uterine horns.

coronary band   the fleshy, hair-covered band just above the horny hoof.

coronopedal contraction   unnatural elevation of the heel due to excessive and continuous pull of the deep digital flexor tendon, resulting in a so-called clubfoot.

corpus luteum   a yellow glandular mass in the ovary formed by an ovarian follicle that has matured and discharged its ovum; produces progesterone, which is thought to maintain pregnancy.

corynebacterium equi   a gram-positive bacillus that is a soil inhabitant and the causative agent of foal pneumonia and (usually) abscesses found in the gastrointestinal tract and throughout the body.

court   the group of mares for which breeding contracts to a stallion have been signed each annual breeding season.

cover   the act of breeding a stallion to a mare.

cow hocks   bowed or bent in an inward curve.

cryptorchidism   hidden or recessed testicles that do not descend into the scrotal sac.

curb   protrusion of the plantar ligament at the back and bottom of the hock; such swelling usually causes lameness only when first developed.

dam   the female parent.

deciduate   characterized by shedding.

defecation   discharge of feces from the rectum.

degeneration   usually irreversible deterioration of specific cells or organs.

dehydration   excessive loss of water from a body or from an organ.

diffuse   widely distributed; not definitely localized.

distal end   the reverse of proximal; located far from the point of attachment.

dorsosacral   dorsal surface of foal's spine when aligned with the sacral vertebrae of the mare's spinal column; the normal position for any foal in preparation for delivery.

dressing   (said of feet) trimming and balancing of the horny hoof.

dystocia   a difficult birth.

edema   excessive and abnormal accumulation of fluid in the tissue spaces, originating from the capillaries.

EEV   abbreviation of Eastern Equine Encephalomyelitis vaccine.

electrolytes   the ions of the various salts of sodium, potassium, calcium, magnesium, iron, etc. found in the body fluids in precise amounts. During stress or illness replenishment by IV and oral administration is relied upon.

embryo   unborn; the early or developing stage of the product of fertilization from the moment of conception until appendages, head, and neck are defined; thereafter it is called a fetus.

embryotomy   dismemberment of a fetus to facilitate delivery.

endocrine system   ductless glands whose internal secretions influence appropriate target glands that, in response, further react upon *their* target glands.

endometrium   inner lining of the uterus.

endoparasitism   invasion of a horse's body by parasites that live within the internal organs.

entity   a particular and separate thing (pertaining to disease).

epiglottic closure   closure of the trachea by reflex action; among other functions, it permits the mare to increase the power of her contractions during delivery.

epiphysial   in the young animal the end (extremity) of the bone is called the epiphysis and is separated from the shaft (diaphysis) by the zone of growth (epiphysial plate or line), which closes at maturity.

epizootic   a rapidly spreading disease attacking a large number of animals simultaneously over a wide geographical area; the animal equivalent to a human epidemic.

erythrocytes   mature red blood cells responsible for oxygen transport to and from the lungs to tissues and organs.

Escherichia coli   a species of organisms constituting the greater part of the intestinal flora of animals (and man).

estrus or heat   the recurrent, restricted period of sexual receptivity in female horses.

etiology   the study or theory of the cause of any disease.

eustachian tube   a cartilaginous tube through which the tympanic cavity of the middle ear communicates with the pharynx. It transmits air to the tympanic cavity and equalizes the pressure on the two surfaces of the tympanic membrane.

evert   to turn inside out.

excursion   movement of the rib cage in order to breathe out (exhale) or breathe in (inhale).

exudates   material such as fluid, cells, or cellular debris, that has escaped from blood vessels and been deposited in tissues or on tissue surfaces, usually as a result of inflammation.

"falling" weather   anything that falls from the sky, such as rain, snow, sleet, etc.

FDA   Federal Food and Drug Administration.

femur   the bone between the pelvis and the stifle.

fetal anasarca (hydrops amnion)   general accumulation of fluid in various tissues and body cavities.

fetus   *See* embryo.

finding   an observation; discovery of a condition.

first milk   *See* colostrum.

flaccidity   reduced tissue tone.

float   to remove protruding surfaces and edges of teeth by friction, as by a file.

foal heat   the first estral cycle experienced by the mare; usually occurs 8 to 12 days following delivery of a foal.

foal scours   foal diarrhea.

follicle   a small sac located in the ovary that contains the egg or ovum.

founder   inflammation of the laminae of the feet (the vertical leaves or structures attaching the sensitive *os pedis* to the insensitive hoof wall); there are many degrees of laminitis, but all are grouped within the term "founder."

free-choice feeding   to make food available at a rate to be selected by the individual animal.

genes   the elements by which hereditary characteristics are transmitted; such characteristics are of two kinds: dominant, the major and overriding characteristics, and recessive, those that appear in the absence of the dominant genes; the biologic unit of heredity, self-producing and located in a definite position on a particular chromosome.

get   progeny, offspring.

glottis the space between the vocal cords at the upper portion of the larynx; structures around the larynx.

gluteal muscles large muscles of the buttocks.

gonad the sexual gland, either ovary or testicle.

gonadotrophic any hormone that stimulates the gonads in the body.

gravid pregnant, containing developing young.

gross coarse or large; macroscopic.

guttural pouch a large mucous, membranous sac; a diverticulum (or pouch) of the eustachian tube, peculiar to the equidae (horse, zebra, and ass; a single-hooved mammal); thought to be pressure regulators in the airway.

hematoma a localized swelling usually full of clotted blood from a ruptured blood vessel or vessels and confined within an organ or tissue space.

hemolytic anemia anemia caused by destruction of red blood cells, usually resulting in loss of hemoglobin.

hereditary inherited from parents; genetically transmitted from parent to offspring.

herpes virus the causal viral agent of herpes simplex (an acute viral disease marked by groups of watery blisters of the skin and mucus membranes); thought to be responsible for rhinopneumonitis in mares that results in certain abortion.

husbandry careful management.

hydrocephalic abnormal accumulation of fluid causing enlargement of the cranial vault and subsequent compression and atrophy of the brain, mental weakness, and convulsions.

hypoplasia defective formation; incomplete development.

icterus (jaundice) hemolytic icterus is jaundice in the newborn (usually called neonatal isoerythrolysis).

IM abbreviation for intramuscular or injected within the substance of a muscle.

immunoglobulin serum proteins capable of conferring immunity.

inappetence lack of appetite.

induction area that space in an equine clinic in which the patient is given the final anesthetic that induces unconsciousness.

infectious cause of infection (by microorganism) with or without actual contact.

ingesta food or substances taken into the body by mouth.

inguinal pertaining to the area of the groin.

interventricular   concerned with a small anatomical cavity, as of the brain or heart.

interventricular septal defect   a defect of the wall between the two ventricular cavities of the heart.

intranasal   within the nose.

intrauterine   within the uterus; *in utero*.

intravaginal   within the canal leading from the vulva to the uterus.

involuted   the reverse of evolution; return to normal size after enlargement by birth, relative to the uterus.

isoerythrolysis   destruction of its own erythrocytes by its own antibodies.

isoimmunization   the body's own development of defending antibodies against a mare's own pregnancy.

IV   abbreviation for injection (intravenous) within a vein or veins.

jaundice or icterus   a yellowish discoloration of tissues and body fluids; the result of hemoglobin destruction of the equine's red blood cells or erythrocytes.

joint ill   hot, swollen, painful joints most commonly caused by streptococcus infection.

keratitis   generalized inflammation of the cornea of the eye.

killed-virus vaccine   a dead virus capable of stimulating an antibody response in the horse's body.

Klebsiella equi   encapsulated microorganism found in the respiratory or intestinal tract, frequently associated with diarrhea and pneumonia in foals.

legume   food plants that efficiently utilize nitrogen from the air; legume hay is alfalfa, clover, or soybean.

lesion   a pathological alteration of tissue; a wound or injury; loss of function of a part.

ligate   to tie, bind, or strangulate a vessel or part by thread, gut, or wire.

liter   the basic unit of capacity in the metric system; it is equivalent to 1.0567 quarts liquid measure or 1,000cc.

live-viral vaccine   a living microorganism contained within a laboratory preparation administered to prevent, ameliorate or treat disease; a *killed* vaccine retains its antigenicity; an *attenuated* viral preparation has had its pathogenicity reduced by means of passage through other animals in order to diminish its virulence and enhance safety of inoculation.

lumbosacral   pertaining to the loins and sacrum.

luteal phase   that phase in the reproductive cycle relating to the development of the corpus luteum and progesterone production that occurs in both barren and pregnant mares.

lymphocyte a type of white blood cell formed in the lymphoid tissue throughout the body.

lymphopenia reduction of circulating white blood cells, specifically the lymphocytes, which are important to the formation of immune responses of the body.

malpresentation faulty or abnormal fetal presentation at time of delivery.

mammary pertaining to the milk-producing glands.

mandible the bone of the lower jaw.

meconium an accumulation of semisolid material in the fetal intestinal tract during intrauterine life; thought to be associated with the embryonic ingestion of amniotic fluid.

metacarpophalangeal that part of the leg from below the knee to the sole of the foot.

microorganism a minute living organism, usually microscopic. Those of equine medical interest are bacteria, spiral organisms, rickettsia, viruses, molds, and yeasts.

monestrous possessing only one estrous cycle annually.

monorchidism lack of proper descent of one testicle.

motile the inherent power of motion; having the power to move spontaneously.

mucopurulent containing both mucus and pus.

multipara a mare that has had two or more foals, whether or not the foals were alive at birth.

navel point of attachment of the umbilical cord to the body of the foal.

navel ill bacterial invasion with subsequent infection of the navel stump in young foals. Streptococcal microorganisms are commonly the causative agent.

nematode any parasitic worm possessing a threadlike, unsegmented body (roundworms or threadworms).

neonate a newborn.

neuromuscular pertaining to nerves and muscles.

neurotrophic having an affinity for nervous tissue or exerting its principal effect on the nervous system.

nictitating membrane the inner or third eyelid.

nidation implantation of the placental membranes enveloping the fertilized ovum into the endometrium of the uterus in pregnancy.

occlusion the proper relation of the upper and lower teeth during the act of chewing.

os pedis coffin bone in the foot or third phalanx.

osteoarthritis chronic, multiple degenerative joint disease, usually of traumatic or physical origin in the equine.

osteomyelitis inflammation of bone caused by a pathogenic microorganism.

ovariectomy surgical excision (removal) of an ovary or ovaries.

ovulation discharge of mature, unimpregnated ovum from the follicle of the ovary.

palpate to examine by hand; to feel.

paresis partial or incomplete paralysis.

parotid area below the ear and behind the curve of the jaw.

parturition the act of giving birth.

patella a flat triangular bone located at the front of the stifle joint.

patent apparent, open, unobstructed.

pathogens any disease-producing microorganisms or material.

pathonomonic the indisputable symptom or group of symptoms that are diagnostic.

pedigree a chart of ancestors; a record of recorded line of descent.

Pen-Strep any combination of penicillin and dihydrostreptomycin.

perinatal immediately after birth.

perineal area the associated structures occupying the pelvic outlet.

peristalsis involuntary movement that propels ingesta through the gastrointestinal tract.

peritoneum a serous sac encasing the abdominal contents.

pervious urachus a permeable or leaky navel.

pharyngitis inflammation of the pharynx.

Phenothiazine a compound widely used to combat intestinal nematode parasitisms of the horse; popular for many years, it is presently being replaced by newer anthelmintics.

photophobia abnormal intolerance of light.

pituitary gland the endocrine gland which controls the other endocrine glands, influences growth, metabolism, maturation, and parturition as well as the entire reproductive cycle.

placenta the developed organ within the uterus which at conception establishes life-sustaining communication between the mare and embryo.

placenta previa a variation of placentation that occludes the internal surface of the cervix; abruptia placenta—premature detachment of a normally situated placenta.

placentation the manner in which the placenta is attached. Type of placentation varies greatly with the different species.

polydactylia a developmental anomaly characterized by the presence of more than the normal number of limbs (appendages).

polyestrous possessing two or more reproductive (estrous) cycles annually.

postmortem autopsy; surgical exploration to determine the cause of death.

postpartum immediate period after birth.

predisposition tendency or inclination; latent susceptibility to disease which may be activated under certain conditions, as by stress.

preformed (relative to antibodies), manufactured, biologic serums which confer passive immunity to an individual after injection of specific antibodies produced in another individual or other tissues that provide immediate protection to the recipient.

preparturient previous to delivery.

"prepped" antiseptically prepared for surgery by preliminary sedation and sterilization of the operation site.

prepuce a covering fold of skin at the end of the glans penis.

prima a maiden mare that has never produced offspring.

profound extreme, great.

progeny offspring, descendants.

prognathia (sow mouth) abnormal shortness of upper jaw *or* abnormal elongation of lower jaw.

progesterone a hormone produced by the corpora lutea, thought to be responsible for preparation of the uterus for the reception and development of the fertilized ovum by glandular proliferation of the endometrium.

Prostiglandins a new, injectable hormone that possesses a strong luteolytic action upon the gonads of the mare.

Providone-iodine a disinfecting agent.

pseudocyesis false or spurious pregnancy.

pyogenous producing or caused by pus.

rectovaginal tear tearing of the tissues separating the vaginal (birth) canal from the rectum.

reduce to restore to the normal place or relation of parts; as, to reduce a fracture.

resect surgical removal of a considerable portion of an organ or structure such as bone.

reticuloendothelial   pertaining to the tissues having both reticular (netlike) and endothelial (cells that line the cavities of the body) attributes concerned in blood cell formation and destruction that play a defensive role against inflammation and help in creating immunity.

rhinopneumonitis   viral infection of the upper respiratory tract in young horses; invariable cause of abortion in mares by attacking the placental membranes and causing viremia in the fetus, followed by fetal death.

rounded hock   to the lay person, any deviation from normal in the structure of the hock.

sacrosciatic ligaments   ligaments attached to the sacrum and the ischium (the inferior dorsal part of the hip bone).

schistosomus reflexus   a fetal monster.

scoliosed or scoliotic   abnormal curvature or crookedness of the spine.

scrotum   the external pouch of skin enclosing the two testes and their accessory organs.

season   condition of a mare receptive to the act of breeding.

septal   pertaining to a septum (a dividing wall or membranous partition) between two soft masses of tissue.

septicemia   blood poisoning due to bacterial invasion of the circulatory system.

service   a stallion's copulation with a mare.

settled in foal   pregnant; acknowledged presence of a conceptus.

Shigella equi   one of the microorganisms that causes foal septicemia.

sickle hocks   shaped like a sickle; these hocks bend in a backward or posterior curve.

"silent" or "spec" mare   a mare that shows no outward sign of being sexually receptive.

sleeve   a sterile, plastic hand and arm protective shield for gynecological examination purposes.

stary   dull, lusterless (as of a horse's coat).

Staz-Dri   trade name for a commercially manufactured bedding material that horses will, we hope, *not* consume.

stenosis   narrowing or stricture of a duct or canal.

stock up   swelling of any of the lower legs because of interference with circulation or bruising of the tissues.

strangles   an acute infectious disease caused by *streptococcus equi*, characterized by enlargement and suppuration of the lymph glands of the head and jowl.

strongyles   *See* nematode.

subluxation faulty articular processes of a joint or joints; an incomplete or partial dislocation.

supernumerary digit extra accessory; more than the usual number of limbs.

suppurate to fester or form pus.

supraorbital ridge the bony prominence above the cavity that contains the eyeball.

symphysis a site or line of union of bony surfaces by means of a plate of fibrocartilage.

syndrome a group of signs or symptoms that collectively characterize a disease.

tease to induce symptoms in a mare of heat or to determine her receptivity.

term the end of a normal pregnancy.

thrifty growing vigorously; thriving.

tibia the bone that extends from the stifle to the hock.

titer the minimum volume needed to cause a particular result in the titration process by means of standard solutions of known strength.

topical applicable to or pertaining to a particular part of the body.

torticollis wry or contorted neck muscles that produce an unnatural position of the head. Found in intrauterine contraction.

transect a cut across a long axis; a cross section.

trochlea a pulleylike structure, as the part of the distal end of the humerus that articulates with the ulna.

tuber ischii a large elongated mass on the body of the ischium (part of the hip bone) to which several muscles are attached. (*See* also whirlbone.)

turbid cloudy or dense.

tympany tightly stretched or distended by air.

ulna bone in the foreleg that corresponds to the human bone from elbow to wrist on the side opposite that of the thumb.

uremia an excess of urine and its constituents in the blood and the toxic condition produced thereby.

urethra the membranous canal through which urine is discharged from the bladder.

vector commonly, a bloodsucking or biting insect; an organism that carries pathogens (infective agents) from one host to another.

VEE abbreviation for Venezuelan Equine Encephalomyelitis vaccine.

ventral abdominal or lower surface of the body.

vertebral column backbone or spine.

vesicle small bladder or sac containing liquid.

villus a tiny protrusion from the free surface of a membrane; one of the thread-like projections growing in tufts on the external surface of the chorion (covering of the fertilized ovum that later forms the embryonic portion of the placenta).

viral caused by or pertaining to a virus.

viremia the presence of viruses in the blood.

viscera internal organs of the body contained within the abdominal cavity.

vulva external entrance to the female reproductive tract.

wax a viscous, honey-colored substance that seals, and may or may not drip from the teats; the precursor of first milk or colostrum; diameter varies from the head of a pin to a golf ball; almost always present, it is produced by the activated ducts and tubules of the milk glands.

whirlbone posterior part of the bony pelvic structure. (*See also* tuber ischii.)

wobbles ataxia, with weakness of hindquarter motion initially, and characteristically pain-free lack of control of the hind legs.

wolf teeth extra teeth in the upper jaw that interfere with the position of a bit and result in pain when the bit is forced backward against these small, useless premolars; a functionless, rudimentary vestige of evolution; canine or bridle teeth are found in both upper and lower jaws in males and are absent in the female mouth, although anomalies do occur.

Index of Signs and Symptoms

SIGNS

SYMPTOMS

263

Index